RADICAL PASSIONS

RADICAL PASSIONS

A MEMOIR OF REVOLUTION AND HEALING

Kendall Hale

iUniverse, Inc.
New York Bloomington Shanghai

Radical Passions
A memoir of revolution and healing

iUniverse books may be ordered through booksellers or by contacting:

iUniverse
1663 Liberty Drive
Bloomington, IN 47403
www.iuniverse.com
1-800-Authors (1-800-288-4677)

Because of the dynamic nature of the Internet, any Web addresses or links contained in this book may have changed since publication and may no longer be valid.

The views expressed in this work are solely those of the author and do not necessarily reflect the views of the publisher, and the publisher hereby disclaims any responsibility for them.

ISBN: 978-0-595-48387-7 (pbk)
ISBN: 978-0-595-71941-9 (cloth)
ISBN: 978-0-595-60478-4 (ebk)

Printed in the United States of America

This book is dedicated to my ancestors, parents, sisters, my husband, my children and to the great extended family of courageous friends who followed their hearts.

PASSION

1. suffering or agony, as of a martyr.
2. the state or power of receiving or being affected by outside influences.
3. intense emotional drive, or excitement; specifically.
   a) great anger; rage; fury.
   b) enthusiasm or fondness, as for music.
   c) strong love or affection.

RADICAL

1. proceeding from the root or root like stem
2. original; fundamental; reaching to the center or ultimate source
3. one who advocates sweeping changes in laws and methods of government
   with the least delay

Webster's New Collegiate Dictionary, 1961 edition

"To Kendall,
With love on her twelfth birthday
From Alys and Myron
April 26, 1962"

A Note on Usage

In order to protect their privacy, I have altered the names and characters of the people in this narrative; in most cases I have used first names only. Any resemblance is coincidental.

Contents

Introduction

I never intended to write the story of my life, especially at age forty-five, on a vacation in Florida with my husband, Steve Norris, and our two children. Walking the beach, Steve casually mentioned that he had been invited to write an anthology with other grassroots activists, ordinary people who had been 'written out of history.' Instinctively I asked, "Can I join?" It turned out this was my chance to get written into history, as well as to give meaning to a life that had often felt overwhelmed by external events far larger than I. Together over the next few years, we made several trips from Asheville, North Carolina to our former home, Boston, Massachusetts, furiously digging out the past, re-living our activist lives with other 'rad writers,' as I called them. Eventually all four of them came to Sharon Spring, our new home in the Blue Ridge mountains. Stimulating conversations unfolded my memory from images into words that filled page after page, to the end of that project. By then writing had become a habit.

Left alone I continued to journal new stories of middle age adventures—rural living, spiritual seeking, death and healing, and yes, more activism, all in a community light years away from the early chapters. So what began as a collective endeavor deepened into an individual exploration: an autobiography. Although I studied history at the University of Wisconsin, my life choice was to make it, and that product is this book, my story, Herstory.

ON THE BARRICADES IN MADISON

1989 Madison Reunion

"Would you believe my little sister and my Mormon grandmother were both visited by the FBI looking for me after the bomb blast?" I said as I laughed with the other grownup radicals sitting around our table in the reception hall. I felt triumphant with two hundred leaders of the sixties liberation struggles at our 20-years-later college/movement reunion organized by a core of activists from the Days of Rage at the University of Wisconsin. "Frieda," I said to my former college roommate, "we are true survivors of the youth movement." My eyes roamed the room searching the faces of the 60's street fighters. Two tables away sat Helen, once a hippie-freak without a bra and tie dyed bell bottoms, now a lawyer with the American Civil Liberties Union. Next to her sat Gail, a peacenik physician with a familiar-looking, hand carved wooden peace symbol around her neck. There was crazy Peter, a long hair who carried the anarchist flag, now an environmental science teacher.

But then I thought of Robert Fassnacht. Several hundred people fell quiet as all eyes riveted on Karl Armstrong walking to the podium. Before his wild brown hair reached his shoulders, now his balding head marked the passage of time. The weekend had been confirmation of all that was right about our battle. Everyone here had work or a lifestyle related to values expressed in our college years. But now the ex-prisoner, ex-bomber whose truck of dynamite had killed Robert Fassnacht spoke.

"I want to apologize for what I did. It was wrong."

No one moved. No one spoke. Then, a ripple of clapping grew thunderous.

August 23, 1970

What was that? It was 3a.m. on Sunday, August 23, 1970, and I sat up in bed, dazed, blinking at the glass fragments piercing the sheet. Had there been an explosion? Then I felt air flowing over my head and shoulders. There was a star shaped hole in the window over my head.

Alone, I sat there and wondered if Madison had been attacked by nuclear weapons. I was reminded of all the childhood drills in my elementary school, when we marched into the school halls and crouched, covering our heads with our hands, or hid under our desks.

The inch-thick wooden desktops would protect us from radiant holocaust. Our teachers seemed to think so.

"Help me," I croaked, running outside onto Bassett Street. Dozens of other people who lived in the student ghetto were also out in the dark, walking toward the university. A girl I didn't know turned to me in the crowd. "It's got to be Sterling." We soon knew the blast had come from Sterling Hall, the building that housed the Army Math Research Center (AMRC), the focal point of the campus antiwar movement.

Sterling, bombed? All right! But I felt a mixture of horror and glee from the pit of my stomach as we approached the police cars and barricades. Lights whirred over emergency vehicles, blue white blue white blue white, and I smelled acrid smoke. I stood there in the crowd for an hour, watching, then shuffled home, hoping to find a friend.

The following day I learned that Robert Fassnacht, a physicist, had been killed in the blast. Poor guy, I thought. But everyone knew the research in those labs was funded by the military. Why was he experimenting at 3 a.m. on a Sunday night?

Getting Radical

> "We walked up the rise behind the Washington Monument to the sight of thousands of people already gathered. It was at that moment the sense that this was to be a remarkable, historic event claimed us. The remainder of the day was marked by exquisite courtesy and kindness. It was like the millennial dream of peace and brotherhood which later in the day was perfectly enunciated by M.L. King's 'I have a dream' speech."
>
> *Alys Miles Hale, my mother*
> *Columbus, Ohio*
> *August 28, 1963*

Author Harriet Beecher Stowe and abolitionist Harriet Tubman were two of my mother's heroines, so it seemed natural that Mom and Dad would go with other civil rights activists to hear Dr Martin Luther King speak at the March on Washington. It was August, 1963. I was thirteen and thrilled to hear the details.

It was a twelve hour ride from Columbus, Ohio on the little bus with straight hard seats and folding chairs in the aisles for overflow passengers. My parents were the only white people on board. Mom had worked with a civil rights group to get a fair housing bill passed by the Ohio State Legislature. The bill made it illegal to keep blacks from buying or renting housing in white neighborhoods. Through the NAACP, they made a reservation on the Reverend Fred Shuttleworth's bus. "We must help the Negroes get jobs and better housing," Mom explained to my sisters and I. "We'll go on a school bus with food and two canteens of water."

Forty years later, in 2002, the local newspaper in West Lafayette, Indiana interviewed my parents. "It was the high point of my life. My children are sick of hearing about it. I don't cry much, but it was unbelievable," Mom told the reporter. "I don't want to say it was a religious experience, but it was so quiet as we all listened to this man. He moved everyone." Dad recounted, "When he started and said 'I have a dream,' and talked about what he hoped would happen, his dreams for America, it was moving, believe me. After serving in World War II, I'm not easily moved by events, but this was moving. You could have heard a pin drop."

Heady, inspiring stuff for a thirteen-year-old. As the child of these two, how could I not be an activist?

Four years after the March on Washington, I was watching the 6:00 news. My mother was cooking dinner while as usual, my father and I sat in front of the television, following world events and preparing to discuss them over the evening meal. On our little boxy, black and white TV, there was a big antiwar demonstration with students carrying crosses. I said to Dad "That's where I want to go to school. Look at that! All those people are against the war in Vietnam!" "Is the University of Wisconsin a good school, Dad?"

Mom and Dad wanted me to go a good college but didn't pressure me much about it. We spent a lot of time sorting through *The College Handbook*: "Too far away. Too expensive. Not good enough."

In the late 1960s, high school in Columbus was one grayish grind, day after day of increasing alienation and growing anticipation of leaving home for a more political, sophisticated world where I would find my place. But I was nonetheless a teenage girl, too. Longing to be popular, I ached for the fashionable prep school clothes my classmates wore, a new matching skirt and sweater for each day of the week, and hated my liberal academic parents for denying me what I wanted. Because my father was a political science professor at Ohio State University, I begged to attend the private university high school offered to professors' children for a minimal fee. There, it was cool to express discontent by wearing protest buttons and Joan Baez-style sandals. I despaired at my parent's constant answer,

"We don't have enough money."

Feeling hollow and defeated, I stopped talking at school. Playing the violin became my sole emotional outlet, but even the music could not calm all my anger. So I routinely hit my stand with my bow, shedding horsehair all over the rug. I clung to the belief that nothing could be worse, so life would likely get better.

I sought meaning in the works of Jean-Paul Sartre. Being and nothingness and existentialism—red meat for a discontented teenager. My father gave me mind-boggling and confusing books, too. *The Communist Manifesto* and *Quotations from Chairman Mao*. (although years later he argued that I gave Mao's Red Book to him)

What planet had these two parents of mine come from? After the Second World War, six months after my birth in Salt Lake City, Utah in 1950, they left Zion, their pioneer Mormon community, so Dad could attend graduate school at Columbia University where he studied political theory. It was in Shanks Village, a large housing facility of converted army barracks (sprayed pink, green or yellow) for World War II veterans attending universities in Rockland County, New York, where the seeds of my life long quest for communal living took root.

Shanks was remarkable not only for the community-run carpool, food co-op, nursery school, newspaper and theater, but for being a fully integrated community where families of all races and backgrounds lived, worked and played together. I was never surprised as a young girl when I saw people with different color skins. But Shanks life also had its pioneer hardships—the barracks weren't insulated, had no storm windows, ice had to be brought in to keep the leaky refrigerators cold, and electric fuses often blew when too many appliances were used. All laundry was hung out to dry. (now, of course, with climate change, it's politically correct to sun-dry laundry) I can vividly remember the monstrous brown space heater that had to be filled several times a day from an outdoor oil tank.

The government paid a married student ninety dollars a month, and thirty dollars for each child. No one had much, which helped foster a strong resourceful network of friends and neighbors. With money from the GI Bill, (Mom and Dad were both veterans) my mother found cheap, used furniture and household goods, and Dad used scrap boards and bricks to make bookshelves and empty orange crates from the market for end-tables by the couch and beds. An old army barrack was a great place for a kid to be—Dad drilled holes in the ceiling for a swing above my bed and Mom taught me to draw and paint on the walls. My younger sister and I took baths in the kitchen sink since there wasn't a tub and my father used a 3x3x 6 foot closet for a study. *The PhD closet.* I can still hear the sound of the black typewriter keys clacking away night after night as Mom put me to bed.

When it rained, I raced outside in my underwear to splash with all the Shanks kids, or jumped into a plastic pool with ten other children in the common yard. Mom showed colored slides of this community to us until the day I came home with modern children who demanded television and video.

People tell me my Dad was the resident expert on politics and government. In 1952, when Eisenhower beat Adlai Stevenson for president, Dad said the country had survived a lot of bad and mediocre presidents and would continue to do so as long as the balance of power established by our Constitution was maintained. By the time George Bush was elected in 2000, Dad was too old to understand that we almost lost it. The balance, that is.

In 1956, Mom cried when we drove away from her beloved Shanks Village to my Dad's new university job in Austin, Texas, home state of the future burning bush.

Late Sixties

My mother was the one who bore the brunt of my restless longings and daily, violent outbursts fueled by my isolation from my peers. I knew from an early age that being a professor's wife did not fulfill her intelligence. She made it crystal clear. From the kitchen stove, jabbing a pan of sauce with a spoon, she complained to me: "I should have finished my graduate degree. If only I had become an anthropologist or historian." The sad refrain's lost career would change from year to year. But the if-only longing and bitterness remained constant.

I was so full of youthful, anxious pain, I hated seeing hers. Mom had watched her own mother experience the Mormon Church's enforcement of female inferiority and discrimination. My college educated grandmother who wrote, acted and taught school, struggled with Mormon dogma—church law made her quit teaching as soon as she married my grandpa She eventually left the Latter Day Saints, but lost her mind to depression in a culture that treated gifted women like mental patients. In the end, it was easier just to forget, and float around her neighborhood of thirty years in her lacy white nightgown like a lost dandelion puff. I know it wasn't Alzheimer's disease. It was grief, plain and simple. And the teenage me sure didn't want to end up like Mom or grandma.

As it turned out, a few Mormons, Mom and I included, needed and wanted change. But she looked stuck and I was shedding my skin. The protesters I saw on TV presented me with what felt like my very last chance: college and rebellion.

The greatest psychic in the world could not have seen how great my mother's suffering would become as America went to war with itself.

By the end of my senior year in high school, I was sure that more time in this part of the Midwest would kill me or drive me to suicide. My alienation was so intense that I refused to apply to Ohio State University, but was rejected by all the private eastern schools I longed to attend, despite a 3.7 average. Hope began when I opened the acceptance letter from the University of Wisconsin: I was in!

My excitement temporarily deflated when Dad was hired at Purdue University, which meant uprooting and re-adjusting for three months in West Lafayette, Indiana, before the fall semester of college. "God, why wasn't it somewhere in the East or at least Chicago," I muttered everyday all summer long, dreaming of the Madison campus.

After our family's move to Indiana, I met Frank, a long, lanky perennially stoned Purdue freshman who was transferring to Wisconsin for his sophomore year. He introduced me to acid rock, marijuana, and rebellion. I no longer wanted to be a virgin, so one evening sitting in the haze of pot smoke and candles at his student apartment I made a feeble attempt to seduce him by putting my head in his lap. But Frank continued to talk excitedly about the upcoming Democratic Convention in Chicago, his eyes widening at the thought of the planned protest demonstration through the streets and into the hall.

"All the big, important radicals will be there, Kendall. Everyone who's down on the system, SDS—you know, Students for A Democratic Society."

"Hey, maybe I'll go too," I exclaimed. "I wonder if my parents would let me?" Obedient Kendall, virginity intact, contemplated asking parental permission to overturn the American political system.

He laughed. "Don't ask. Just go. Come with me."

I made a face, and sighed, "I've never done anything they didn't know about."

"What do you mean? They don't know you are here with me, do they?" He turned over the Jimi Hendrix record.

He had a point. But it looked like Frank didn't want to sleep with me, so I left, pondering protest instead of sex, I saw myself participating in the biggest organized confrontation I could imagine. I had been on picket lines with my parents to protest segregated housing in Columbus, and the March on Washington was family legend. I thought about Chicago for days, but my father wasn't too excited about my attending and I wasn't ready to plot against him. Instead, Dad and I watched the 1968 Convention on TV. Lines of cops in black jackets and white helmets advanced in unison toward the protestors, then charged, batons battering anyone they could reach. Nightsticks swung randomly, rhythmically onto skulls, and I could lip-read their curses. Four uniforms threw a woman bodily through the air into the back of a paddy wagon. The cameras closed in as people held their hands to faces streaming with blood and tears I screamed, "Look at those cops, Dad. Look!"

My body was shaking as I paced back and forth. "They're clubbing those people! That could be Frank! And the Students for a Democratic Society. My God, I don't believe it. Why? Why?" Angrily I asked, "This is a democracy isn't it? Why can't they protest?" I knew we had a right to voice opinion without being brutalized.

My stunned father was speechless. Walter Cronkite's urgent voice sounded as if he believed we were living in a police state.

Even though I knew next to nothing about SDS, I knew a lot about Vietnam, and the history of US involvement, and had been persuaded by my father that the war was unjust because the US had blatantly violated formal agreements. Now in Chicago, two hours away from my bedroom, young people just like myself, angry at makers of US foreign policy and the inequality in American society, were being beaten, their skulls cracked by a bunch of cops following the mayor's orders. I was furious. That night I closed my eyes but still heard and saw the sounds and images of bodies being dragged through the streets, of tear gas and screams. And a neighbor's bumper sticker, "America, Love It or Leave It".

Madison, 1968

I had not died, I had not committed suicide, and I was finally escaping to college. As my Dad and I drove into the Gary, Indiana, smog towards Madison, I was rattled by my mother's last frightened, sad expression. There were no words of support, encouragement, or even good luck, just simply her deep sorrow and lingering words:

"Once they leave, they never come back."

And she was right. I never did come back; not because I didn't want to, but because the movement, the energies of change that were shaking America, propelled me into a new world she did not, could not, and would not understand. This same movement engulfed my total being and turned me inside out, rendering me unrecognizable. It was transformation by fire.

My mother and I lost each other in America's second civil war, connected only by the go between efforts of my father, who suffered silently between us. I had no compassion for my frightened, anxious mother who directed blame at me instead of Richard Nixon for the darkness in America. Trapped in suburban despair, she criticized almost every action and decision I was to make for the next fifteen years. Consciously or unconsciously, she saw her lost opportunities embodied in me, and I had walked out the door into the larger world. I was physically free, but I was carrying some big, heavy suitcases of guilt and resentment when I arrived on campus in Madison.

Naomi. My brilliant, crazy, wild new friend. Naomi drew me out of a long, deep, depression into joy and freedom. In Madison, she drew me from our dorm room into as many parties as we could find. She wore old blue jeans and moccasins, and her thick, stringy hair hung down like a curtain as she fired up the next joint, which was frequently. Fearless, she led me in and out of the student union, up and down streets in student neighborhoods, stoned with pleasure, frolicking, laughing, dancing, rolling on floors. The University of Wisconsin was far from the cozy, cloistered college campuses back east that I thought I wanted. On the Madison campus there were two choices: You either drank beer with the fraternities and sororities or smoked dope with hippies and radicals. The healing water of beautiful Lake Mendota gave all 40,000 students our common bond: we swam, canoed, sailed, and skated. In the winter, some of us demonstrators even escaped from tear gas onto the frozen lake.

My new life was joyful, but first semester classes were a terrible disappointment, dull repetitions of high school memorization and regurgitation. Where were the encounters with authentic political and social movements, the changes that were roiling America? So I found intellectual stimulation from meeting people at parties and demonstrations. I threw myself into what I thought of as a movement that would force us to re-examine everything we had ever been taught.

One of the first pamphlets I read was *Student as Nigger,* an angry, bitter attack on the students' powerless position in the university. This was just the beginning of an onslaught of flyers, pamphlets, speakers, rallies, student union debates, and sidewalk preachers that stimulated me to insomnia night after night. After tossing for hours, I would calm myself by taking a plastic flute, a cup of warm milk, and a stack of reading material to the laundry room floor. Here I pondered these wondrous concepts until I got sleepy at sunrise. "This is the dawning of the Age of Aquarius" the lyrics sang to me with joy and hope. The new astrology promised that now was the last of the dark ages, the end of a Pisces-cycle era of war, divisions, and patriarchy. And the birth of a new era. My era.

Second semester. The University of Wisconsin teaching assistants were striking for better working conditions, smaller classes, and higher salaries. I joined the picket line, of course, proudly wearing my red and black RESIST button. This strike took me into the next one, led by black students demanding a Black Studies program. In the bitter cold February of 1969, with a copy of Eldridge Cleaver's *Soul On Ice* under my jean jacket, I closely watched the protesters wearing berets and leather jackets and realized that they wanted nothing to do with white people.

As I watched them marching in rhythm, chanting "Black Power!" and terrifying most of the white students, I knew they were right. After all, these were real Black Panthers from Chicago. Malcolm X had come alive! Slogans about guns and armed struggle, echoed through library mall and appeared scrawled on campus buildings, sidewalks, and bathrooms. "Seize the Time!"

"On Strike, Shut It Down, On Strike, Shut It Down!" Our voices reverberated off Bascom Hill, the center of campus. Within days University President Fred Harrington called the governor, who brought in two thousand National Guardsmen armed with machine guns, automatic weapons and grenade launchers.

In response to Harrington's move, 10,000 students rallied, waving signs and chanting.

"Pick up the Gun! Seize the Time! Off the Pig! Off the Pig!",.

"All they want is black teachers and counselors and scholarships!" I yelled furiously at an armed guardsman standing in front of me. His frozen white face didn't get it.

"Power to the People! Right On!"

So new! So exhilarating! I thought everyone was saying "Right Arm!" So I punched my right fist into the air. If only the people I knew at high school could see me now, I thought, surrounded by hundreds of people like me, expressing our rage! Demanding justice! I felt a rush of high-octane energy surge through my body. I was no longer scurrying through locker-filled high school hallways, mouse like and isolated, wearing my protest buttons that no one cared about: "Black = White," "Eugene McCarthy for President," "US Out of Vietnam," "Don't Trust Anyone Over Thirty," buttons that no one noticed or cared about. I was in my true element, with my people.

I threw my fist into the air again, "Power to the People, Right Arm!"

Apparently, the days of begging for an equal piece of the pie had ended. Non-violence seemed impotent in the face of armed police and war. As the university and the government escalated tactics, students did too. The Black Panther Party meant business! To them political power came out of the barrel of a gun!

"Pick up the gun!"

Was that really *me* saying those words, a white middle class girl from Columbus? I was frightened and intrigued. Fred Hampton, a militant Black Panther, preached revolution and drew thousands when he spoke at the Memorial Student Union. At twenty-one he was a charismatic leader and an orator, so powerful the auditorium pulsated as he described how the rich and powerful at the top of the hill would be brought down by the poor at the bottom. All chairs emptied for a standing ovation that shook the hall. The same moment that thrilled us rattled the FBI. Hampton was winning allies for the Panthers' political platform among the white middle class students who responded with anger and rage at his description of racism and class exploitation. A year later, in the winter of 1969, the Chicago police riddled his apartment with 100 bullets. Fred Hampton was murdered in his sleep.

Overnight after the murder, all the young white men who considered themselves revolutionaries began wearing black leather jackets and berets. A week later as I sat in an anthropology lecture hall, one of the white SDS leaders and two black militants ran down the aisles, jumped up on the stage, knocked over the professor's desk and smashed the glass cover to a fire extinguisher. "Avenge Fred Hampton! Black Studies now!" Throwing chairs around, they disappeared as fast as they had come. I pitied the professor as he vanished backstage. Quaking and confused, I sat holding onto the arms of my chair. Those of us sympathetic to the rebellion saw looks of contempt and fear on most people's faces as they filed out into the sunlight. But that didn't stop me.

"Avenge Fred Hampton!" I screamed at a girl scurrying by.

From then on, boycotting classes became the norm. I stopped opening my textbooks to embrace the movement, but never questioned its logic. I realized that our educational system was racist and each of us was being confronted personally and challenged to take responsibility to change the university. Black people had a right to learn their own history and heritage. Acts of violence in and of themselves were meaningless, but I began to believe that violence was necessary when connected to a political or social cause.

I felt connected to the rest of the country and the world when The San Francisco Mime Troupe, the Weather Underground's Bernadine Dohrn, and a multitude of other famous radicals visited the Madison campus. I can still see the red and white face paint smeared on Abby Hoffman and Jerry Rubin, two of the seven Chicago Conspiracy defendants, as they waved to throngs of students crowded onto Library Mall. Leaders of the International Youth Party, better known as Yippies, Abbey and Jerry described Judge Julius Hoffman's courtroom and the three-ring circus confrontation that exposed the judge's "fascist soul."

"Our strategy was to give Judge Hoffman a heart attack. We gave the court system a heart attack, which was even better," Jerry grinned.

The Yippie leaders laughed at sick Amerika (with a k, not a c, Nixon's country being a fascist county) and cheered on revolution, talking to the thousands listening about their own feelings of emptiness, pain, anger, and their contempt for a corrupted political system with no answers to their questions about Vietnam or social injustice. It was thrilling.

The antiwar agitation mounted and focused on the Army Math Research Center working under a contract that the University of Wisconsin had won from the Defense Department in competition with many other universities. Army

Math was suspected of research and development of chemical warfare being used in Vietnam. Our campus could be housing the same people who produced the napalm that descended on thousands of innocent villagers, burning and maiming in a fiery horror. Student groups picketed, leafleted, and performed guerrilla theater day after day to raise consciousness about the university's contract with the military. I was a dedicated protester by this time, becoming more and more horrified at the atrocities being committed against the Vietnamese, especially the use of napalm. The meaningless death of the US soldiers whom I considered both victims and agents of imperialism haunted me day and night. Thinking that this might be the direct result of a University of Wisconsin physicist's collaboration with the US Army tormented me even more.

By the end of the second semester my life had become one continuous protest from dawn till dusk, marching behind Vietnamese flags, anarchist red and black banners, and a multitude of organizational signs. "Ho, Ho, Ho Chi Minh, The NLF is Gonna Win," we cried. Many demonstrated stoned, but I got high on my friends, my own convictions and adrenaline. Night after night I fell asleep exhausted from running from Bascom Hill or Library Mall down State Street to the capitol building, choking from tear gas the cops used to break up the crowds of thousands. Pandemonium followed each police attack, making it necessary to function in affinity groups of four to five people for personal safety and to avoid being arrested by plainclothes cops.

Covering our faces with bandannas, we escaped wherever we could from the toxic gas, into bars or sliding onto icy Lake Mendota, all the while chanting, singing, stomping, clapping. Groups with names like "The Motherfuckers" and "The Stone Throwers" dodged police on their way to attack ROTC, the Land Tenure Center, AMRC and other scientific/military targets identified in leaflets distributed by organizers. As the demonstrations grew larger and larger, and the US government continued the bombings and raids in Vietnam, our tactics became more violent. The inhumanity of the death and destruction in Vietnam so gripped me that watching my fellow students smash windows on and off campus didn't bother me. What was a window? I had come to believe that this war had to be stopped at all costs including the demolition of public and private property. Nothing else mattered. I had become a student of the revolution.

There was a sexual element to the ferment too. The male heavies in SDS appeared almost like angry gods, frightening but attractive, and the women close to them intimidating. At SDS meetings, I was almost awestruck by how articulate and intelligent each speaker sounded, but never ventured a word myself. Meetings were run by men, and only the most aggressive women or those sleeping with the most powerful men were permitted control. So I settled for Jerry, a poetic,

Jewish leftist with black curly hair, who sympathized but kept his distance from the heated core. A friend introduced us and immediately I wanted his calm protection. His off-campus apartment and gentle love gave me my first caring relationship with a man. Not to mention, losing my virginity on his living room floor—a huge bonus.

Being a hippie and being a radical held no contradictions for me. A wild acid-taking, music-loving, group of political young men who lived communally on one whole floor of a dormitory became my closest friends. I moved across campus to be roommates with some women who were friendly with these men. Through them, we had access to all the experimental drugs circulating on campus, and soon I had to decide whether to try LSD.

Scary LSD stories frightened me, but when my roommate, Regina, a good student whom I respected "dropped" and lived, I did too. Turning on, yes, tuning in, yes, but dropping out for me meant becoming an active revolutionary. Mind expansion and politics went together. In order to believe we could confront the power structure we needed to suspend our own limiting beliefs. Taking pure psychedelics forced me to reach deeper into my imagination and to create a reality worth living for. High, I watched the Madison state capitol dome vibrate in the heavens, trees oscillate over sidewalks, age lines on the stump of a tree squiggle and breathe, sticks turn into snakes, all of life reveal itself down to its component parts under the giant microscope of LSD.

Though I'd thrown myself into the movement with the fervor of a new initiate ("Right Arm!"), I'd gathered some perspective on what I was doing. Here is a letter I wrote to a childhood friend after my freshman year:

August 1969

Dear David:

… My first year at the University of Wisconsin was really a mind-blowing experience. I really fell for the radical rhetoric and felt at times that life wasn't worth living unless I was involved with the movement. I didn't miss one SDS meeting, and attended every rally …

I figured out that many radicals are really disturbed idealists seeking refuge from reality on college campuses. They spend all their time writing ON STRIKE SHUT IT DOWN on cement walls or throwing bricks and smashing windows. A martyr complex wanting to get busted. I know how fucked up things are, but parading around forever on a campus won't change much. Maybe we should work within the system, just a tiny bit. Maybe?

... I'd been smoking grass all year then graduated to acid, mes-caline etc. Drugs are so big in Madison, but I guess now there isn't a college anywhere that is completely straight. Just wish freaks would use them a little more cautiously. Popping any capsule for kicks is insane! My acid trip was unbelievable ... It was another dimension, another reality. Thoughts rushed through my brain ... truly mind expanding. although I think they weren't as profound as I imagined at the time ...

Well, I'm living on Bassett perpendicular to Mifflin. The news-papers call it the "hippie ghetto." Yeah it's communal living, but at times feels like a permanent sex orgy. It's all right to sleep around if that's what you want, but all it takes is one kid with VD and wow ... bad scene.

Sometimes, David, I really want to believe in the revolution and I do, but at other times I laugh at myself for being so naive. Then again, which revolution? Black, radical, drug, gay? Tell me David!

Love, Kendall

In my sophomore year my interests in history and sociology converged as I sought out leftist professors and sat with hundreds of other students absorbing the lessons of prior revolutions and radical social theory. Harvey Goldberg was the best. A strange, brilliant, almost deranged looking man with messy hair, blinking eyes, and a hooked nose, Goldberg was also a story teller and dramatist who could keep a lecture hall of almost 1,000 students perfectly quiet. Professor Goldberg collapsed time, catapulting our minds back to the lives of Rosa Luxembourg, Kropotkin and Bakunin, Lenin, Trotsky, anarchists, socialists, communists, and social democrats, then fast-forwarding us into the cyclone of the current American drama playing on the campus and streets of Madison. It was like being sucked through a worm hole into another time-space dimension, a dimension in which we were present on the battlefields of Cuba and Che Guevara, Latin America and Regis Debray, Southeast Asia and Ho Chi Minh, China and Mao Zedong. American blacks, women, workers, homosexuals linked America the world and its oppressed peoples.

"Revolution is the way to lasting peace," I recall Goldberg saying, one hand on his forehead, the other waving his thick black glasses over our heads at the end of the lecture.

My fellow students and I considered Communism. Were they achieving that dream in Russia? Where was utopia? Certainly not here in Amerika. Not in Europe, based on what I knew about European protest movements and the eight million worker-student uprising in Paris against the system, led by French university leader "Danny the Red." Thus continued my endless search for truth, among Marxist study groups, guerrilla theater troops, student co-ops, women's consciousness raising groups, weekend rock festivals, and spontaneous travels to the West coast.

Anyone who did not believe that violent revolution and bloodshed were better than living under a corrupt social system was an idiot. Becoming a revolutionary was my only goal; the idea of becoming a professor or violinist laughable. I saw myself armed in the jungle, fighting or perhaps dying in the mountains of South America before adulthood. Money was a bourgeois evil, so even my parents were part of the enemy, and might have to die in the class struggle on behalf of the proletariat.

By now, my gentle Jewish poet had transferred to a more subdued atmosphere at Reed College and I was dating Alan, a twenty-six-year old graduate student who took me to Chicago the same October weekend the Weathermen crazies attacked downtown. The Weathermen were a group of students driven by magical fury who had given up on the white working class as an agent of revolution. They were going to do it themselves. Driving around in his VW bug we, viewed the aftermath of the Four Days of Rage. Two or three hundred students and ex-students equipped with chains, pipes and clubs had trashed cars and windows, and smashed into police lines.

The broken glass, boarded up windows and property damage reminded me of the newspaper photographs of the 1965 Watts race riots. Shaken by the destruction, I asked, "Do they use clubs and shields to fight the pigs like the Japanese students do?"

"Yeah, man," Alan grinned. "Three hundred of them did this shit. And they have guns and explosives too." His black eyes darkened. "And fuckin Mayor Daley said, shoot the looters to kill." I nodded quietly, alarmed by the rampage.

Back in Madison, I attended a meeting with a Weatherman boyfriend. Though I professed a belief in violence, the pillage of downtown Chicago was all too real. Off the pigs? No. I was not prepared to use the weapons or tactics of violent revolutionaries. The broken windows of Chicago had made it real. *Too real.*

The War Comes Home

In my sophomore year, I moved off campus to live with some women friends on Basset Street near the heart of the counterculture-student-hippie ghetto on Mifflin Street, better known as Miffland. Our area's city council representative was a declared socialist, and Tom Hayden also proclaimed Miffland one of America's seven liberated zones, a region of freedom. The revolution had its own cuisine; we shopped at the new Food Co-op, where I bought brown rice and ate delicious oatmeal-raisin "guerrilla cookies."

Free love bloomed, and everyone could share a bed with a different person every night. Since crabs and VD (still curable with a shot of penicillin) were the worst consequences of this pre-AIDS lifestyle, non-monogamy became an attractive option, a way for me to avoid a committed relationship and eventually experiment with bisexuality.

In the spring of 1969, Miffland was denied a block party permit by the conservative mayor, William Dyke, or Bull Dyke, as the male movement heavies called him. Block parties were held every spring in different neighborhoods, but the mayor refused to grant us a permit. Defiant and angry, we held the Miffland block party anyway. Anticipating a confrontation of some kind, organizers plastered posters all over Madison, bands were brought in, and we all prepared to "Bring the War Home," literally a block from my doorstep.

On a brilliant green, spring day, hundreds gathered on the corner of Mifflin and Basset Streets to celebrate youth and flower power, an affirmation of our own culture of peace, music, and dance. All was well for the first few hours, and then the police marched in with a pepper fogger. This new piece of equipment was capable of shooting tear gas the distance of a city block. The city fathers were out to crush and destroy all that we stood for, whether in Vietnam, the black ghettos, or on Mifflin Street, so I began dancing to the Rolling Stones "Street Fighting Man" blasting from a porch stereo. In front of me, a pink and white paper-mache pig's head waving wildly on a stick. *Whomp!* When the tear gas exploded, my eyes burned red, first with blood, then with tears. Nearby friends vanished into the thick smog now enveloping our neighborhood. Screaming and choking, I lowered myself to street level coming face to face with a young man bleeding from his head. He was being attacked by a policeman.

"Oh my God, it's the Gestapo! They're killing us," I screamed and reached to help him. But I slipped sideways into the gutter as the cop's club swung up and down. "Run," the boy grunted, "before they get you too." So I ran in the direction of the university.

By the end of the afternoon, a new battle line had been drawn, and Amerika was no longer my country. I'd sneaked home from campus. Back on my front porch, I saw flames in front of the food coop and heard Jimi Hendrix's anguished version of the "Star Spangled Banner" playing sadly over the trees in blossom. Huddled together, my friends and I cried. We cried at the hatred and horror that we had thought our flower power would heal. The Age of Aquarius was really a bad moon rising, as the Credence Clearwater Revival band had predicted. A little later I wrote an anti-anthem:

> *Amerika, Amerika where are your specious skies?*
> *But clouded with pollution, tarnished black with lies*
> *Purple majesty and amber grain waves*
> *Created by workers, created by slaves*
> *Broad stripes and bright stars fly low on the mast....*

Kendall 1969, 19 years old

In Miffland, the war came home more than once. This was about force and economics. A second near-blood-bath was the battle between the C.C. Riders biker gang and rent strikers who were protesting substandard housing. Recruited by a slumlord, the motorcycle thugs confronted young students who called themselves the Madison Tenants Union and had occupied several houses on one block of Mifflin Street. I did not know that a group of Mifflander men had stockpiled guns in preparation. Early one morning, the C.C. Riders showed up in the neighborhood and were met by hundreds of young people waving North Vietnamese flags, shotguns, and garden tools. I heard the shouting and ran joyfully to join the throng, completely unaware that my comrades in the houses were prepared to shoot if necessary. The bikers stared in disbelief, then sped away to the sound of our cheers.

In the fall of 1969, I went to Washington, DC. Thousands of antiwar protesters assembled with bandannas over our faces, while huge helicopters swept over our heads. Gradually the smell of tear-gas filled the air, and the police began sweeping the streets arresting everyone in sight. An army tank rolled toward the intersection. *Pop! Pop!* Canisters blew up in circles in front of the Justice Department. I knew that hundreds of students and leftists had already been arrested, and thousands had camped out at the Washington Monument, in the largest national mobilization then seen against the war. My anger at the US government was at an all-time high, my studies at an all time low.

Antiwar violence was now an everyday occurrence in Madison. In May 1970, Nixon invaded Cambodia, resuming the bombing of North Vietnam. In response, students all over the country ransacked and burned ROTC buildings and stepped up a wave of demonstrations, boycotts, and strikes. When I learned that the National Guard had killed four students at Kent State and two at Jackson State I became convinced that it was time to "smash Army Math" at any cost. One afternoon, 2,800 of us battled 250 local and county Madison police knowing we might be shot or killed. I imagined my body returning to my mother and father wrapped in a Viet Cong flag. Part of me envied the dead as I hurled myself onto the barricades.

As Amerika deteriorated, I hoped my Garden of Eden might exist in Cuba. The Venceremos Brigade in Madison had started recruiting and sending students sympathetic to the Cuban revolution to cut sugar cane and see socialism first hand. I began reading about the history of pre-Revolutionary Cuba, a country strangling under US economic control. Filled with facts and images of poverty, crime, and illiteracy, I eagerly listened to details about the current conditions from wide-eyed, young North American *brigadistas* with enthusiastic stories of the Cubans' support for their new government.

Once a vacation land for tourists, gamblers, and prostitutes. it now sounded like the vanguard of world revolution, with free medical care, free universities, no starvation, no commercial billboards, and the highest literacy rate in Latin America. Batista was the evil dictator, not Fidel Castro. This hairy, cigar-smoking man had been portrayed as our dreaded enemy by both the government and the media, but Castro became a hero of third world liberation. Che Guevara's image now hung on every radical's wall, looking bold and handsome, a symbol of freedom for our sisters and brothers suffering under US imperialism.

When I attended the International Youth Festival in Cuba nine years later, in 1978, social conditions appeared so superior, I became convinced that the government had created a new society and a new socialist human being. The artistic billboards promoted public health, and the people I saw and spoke with looked healthy and happy. Almost twenty years later, Che became my son's middle name. Thirty years later, the CIA confessed to having murdered and buried our hero under an airport runway in Bolivia.

Love is a Gun

By the end of my sophomore year in 1970, I saw no point in the university as an institution, with its thousands of students and distant, all male teaching hierarchy. My only goal was to organize "The People" to overthrow capitalism. Confusion about myself as a woman emerged and deepened as I participated in women's meetings, analyzing sexism and its pervasive and insidious role in society, the university, and the movement. As an activist I had to look at my own oppression, a long, painful process that lasted well into my forties. Relationships with men and lovers got angrier and more distant as I found myself deeper in the women's movement. I gravitated toward socialist-feminist theory and a collective of women, most of whom were graduating and looking for a way to help liberate women from chauvinist husbands and boyfriends. It was imperative we participate as equals in the future party and new society. Romantic love was now impossible. All women were members of a "Fourth World" that limited their personal and economic freedom. Robin Morgan's book, *Sisterhood Is Powerful*, and our battle cry "Free Our Sisters, Free Ourselves" united young women around the country.

Once, during a rare moment while I was cleaning my apartment, my then-boyfriend Alan walked in with a smile on his face. "Hi, Kendall," he grinned cheerfully. Without looking up, I furiously yanked the vacuum cleaner across the tattered rug rattling dust in his face.

"Men are the enemy, Alan! Women have been exploited for centuries by you guys," I roared at him over the noisy machine.

"Uhh, would you like to go for a walk or for a sandwich?" he calmly asked.

"No, Alan. You exploited me! You're no better than the rest! It's over!" I continued without looking up, concentrating on the floor.

"You mean that's it?" He seemed shaken.

"Yes. I don't want to see you anymore. Go struggle with your sexism." I shot visual darts at him over the vacuum handle.

"OK, Kendall." He turned slowly and closed the front door. I never saw him again. He had once told me he'd never touched anyone as beautiful as me. But at that moment, being a sister in the struggle was all that mattered.

A splinter group from the Weathermen was recruiting members from Madison to form political collectives in Milwaukee and Racine to work in factories with the industrial proletariat, as defined in Marxist-Leninist theory. I remember visiting the homes of these young radicals, now working as members of trade unions, and publishing radical grassroots newspapers. Many were red diaper babies, children of American Communist party members (CPUSA), who believed they were picking up where the party had failed after the Stalin era and its descent into revisionism.

Awestruck by their courage and integrity, I told myself "This is the next step, Kendall." But I noticed that the women were, again, in fairly serious monogamous relationships. Part of me was jealous and wanted to be comfortable and cozy with a man and a political party that had the right answers, but I also questioned their labeling of feminism and homosexuality as "bourgeois decadency." I had plenty of anger to go around, as I wrote to my parents in 1970:

Dear Mom and Dad:

I have become one of the people you warned me about. The military industrial complex—the Bank of America, Standard Oil, IBM, Mobil now hold 95% of the world's wealth and profit from the rape of the Third World by Nixon and the warmongers. Here in Wisconsin, monkeys in the zoo are allotted 58 cents per meal and welfare mothers are expected to live on 16 cents per meal!!!! The only solution is revolution. Armed revolution.Unfortunately, since you are members of the middle class and the silent majority, our People's Army will have to fight anyone who stands in our way. This means I could be face to face with you and have no choice but to shoot. I will not be coming home this summer.

Kendall,

DARE TO STRUGGLE, DARE TO WIN!

It was unthinkable to go home in the summer of 1970 to bourgeois middle-class Indiana, so I stayed in Madison. And that summer, my political awareness found a comfortable alignment with my personal beliefs as an emergent feminist. Living in Miffland, I joined a political guerrilla theater troop of about ten students that performed for people in Madison and nearby towns. Our bold, adventurous surprise appearances in shopping malls, parks and beaches attracted crowds with drums and music. With simple props and ten minute skits we stimulated heated conversations about racism, sexism, and imperialism. Our women's liberation skit featured a female character who became a wind-up mechanical puppet controlled by her boyfriend. The anti-imperialist skit featured Uncle Sam as an evil character who propped up dictatorships in South America.

We drove all over in a bumpy VW van with no air conditioning, and for three months I felt calm, focused, creative, and relaxed with my family of political friends. In this setting, women were not only respected, but were in the leader-ship. Men were sensitive and occasional lovers.

Enchanted by the success of our collective creativity, by midsummer I had decided to drop out of college, leave Madison with a women's collective, and stop shaving my legs, a radical act in 1970. I was most comfortable expressing myself in an all-female setting, where I felt valued for who I was, not overrun, dominated, or awed by arrogant male political heavies. They no longer dazzled me and their sexism pushed me to a political belief that women needed to live and work separately from men. I believed I had no positive female role models. The only women I admired or respected were revolutionaries. Who could I turn to other than my sisters in struggle? My parents were relieved to hear I was doing theatre, but dropping out was the end of the world. Worse than wearing the same old blue jeans for four years.

Six of us, all under the age of 24, decided to form a collective to organize working class women *to take control of their lives.* A clear, easy goal. Four had graduated from the university and two of us were dropping out. We divided into three groups, each picking a different part of the United States to visit and observe the political/social scene. We agreed to return to Madison later in the fall with a report from each group, and determine where to sink new roots and build a working class women's movement. I grabbed Miriam, a tough minded, spunky graduate, and we decided to go West.

To celebrate my decision I went to a local Woodstock. A county farmer sympathetic to the student movement offered his land for a rock festival that drew hundreds of young people, and our guerrilla theater troupe intended to perform. But huge amounts of LSD were dumped into a bottle of wine circulating through the crowd, creating one collective acid trip that included the police. Rows of people stood facing the music while I danced ecstatically, weaving in and out, inviting them to follow.

It was here that I freaked out and charged past the security guards to the stage. I sat on a piano bench transfixed by the musician's long black fingers, then jumped to the ground and ran into the woods, screaming, sliding down slope into a streambed. Floating away, I felt joyous at leaving this world. Covered in soft, oozing mud becoming weaker and weaker I almost lost consciousness—until I got hungry. Thank God for survival instincts! I needed food. You can't live on your own in the woods a voice told me. I screamed.

"Help, won't somebody help me?" And the tribe heard. A few tripped out kids carried me up the slope to a police car. Can you believe they put me in the enemy's hands. The pigs! Or as the Beatles called them, the blue meanies. Especially when I was out of body!

"Take her to a hospital," some mature, hairy, naked freak yelled. But the cop was so stoned, he drove his squad car off the road into the forest.

At this point, my consciousness quit hovering and reentered my body, and I jumped out of the car. As I ran through trees toward the sound of the music, I stopped to lean on a tree trunk. Spontaneously the sound *OM* welled up in my throat and out of my mouth. I had never heard or read about this word, about its use as a meditative chant by wisdom traditions that believe it to be the sound of the primordial universe. But I uttered it, mystically and magically, once, twice, and again. OM, OM, OM.

Then I turned to look behind me, and there stood a boy with a copy of *The Little Prince* by Antoine de Saint-Exupery. He looked into my eyes, handed me the book, and while wrapping a blanket over my shivering body said, "*You* are my little prince." Momentarily I felt protected, back on earth, ready to re-enter, leaving the mystical search for my lost vision for another time. Like until I was fifty.

"Thank you," I whispered, grateful for his tender contact. Moments later he disappeared.

It had been the happiest summer of my life. Then on August 24, 1970 and anonymous phone call came in the middle of the night to Madison police headquarters.

> *Listen Pigs, and listen good. There is a bomb that is going off in Army Math in five minutes. Clear the building. Warn the hospital. This is no bullshit man.*

And then the bomb blast shattered the window over my head.

The bombing of the Army Math Research Center split my memory of college into before and after, forever. Before the explosion of 1,700 pounds of nitrogen fertilizer soaked with about 100 gallons of fuel oil, and after. It reverberated around the country, giving Nixon's White House, J. Edgar Hoover's FBI, and John Mitchell's Justice Department the excuse to wage all-out war against the Left. An innocent physicist had been killed.

A week later our guerrilla theater troop spoke on the student union terrace. Our topic was the bombing and Robert Fassnacht's death.

"No, he didn't deserve to die. There was a phone call to the cops. It was their fault for not evacuating him," my friends and I told stone-faced physicists sitting on the union terrace. "It was an accident," we pleaded, passing around a leaflet explaining that Army Math had been an antiwar target for several years.

"SsssssssssSSSSSSSSSSSSSSS."

The hisses rose, as we quietly retreated. For the first time in my life I felt myself the object of complete contempt. Radicals were now completely ostracized. My summer was transformed into another tortuous debate within myself about violence, war, and death, one that drove me west, looking for meaning, hope and the path to my dream of peace.

Search for the Working Class

My women's collective sister, Miriam, and I hitchhiked across the country with strangers, mostly men who were fascinated to meet real live hippie chicks and to listen in what must have been fascination and disbelief as we talked to them with the revolutionary fever of the guerrilla theater troop.

Each driver who motioned us into the car became a potential convert to our cause, a prisoner trapped in his own vehicle with two socialist women. Some might have been thinking about free love, but Miriam and I were all politics. We left Madison in the fall, where it was still warm enough to stand on the corner with our thumbs out, and headed straight into the freezing winter of South Dakota. To this day I am thankful for those honest, hardworking truck drivers who sheltered us from the cold, dangerous highways, driving us hundreds of miles, letting us sleep in and under their trucks, sometimes buying us food and listening to our story. Rarely did they proposition us; they never harmed us but simply wanted company on their lonely long distance drives. We didn't think that two young women on the road needed protection. We believed we were invincible because we were revolutionary and righteous.

As we approached Berkeley, my heart thumped wildly. I knew California was a landscape for seekers, a mixture of head shops, crash pads, be-ins, demonstrations, concerts, free clinics, and street theater, a refuge for alienated hippies, yippies, radicals, draft dodgers, anyone wanting to break with tradition or live on the fringes. My kind of town. We spent the next few weeks immersed in the counterculture, enjoying each other's company and reveling in a new world of bizarre freaks from all over the country. I had a little money from my parents and from a job in the student union cafeteria, but counted primarily on free rides, free shelter in churches, parks or communes, and free food wherever I could find it. This 24-hour-a day street festival was home to the Diggers, Mario Savio and the Free Speech Movement, Huey Newton and the Black Panthers, Joan Baez, The San Francisco Mime Troupe, flower children, and Route 1, overlooking the most spectacular ocean cliffs in America. Particularly spectacular if the viewer was stoned. San Francisco won my heart, but Miriam felt overwhelmed.

Our next destinations were Eugene and Portland, Oregon, where we visited various political collectives. Since Portland had not yet been infiltrated by radical fringe groups, Miriam argued it would be an easier city to organize without the competition, so we persuaded the other collective members to move there.

In the midst of waterfalls, ocean, and mountains, the six of us hung out with each other and other local activists, traveled around Oregon, and participated in a May Day antiwar demonstration in solidarity with student protestors who shut down Washington DC for a whole day. I joined a rock band, began playing electric violin and composing music. I met a lesbian couple who lived in the same house with a heterosexual couple and learned they were just as normal.

Each day I woke up wondering how all the theory we learned in Madison applied to the real world. Slowly I experienced the sufferings of real life. I worked briefly in a nursing home, but was fired for handing out the local radical newspaper and inciting the patients. Then, Tracy, a sixteen-year-old runaway from California, moved into our living room. Next, our house was broken into and my violin was stolen. And then I was raped.

Three black men had picked me up hitchhiking to a bookstore. Completely naïve and flattered by their offer to smoke a little weed, I naively believed they were fellow militants. Before I realized what was happening, we arrived at a middle-class house in the Portland suburbs, with photographs of smiling white people on the mantle. After a few puffs on a joint, I expected a discussion to follow, as often happened with university men. Stunned when they asked me to remove my clothes and dance on the coffee table for them, my instinct told me to get out quick. For the last two years on campus, I had partied with men and never been treated like a sex object. I didn't even know sex was all they had in mind.

"I didn't come here to parade around in front of you," I said fiercely folding my hands.

"I believed exactly what you said. I came here to smoke and rap"

One of the men sitting close to me on the couch raised his eyebrows. "Well now, let's rap for awhile. What's your trip, baby? Alcohol, drugs, the revolution? Now, me, I'm an athlete. Football is my game."

"What do you think of the Black Panthers," I butted in.

"Well," he rolled his eyes. "I can dig them. Huey and Eldridge, they're doing a fine job with their breakfast program and all. What do you think?" He swung his right leg over my right thigh. I quickly lifted it back over his left leg. "I have some friends in Wisconsin who have a breakfast program like the Panthers. They've also started a bookstore and a newspaper."

The man leaned over and shoved his hand down the front of my tee shirt, squeezing my breast and pulling at my nipple.

"Stop it!" I felt like striking him hard and fast and bolting outside. Instead, I stood up, side stepped the man on the couch and calmly walked to the front door. A man in dark glasses clapped his hands. "Let's get this show on the road." Quickly I was overpowered and dragged upstairs. My heartbeat tripled. I knew they were going to kill me. I was raped three times, one after the other. Breathing rapidly, each man promised, "I'll give you the best you ever had it, baby," fantasizing a scream of ecstasy or at least a moan of pleasure from my lips. Realizing it was futile to resist, I prayed silently that passivity would save me from physical violence, but expected a punch, a knife, then, the trickle of blood over my ribcage. I felt like Mia Farrow in the *Exorcist*, clawed by the devil.

"Stop, stop, stop, it hurts," but the third man continued his harsh grind, pinning my head to the floor crushing my spine. Dazed, I dressed quickly as the three rapists joked, drank another beer and drove me back to town. In the middle of Portland I got out of the car, numb, feeling lucky to be alive, not knowing in what direction to run.

I didn't report the rapes because, illogically, I was afraid the rapists would retaliate. Passivity had saved my life once and maybe it would again. When I told the women I lived with and shared my story with a larger community of women, no one had clear advice. Since this was before rape crisis centers and counseling existed, it felt easier to try to forget it happened than to ask the male authorities for help. When men became the enemy, I'd thrown my birth control pills out with my razor blades. Pills had dangerous side effects anyway. Me pregnant? No way.

In 1971, violence against women was blamed on women's bad behavior. On the phone from Indiana, my mother expressed anger at me for getting into a car with strange men.

"Let me talk to Dad—Dad ... Dad, I've been raped." No comment ... Silence.

"Dad, are you there?" I heard a muffled cough.

I knew rape was a criminal offense, but our feminist communities' confusion coupled with my parents' lack of empathy or assistance left me unable to act. My hatred of these men did not translate to all men or all blacks, though for weeks I crossed the street every time I saw someone of the male gender approaching.

Twenty years later, I finally asked a therapist why I still feared being alone in empty houses and jumped when a cat walked behind my chair.

"Were you ever sexually abused? She watched my face closely.

"No, not that I remember ... well, there was that assault in Portland, but that's all," I shrugged, twirling my glasses, tapping my finger.

Shortly after my rape, I met with a contingent of Vietnamese women representatives from the National Liberation Front in Vancouver, Canada. I touched their hands and gave them flowers, trying to comprehend how these tiny, delicate people were considered our government's enemy. I had seen pictures of women guerrillas armed in the rice fields defending their children and homes. Knowing how much these women had suffered, made the violence of my rape seemed small in comparison. As tears streamed down my face, all I could feel was a tremendous sense of shame for Amerika. I could hardly believe their warmth and acceptance of us, as human beings first, and Americans second. When I later visited Cuba and Nicaragua, I experienced first hand how many people still reached out to embrace the people who came from a country considered an enemy.

Our Portland collective fell apart and with it our dream of organizing women *to take control of their lives.* Our experiment crashed the limits of theory and the generation gap finally caught up with us. Floundering and confused, we were all suffering from different versions of post-traumatic stress syndrome. Big ideas need money, a mission statement, structure, and the women leaders over thirty, red baited out of history during the McCarthy era. We needed Mother Jones, (a celebrated agitator and organizer) but she died in 1930. I watched my sisters whom I looked to for strength fall into depression and despair, leaving us with no focus, organization, or sense of direction.

My father had been sending me money, but I knew I had to make an individual decision. One of us went to nursing school and one went back to New York where she had grown up. Returning to the university looked like the only option for me. It felt like a major defeat. Was there no place in the world for me, or my beliefs? From the west coast, Madison looked like home in my frenzy to ground into some kind of reality that I knew and understood.

Once I decided to leave for Madison, I met Sarah, one of our collective members in San Francisco, who was planning a visit back home to Milwaukee. Much of our common philosophy had stemmed from the Yippies, who advocated ripping off the system whenever possible. In the Bay area, Sarah had managed to buy some stolen plane tickets for $10 a piece. It took no convincing to get me to travel by air rather than by thumb. We took on false names, feeling exhilarated as we boarded a plane for the Midwest. But we were discovered before takeoff. Perhaps we looked like victims—young, innocent, middle class girls—because our story of how we bought tickets from a stranger in Berkeley, got us off the hook with no charges. We were only disappointed that we had to hitchhike. Abby Hoffman's *Steal This Book* convinced us we deserved life for free. After all, the system was corrupt and we were working for the good of humanity.

Sarah went back to Portland. A week later I left with runaway Tracy, her German shepherd, and Ryan, my newest love, an irresistible college drop-out mechanic. He wanted to visit family and friends in New York. The three of us decided to pass through Salt Lake City, my Mormon birthplace. Granny Otelia Hale was taken by surprise when I called asking for shelter on my way back to Wisconsin. I don't think I had seen or spoken with her for years, but she didn't hesitate. Orphaned at twelve and raised by relatives, she had run away from Kansas to Oakley, Idaho, where she joined the Mormon Church. My adventure must have resonated with her spirit of escape.

"Of course you can stay here, Kendall," Granny said sweetly from her old black dial phone. "But tell me one thing. Why is the FBI looking for you?"

After we arrived, she was relieved to know that Ryan was a doctor's son. That seemed to make everything all right, despite the FBI telling her I was an Army Math bombing suspect. Other relatives, including my younger sister, received visits by agents. I found this humorous, (my uncle worked for the FBI) exhilarating (Wow, Kendall Hale, wanted by the FBI) and a teeny bit frightening, knowing that I was innocent of any connection to the bombing, but incredulous that the government had these resources and would waste them on a "little" person like myself. I didn't make the connection that my sudden disappearance from Madison might have looked suspicious.

"Granny", I said, "I didn't do it. Honest. But I was a protester."

She sat quietly, her sharp blue eyes focused on her arthritic gnarled hands quilting tiny stitches on an orange and green flower. She had sewn hundreds of quilts for all her children and grandchildren.

"Granny, do you remember when you told me all Hales are related? Granny Otelia and the Mormons loved genealogy.

"Yes, I do."

"Well then, I am a descendant of Nathan Hale, famous American revolutionary. The one who said, "I only regret I have but one life to give to my country."

Her thick, curly, white, head of hair lifted for one second. "Well then." Pause. "I believe you."

The next morning, Granny called one of her sons, who politely took us out to the highway with only one question.

"Are you sure this is what you want to do?" my uncle asked as we stuck out our thumbs like old pros. Nodding yes, we faced the Midwest, riding with the lonely or curious, never doubting our security. When Ryan decided to take a shorter route to New York, I choked back my fear and sorrow. I had hoped he had fallen in love with me. I needed to be strong for runaway Tracy now that I was the older responsible party. Waving good-by to Ryan as he split to the east, with a piece of my heart, I knew he was gone forever. But rides got easier without him though maybe a little riskier and much sadder.

Arriving safely in Madison, after nine months of searching for the working class, I failed to see that I had been in their care all along. At least the male half. Decades later I realized that while our society fought wars abroad, American truckers held us together delivering capitalist goods and sheltering young radicals who dreamed of leading them, the vanguard of the revolution, into a future insurrection. At this time of my life, irony escaped me.

From 1971-1973 the war and the movement were winding down. I spent my last two years of college recovering from the journey of the previous three years. So many of my friends had left or dropped out or transferred away that I returned to a void. I studied for the first time since high school, but it all felt empty. I am still amazed at how little was required of me as a history major, in terms of writing or analysis. Studying the past helped ground me, but offered no answers or methodology to evaluate the turmoil of the student uprising or the critical observations and questions confronting me. The most relevant study group was led by a graduate student who was reading all three volumes of Marx's *Das Kapital*.

Once my father's most respected political philosopher and now one of mine, Marx gave me answers I had not found in Portland. The Army Math bombing had eliminated and obliterated everything: the movement, my friends, actions in the streets. My new and closest companion, Frieda, became my roommate at Nottingham Co-op, an old fraternity converted into cooperative student housing where everyone shared cooking and cleaning jobs, and a spirit of togetherness. I continued to have affairs with various men, and finally one with a woman, which seemed perfectly natural after living in a lesbian-feminist community in Portland. But Frieda. Well, I needed Frieda's sharpness and her bag of tricks—astrology, tarot, yoga—sprinkled lightly with political theory because my life was as frayed as the end of my blue jeans. Marx or no Marx.

The most radical personal action I took during those two years was choosing to spend two nights in jail rather than pay a $25 fine when my puppy escaped from the co-op and trespassed in a park. Ironically, it was the only jail sentence I ever received. I marched in with a copy of *Das Kapital* and read for two days, occasionally exchanging conversation with a local hooker.

My next intellectual marriage was to Chairman Mao. In 1973, graduate students returning from China confirmed the new truth I had found reading William Hinton's *Fanshen.* I wrote a term paper about how Communism and the collective agricultural communes in the new China had liberated women, puzzled over Mao's quotations, and longed to join the Red Guard. To Serve the People. I can still see the poster of the rosy cheeked shipyard worker feeding my dreams of an egalitarian worker-run state. At that time no one knew about the brutality of the Cultural Revolution, about the thousands of intellectuals in forced labor and artists imprisoned and humiliated.

My graduation with a degree in history was anti-climatic. I was completely unprepared for a career and at sea about my future. With faith in the dialectical thinking of the Chinese, I threw coins with the *I Ching* (an ancient divination system) and decided to follow Frieda to New York City, hoping for friendship, support, and direction from her.

On the way East, I visited Indiana, much to my mother's relief. She called me her prodigal daughter, returning from sin and misguidance. I welcomed her love and appreciation, but knew that the barriers had not been overcome. We quickly fell into our old fights and patterns of blame and disrespect.

"But what will you do in New York City? And who is Frieda? Shouldn't you think about graduate school?" She looked despairingly at my five year old jeans. My only pair.

"I'll probably work for Liberation News Service, Mom. Don't worry, Frieda's a New Yorker. She has an apartment for us and everything."

"Well, it looks like everything and nothing to me, Kendall."

I grabbed an old photograph off the mantle, one that had intrigued me only because Mom treasured it so. It was my great grandmother Hannah Hall Jacobsen, with her three children, one of them my mother's mother, Eunice, standing in their 19th century clothing each holding a musical instrument.

"Mom, Hannah didn't listen to her mother. No, she ran away from Sweden—from wealth and status to follow her dream across the ocean. To be a Mormon!" I placed the black and white picture before her on the table. "God, Mom. And what about Annie Smith Miles? The grandmother who lived through the last Indian war in Utah. You're so proud of them!

Before she could answer, I raced to the back bedroom, changed outfits and sprinted angrily out the front door in shorts and jogging shoes.

Mom was still looking for a daughter who wanted marriage and a safe, respectable, professional career. I was still looking for the next radical step. Without a guerilla war to fight for, living my life for the revolution was, well, to be blunt, mind boggling. The war in Vietnam was over, yet I burned with the fever of an anti-war protester without a cause. Who was my enemy now?

A few days later I hitchhiked to New York City with a couple of young guys from Purdue University. The rides went smoothly until just outside Manhattan when the driver suddenly pulled a gun on Mike, with whom he was engaged in friendly conversation.

"I know you're going to rob me. Get out," he ordered waving a pistol at him. From the back, I could see the weapon through the bucket seats. So he is the new enemy? What a ridiculous way to die, I thought, moments before he dumped the three of us on the side of the highway.

WE NEED A UNION HERE

Cambridge, Massachusetts, 1973

"She awes and intimidated everybody," my housemate, Lauren, told me. The "she" was Shanna, six feet tall with huge turquoise eyes, the 26 year old revolutionary, a Marxist-Leninist goddess. She taught us about democratic centralism, a form of government proposed by the Russian political theorist, Lenin. Her goal was to transform us into a modern communist cadre while working on our master's theses at Cambridge-Goddard, a radical experimental graduate program run by Goddard College. It was 1973.

Two mornings a week we gathered in Central Square in Shanna's shared living space, part of a big Victorian house rented by students. With a poster of Lenin above her head in a living room littered with coffee cups and muffin wrappers, Shanna told us: "Lenin won the Russian revolution with a party of steeled, communist cadre of iron discipline. Only a party which has mastered Marxist-Leninist theory can confidently advance and lead the working class forward." On her night shift job at Cambion, a local sweatshop electronics plant a couple of miles outside Harvard Square, Shanna was organizing a union drive for higher pay and better working conditions. One by one she recruited our entire class into the factory. We would work side by side with our laboring sisters and brothers. We would be the vanguard, bringing political theory to the uninformed proletariat. And once enlightened, they would join the party and achieve collective empowerment. Organizing unions was the first step.

So for three months I faced a wall while I did piece work on a plastic molding machine. For $2.30/hour. During one of the two fifteen-minute breaks I got during an eight-hour shift, I approached a woman in my department I considered friendly. Middle aged and heavily made up, she sat silently in the break room, smoking. "We need a union here, don't you think?" I said. Her face looked greenish under the fluorescent light as she exhaled cigarette smoke, blinked, pursed her lips, then nodded. The smoke hung like a curtain between us in the stale air. The next day I was fired.

Rescuing Unitrod

Every day I saw Angie's red beehive hairdo and her bloodshot eyes across the top of the microscope in one of the workspaces we shared. Three months after my dismissal from Cambion I had gotten myself hired at Unitrod, another non-unionized, largely female electronics sweatshop in Watertown. More cautious this time, I cultivated a friendship with Angie for months. She didn't seem likely to squeal. Thankful to be on a rotation outside the acid room, a workspace with open vats of smelly chemicals, I looked forward to the clean air. I slid a chip out from under my microscope and into the last slot of a glass dish ready for heat treatment in the oven. I looked over my shoulder to make sure the engineer was gone.

"Angie, can you hear me? I whispered. "We need a union here. There are women working in the acid room breathing toxic fumes. You have terrible headaches. We're being poisoned."

"Kendall, the people here aren't union type people. They're too scared," she whispered back. "Last time it happened they fired four girls, and that shut everybody right up. You just find yourself a better job, honey, cause I'm willing to bet this place won't never change."

Angie put every ounce of herself into the company. She had sat at a microscope for twenty years, inspecting silicon slices. She still made minimum wage. Hour after hour she sat, never getting up except to visit the bathroom or for the twice-a-day coffee breaks. Married young, Angie had three children before her twenty-fifth birthday and took a job at Unitrod to supplement her husband's wages.

"I thought it was temporary", she sighed standing up to stretch her neck, rotating her shoulders. "Ben was out of work with a back injury so I took a job. He got used to me working and we liked the extra money. At first, I didn't have to work, but nowadays, there's no choice. You can't live on one income." Wiping the sweat from her forehead with a wet hand towel, she wrapped the towel around her neck and sat down again. "My kids are grown up now, so I'd just sit home and eat all day anyway." And with that, she bent to her microscope. Subject closed.

Ola, my favorite co-worker, was a tough, black militant woman with a diamond circled watch hanging on her bosom who pounded her fists at the supervisor whenever he left our station. Ola spoke often of shooting at her husbands' head and cursing the motherfuckin' son of a bitch bigot next door.

"The shock treatments, they's keep me goin', but the pills I just flush 'em down the toilet. Really, Kendall, what's better 'bout being here than bein' in jail? Jesus!" She paused, delicately placing another silicone slice on the baking tray. "I guess I wouldn't see my kids as much behind bars."

I joked, "You'd miss your own home cooking, Ola. Don't you worry, before long we'll have rock and roll and classical music over the sound system, instead of this musak shit. High pay … five weeks vacation."

She snorted a loud, "Pppuhhhh! You'd better shut up baby, before they come give you some electric shock!"

When I arrived at Unitrod, there was already a union drive in its early stages. The Revolutionary Communist Party (RCP) cadre (formed during the student movement) were very self confident, arrogant, but totally inexperienced, much like myself except that being fired from Cambion had put a check on some of my more urgent, adventurous behaviors. The United Electrical Workers (UE) had assigned Mike, a young organizer who was all hot and fired up to unionize, and had the experience to do the job, or so he said. We approached each other cautiously, suspiciously. When he discovered that I was an independent Marxist Leninist, he began pumping me for information about the RCP strategy, meetings, or any leads he could pick up on. I suspected he was a member of the Communist Party, (CPUSA) (the CP founded the United Electrical Workers Union) and I limited my political discussions with him as we drove back and forth from my house in Cambridge to bars and restaurants in Watertown where we met with workers from the plant sympathetic to the union. Dressed like a salesman with chinos and well shined loafers and slicked backed hair, Mike gave condescending lectures about how crazy the student movement and the Progressive Labor Party (PL) had been, which pissed me off. "Kendall," he said wrinkling his well trimmed mustache, "All those hippie anti-war protesters were on drugs. And PL wasn't much better."

I distrusted Mike for several reasons, his taste in clothing aside. My knowledge of the Communist Party was not extensive, but I knew their track record on women and gays was bad. The old guard hadn't notice our cultural revolution. Even worse was their flunkeyism to the Soviet Union. Not only was the USSR a true socialist country in their minds, but a model for all societies. They thought everything had progressed steadily after the 1917 Revolution, Stalin and all. The means justify the end. Soviet workers had real control over production, discrimination and inequality had disappeared, and the Communist Party was a democratic centralist organization with real democracy representing the peoples' true interests! What more could a revolutionary ask for? There was nothing to dispute, so they thought.

Dropping me off one evening Mike leaned toward me and intoned, "There is only one way to organize a union." He held up the United Electrical handbook. "You follow this formula, Unitrode will get organized." He thrust the dog-eared paperback at me. "Two thirds of the workers must sign union cards before we go open. Otherwise the company will start a campaign of attack and destroy us."

Climbing out of the front seat of Mike's Toyota with the book, I felt discouraged about the prospect of a successful drive at Unitrod. The blend of Mike's dogmatism and the RCP's ultra leftism, peppered with large doses of egotism looked like a recipe for an atomic bomb.

The party building movement and all of our sessions with Shanna had taught me that good organizers and true communists sought out open-minded workers with whom to discuss non-economic issues, such as racism. First, find common ground and then find common cause. When my boss, an incompetent, sleepy guy was gone, I ventured away from my work station, amazed to find real, live people on the lower level of the factory performing the very first steps of the operation I performed.

"Management does a good job keeping us isolated from each other," I said out loud sneaking back upstairs, "so we won't know what we are producing or how it is produced." Flabbergasted, I remembered this was exactly what Karl Marx said in Das Kapital! (Capital) This is how corporations get away with producing toxins, pollutants and weapons. Most workers never see the assembled product! I froze. What am I making?

Every day for the next week, I disappeared downstairs on my break scanning the room for someone who looked 'advanced' enough to be fertile ground for some political bonding. I decided to approach the very dark African looking man everyone else ignored. No managers around. No time like the present.

"My name is Kendall. Can I sit down?"

Startled he looked up from his work, "Yes."

"What do you do? I mean other than this?"

"I am a student at Boston University." When I learned that he was from Nigeria and a political science major I knew he was a good pick. I visited him every day after that to escape the noise and the constant surveillance of my boss. It was 1973 and school busing was a very hot issue in Boston. Everyone had strong feelings, there had already been riots in the city and tensions ran high. The factory was no exception. It was much easier to talk with a Nigerian who wanted to hear about my views, than my racist co-workers upstairs.

One afternoon I whispered loudly to emphasize my point, "I support busing for one reason. How else are we going to achieve equality of the races? Blacks have the worst schools in the city." A wet sweeping sound made me turn my head. It was a white worker mopping down the floor behind my chair and I could see I had his full attention.

His face flamed red under his navy Unitrod cap. The name embroidered on his work shirt said *Gerald*. "Them coloreds are running everything now. They have the first choice in jobs and they've taken over the school system!" Glaring at us, he pushed the gritty mop angrily around our shoes. Jerking my feet up and groping for an answer, I pointed to the Rainbow Coalition button on my tee shirt, as he stalked past us down the aisle, continuing to assault the floor with angry jabs of the mop. Like most of the working class in Boston, Gerald's grievances had a black face. Watching Gerald's stiff back as he attacked a defenseless work table with his mop, I thought about another Marxist-Leninist meeting the week before when I watched cadre struggling to understand why minorities were not joining their organization. Using *criticism-self criticism*, a method for correcting individual mistakes used by Mao Tse-Tung and the Red Guard they hoped to 'root out' their own racism. "I overlooked a black worker standing near the coffee machine, and spoke directly to the white worker instead," said George. "I was too scared to challenge a white worker who did not support affirmative action," admitted another.

I knew all white people were prejudiced by our racist culture, but confession in a large crowd felt punishing. To avoid guilt of any kind, I called out to the mopper, "We must all challenge our racism."

Jab. Jab. Slosh. The mop continued to move. All I got was an unintelligible snarl from Gerald. Then mercifully, with a final crash of the mop bucket, he left.

The Nigerian took a deep breath, blinking his large deep eyes. "This is your union?" he asked.

Meanwhile, my co-workers punched their time cards, worked their tedious, repetitive eight hours, some aware of the union drive but most numb to their feelings, waiting for 3:30pm when their time was their own. Mike's union card-signing tactic went smoothly for a few months, despite the RCP's constant griping about his conservative approach. At some point, the numbers stopped increasing. Candy, an eager RCP member working at Unitrod, kept stressing that something else had to be done.

"Kendall, our members think Mike's got to be won over to our point of view. There has to be a leaflet put out soon, or we'll lose the people we have. None of the departments know what's going on outside their own area. We need a vehicle for better communication. A leaflet and a newsletter are the only vehicles that can build momentum to expand the drive," Candy said adamantly. I delivered the message to Mike and he opposed it, but events overtook him.

One afternoon, I walked to the parking lot, fuzzy headed from breathing fumes in the acid room all day, thinking about my poisoned co-workers. When I asked the four older women, "How can you stand the smell in here," they answered, "What smell?" Then I knew their brain cells had been permanently altered.

"Kendall," Candy rushed toward me waving an RCP leaflet. "Read this, we're almost ready to go." she hissed through her proletarian lipstick. RCP cadre tried to look as much like the working class as possible.

My eyes and head hurt but I read the thing. "Fine," I agreed.

But much to my dismay, the leaflet handed out by the RCP at the factory door the next morning had some slight but critical alterations. It read:

"Unions have sold out most working people. Therefore we cannot depend solely on the United Electrical Workers. It is important to form our own rank and file organization to guarantee that our demands are met."

Dammit! Nothing like a split between the organizers to imperil the union drive, I fumed to myself.

But I felt obligated to follow through and pass out my share of leaflets since they'd already been distributed to the first shift. A group of us from each department on the second shift agreed to stand in a line inside the plant, at a spot right before you got to the time clock. We were all scared as we left our cars, and walked slowly toward the entrance. Well, I'd been fired before, I thought. This was the moment we had been waiting for over the last seven months, this precious moment to stand and exercise our right, to say what we believed, to be proud, strong comrades with the workers. The security guard didn't seem to notice the leaflets or see anything unusual. He just sat on his stool waving us through. Nervous, I looked around for my supervisor and the plant manager. Neither were in sight. I took the leaflets out of my black shoulder bag, divided them up among four brave workers and then I dramatically handed one to an older woman in a down coat as she punched in at the time clock.

I was elated as the woman in the down coat squinted at the leaflet, nodded silently, stuck it in a pocket, and rushed past us down the hall. Okay, find someone else. As we handed out flyers, there were no strong reactions from people, either positive or negative. What did this mean? Where were the exclamations of "Aha! Or "At last" or "What the hell is this" Or "The cops are on the way!" I felt—let down.

Then Billy, a maintenance worker and hard core company man all the way strolled over "Well, I thought you were playing games with this union stuff. Guess I was wrong," he said and walked away. My heart pounded—proudly against the last flyer pressed against my chest. My strong, brave chest.

A week later, preparing to leave my apartment for the second shift, I opened my mail box. I was startled to find a letter from the United Electrical Workers Union. The language was direct, and it was the voice of doom. "Because a group of young radicals is trying to take the union drive into their own hands and refusing to follow union leadership, UE will not continue the campaign at the present time"

Disaster. The end. All those months of organizing had been for nothing. Cringing, still holding the letter, I slumped down on the cold concrete curb, my feet in the gutter. My friend Angie of the red beehive was right. I should have found a better job. My conservative sister was right. I was wasting my life in the working class. My artist friends in Cambridge were right. All politicians, including communists of every stripe were manipulators. Screaming and cursing, stomping up the stairs to my house, I grabbed the phone and called the factory.

"I won't be in … *ever again!*" I smashed the handset down on the receiver and ate all the chocolate I could find in the kitchen.

The Revolutionary Communist Party, like the Chinese Maoist Red Guards, couldn't wait for Mike's old fashioned, step-by-step card signing strategy to work. They wanted a newsletter in a hurry. It attacked not only the company but the United Electrical union as well. We had barely convinced a small group of people that a union was a good organization to have. Sure, I didn't like Mike, but he was the union and the RCP portrayed him as an enemy before he'd done anything wrong. While we all continued out word battles along party lines, the union drive imploded.

And Angie sat at her workstation earning $2.50/hour. Waiting for her coffee break.

But I was only temporarily flattened by the Unitrod fiasco. For three more years I continued to work with other leftists under the influence of the new communist party building movement, as a union organizer/worker in electronics factories in the Boston area. Eighty percent of the workers were unskilled, uneducated women, and I hated the capitalists that exploited them. But whatever my higher political goals were, the trouble with these factory jobs was they each destroyed a different body part. By 1976 I had quit or been fired from four sweatshops and already seen several chiropractors and one osteopath for job-related neck, wrist, and back pain. Then my whole body betrayed me. I learned I was pregnant. If my boyfriend, Norman, had asked me to marry him I would have, but his response to pregnancy was exactly the opposite, so I knew abortion was the only answer. Even though the idea of a child and a husband seemed perfect, my mind never entertained the possibility of raising a child alone. Every woman had the right to choose whether to mother or not, and I was not prepared.

I promptly scheduled an appointment at a clinic in Brookline, a long drive from my commune in Dorchester. I was frightened, but not of right-wing terrorists blocking the entrance. My terror was facing this emotionally difficult experience without Norman who refused to take a day off from work to be with me. My housemate, Susan, could not imagine any woman having to face this alone, and without hesitation, drove me to the clinic.

Journal

> Abortion means freedom to continue my own independent existence without interruption, even for someone else's life. When I think about this abortion, I sometimes imagine what my baby might have looked like, but I shut off the fantasy with its slight edge of pain because even though I am certain this pregnancy must end, there is conflict and torment. Why didn't the diaphragm work? Why isn't there a birth control pill for men? If only I had a good paying job. If only there were quality, affordable childcare. If only I could survive easily as a single parent? If only women had true equality which meant being supported as women, instead of extensions of men. I snarled at the strange male doctor, who performed dozens of extraction's everyday from women's wombs. Why couldn't we create birthing communes with collective child raising? These questions flooded my mind as I lay on the table my legs open to a horrible suctioning, a pulling at my uterus strong enough to destroy all the tissues and cells. I am crying. My baby, a part of myself, even though barely alive, is gone, leaving me saddened and angry at society's flaws, yet grateful I did not have to bring forth new life into a life yet unprepared. I remember the time in history when abortion was illegal and the suffering was so terrible, and the deaths numerous at the hands of unsafe, untrained doctors or quacks. When only the moneyed, privileged escaped to Europe or Mexico to exercise control over their own lives.

I was surprised at the depth of my sorrow: my privilege was bittersweet. Losing the baby and splitting up with Norman, pushed me into a deep, dark despair. His rejection was overwhelming, drowning me in major emotional battles, degenerating into physical violence between us. I had invested too much of myself. Loving a man deeply opened my heart, yet in the process, I lost my boundaries, and my self-esteem.

Boston had been my home for several years before my parents visited, and while my life was hard, I rarely turned to them for advise, comfort, or to discuss my political work. Mom and Dad drove from Indiana to deliver my first car, and to meet Norman. They left unhappy but resigned to my troubled lifestyle.

Feeling desperate, sinking in quicksand, now I could call my mother.

"When relationships end, it is like a death," she commiserated. But I couldn't tell pro-choice Mom of the abortion for twenty more years. So I channeled my pain and anger at Norman giving me the strength to heal and forget.

After little success as an organizer in light industry, I decided to join the better organized, male-dominated sector of the working class. Wages were higher and the workers more militant. Maybe I could find a more enthusiastic audience for a revolutionary third political party among them.

During this time, Shanna, the six foot goddess, and several other activists formed an independent Marxist-Leninist organization sympathetic to feminism and gay rights, and I enthusiastically joined. Six of us, two heterosexual couples, myself, a gay woman and two half-time children set up a political commune sharing the rent in a beautiful old townhouse in Boston's South End, with a hammer and sickle tattooed on a third floor ceiling by former radical tenants. First, we shared rent, food shopping, cooking, house cleaning, and marijuana. Second, we read political theory for hours. Then, we organized ourselves into workplace units with other members of our ML group, and got jobs at corporations we believed were strategic to reaching both non-unionized and unionized workers.

"The objective of communist work in the trade union movement is to win the trade unions to the side of communism," we quoted to each other from *The History of the Communist Party of the Soviet Union*. A booklet published by the Bay Area Communist Union, told us that "Aside from communists, the leftist forces of the day are the advanced workers, workers with more class consciousness and greater political awareness."

Our goal was to secure jobs at three of Boston's big corporations: University Hospital, General Motors, and General Dynamics and to recruit advanced workers into discussion groups where we would convince them of the evils of capitalist exploitation and the virtues of socialism. We expected women and minorities, the most disenfranchised and alienated, to be the most attracted to our views, with select white men joining in solidarity. That was the plan, anyhow.

YARDBIRD: LIFE IN THE SHIPYARD

Oh we're feelin' the pain
Of the big man's money game
And that's where you'd better put the blame
If you intend to make a change.

And the plan took me to the shipyard.

Had I ever known the unbearable agony that welding at General Dynamics, the largest shipyard in New England, would cause me, I'm sure I would have renounced my political beliefs for a comfortable place in the suburbs, a professional job, and the nuclear family my parents had dreamed for me. But my life was a dare, and my politics thrust me into situations to cause disruption, discomfort, and change.

With my shield protecting me from the bright orange flame of the welding rod melting steel to steel, I asked myself how I'd gotten to this huge shipyard in Quincy, Massachusetts. It was a bitter, snowy morning in 1976, and I thought back to that afternoon in 1967 when my father handed me a copy of the *Communist Manifesto.* "Here is a really good book you might like to read, Kendall," Dad said emerging from his study, where for seventeen years I usually saw his back bent over his typewriter, his Ph.D. dissertation, or university duties.

"Karl Marx? Who's he?" I asked.

"He was a philosopher who believed that we should create a society where social classes and class differences had been eliminated. A classless society is one that operates according to the principle, 'From each according to his ability, to each according to his needs'," Dad answered, his eyes tired from reading and grading papers. "Marx said if members of the working class stood together against the capitalist ruling class, they could overturn the government and create a new society. Worker solidarity would set them free."

"Free of what?" I asked. I was still in high school.

"Exploitation."

"Oh, I get it," I lied. Yet somewhere my heart understood and carried the message.

And so it went from late 1960s, Marx, and Chairman Mao's *Little Red Book*, to Madison and the student rebellion, and now union organizing.

As the welding sparks flew around my body, I wished my Marxist-Leninist mentor Shanna could see me. After she was jailed for slashing a strikebreaker's tire, I would need something like the shipyard to win my "red badge of courage."

"*Bang*," a thunderous sound reverberated on the steel beneath my boots.

"What the hell was that?" I gasped, catapulted back to the shipyard from my daydream. I flipped back my shield. An eight-foot long plank had landed inches from me. Glancing into the dark staging sixty feet up, I saw two pairs of boots.

"Watch out, you bastards!" I screamed, shaking my fist. "You could have killed me. You knew I was down here!"

Silence. Solidarity, I thought to myself. Worker solidarity?

Walking through the shipyard gates in 1976 was like going to war, with a constant battle between the workers and supervisors, the General Dynamics "white hats," who punished and verbally abused most workers they came in contact with. Every morning I woke up at 5:30, facing blackness and the terror of being late for the 7:00 a.m. shift. The 45-minute drive to Quincy always left me and my co-workers running or hop-skipping into Joe's Lunch for coffee, the only restaurant that serviced the shipbuilders. I tried to blend into the sea of gnarled, weather beaten men who had given twenty to thirty years of their lives to the New England winters, the relentless, ocean wind forever imprinted on their features.

I wore what all the welders wore, a hard-hat, huge baggy coveralls, heavy work boots, and company supplied leathers that covered my shoulders and chest to keep from being burned by welding sparks. After a few weeks, I looked as tattered as the veteran welders, with spark burns on my sleeves and pant legs, along with dirt from lying in garbage heaps inside the tunnels. But my face was young and beautiful, smooth and round as the full moon, as I walked, shaking, past the crowded tables of tough, raucous men, my downcast eyes focusing across the room until I managed to get past the stares coming from all directions. Bottom line: I was female.

There were just fifty women hired at General Dynamics to work on the liquid natural gas (LNG) tankers, a requirement of a federal affirmative action program. Half of us were there because of our affiliation with the new communist party building movement. Women and minority workers walked into the yard to become "yardbirds" for the first time in history, except when women known as

"Rosie the Riveter" had filled in for men at war in the 1940s. We were the other creatures, out of kitchens, bedrooms, grocery stores, and beauty parlors, wearing hard-hats and steel-toed shoes. I knew if I could see just one familiar feature, a nose, mouth, a gesture, while walking toward the coffee counter, I would begin to breathe more evenly, just to be able to say "Hi or good morning," not enough to gain acceptance or be one of the boys, but just enough to connect for an instant. Unfortunately, the morning entrance into Joe's never got comfortable. Familiar, but never friendly.

I had enjoyed the eight weeks of welding school, as well as the attention I received from lots of young men. We started working on the "plats," an area of the shipyard in front of the tankers where the bulkheads were constructed and welded together. But welding school had not prepared us for the lion's den, and I quickly became lost in a maze of metal cranes swinging like prehistoric creatures carrying huge pieces of metal without any safety bell ringing to warn workers when to run for cover. We joked about wearing a hard hat for protection from a piece of huge steel dropped from one hundred feet up. The school instructors had so terrified me of the boats, that I considered myself lucky with the plat assignment. But soon the foreman or white hat (in distinction from the workers who wore different colored hard hats), who never spoke directly to me, grumbled orders to the working leader and had me transferred to a tanker, the length of three football fields. Panic flooded my body, and I protested every step of the way, asking and begging: "Why, why? I was welding just fine. You didn't give me a chance, I was only here three weeks!"

"Well, that's the breaks, sister, GD isn't fair," he answered. "You can handle it."

The foremen were trained to run the yard just like a military machine, barking out commands they carried out according to rigid, inflexible rules. The corrupt Shipbuilder's union was just a name and a card. If a foreman wanted to transfer you, there was no choice. You went.

This transfer, however, was a blessing in disguise, because my new crew had a woman member, Dee. Red-headed, lesbian Dee. She was tough and kind, and she sensed my desperation. We immediately developed a deep rapport, and then I clung to her for psychic, emotional survival. The crew seemed to resent my being her pal and her protection of me, but for a few weeks life was good. This foreman put us on jobs together. Dee taught me how to weld, and we laughed, talked, and created a female dynamic that reverberated through the cold steel into the darkest, dampest, dirtiest holes. We paraded gleefully before the carpenters, burners, ship fitters, and all the male-only groups we were not welcomed to join. With Dee, I felt proud to be a woman and proud we were taking on new challenges together. In her presence my level of fear and timidity was halved. No one bothered us.

On rare occasions on an outside job, high above the decks, when the sky was clear, I had a spectacular panoramic view of the Quincy Bay, with seagulls, boats, blue ocean, and fresh, gentle breezes. On those days, I identified with the young Chinese woman shipyard worker glowing from the socialist poster I had bought in Madison, Wisconsin. In those moments, I merged with my welding rod and felt peaceful, accomplished, and almost happy.

Signs of solidarity frightened management, even two women friends, and Dee and I were separated. A few days after she was transferred to another tanker, pin-ups of naked, huge-breasted women started appearing on and above my toolbox. I seethed at this harassment that must have come from men on my crew. The deeper I worked in the tankers, the more chalk drawings of vaginas and breasts were scrawled on the bulkheads. I knew it was futile to report sexual harassment. In 1978 it was not recognized, just as my rape was ignored in 1971, blamed on women's seductiveness.

The foreman I had been so grateful to had ruined our honeymoon by sending Dee to a different crew and me to jobs I could not do. One of those places was called wing walls, a space so closed in and filled with smoke, noise, gas leaks from acetylene torches, toxic welding fumes, dropping pieces of metal, and burners fumes, that I was absolutely terrified. I had to squeeze into spaces and lie down at angles that my body would not bend, and weld where my arms could not reach. Sometimes I welded upside down so the hard hat offered no protection and my hair caught on fire. Sparks fell into my shoes, burning through my socks and causing me to jump off the job shaking my boots wildly. Welders have lots of tattoos to show for their trade: burn marks dotting arms and chest, noses blackened by smoke. My eyeballs, temporarily dried out by welding flashes, felt gritty, like after a walk on a windy beach.

Our lungs took the worst abuse, breathing in cancerous chemicals that entered throats and air sacs through holes in the aluminum blowers that management refused to repair. Long-term employees developed welders' lung, just as our fellow workers in the mines and textile plants suffered from black and brown lung disease. We were expected to weld wherever we were told, without questions, complaints, or demands, in the darkest, damp, garbage-filled holes often tainted with urine. "How is it that our country has the technology to put a man on the moon, but the management of General Dynamics can't fix our blowers?" I repeatedly asked other workers.

Every day we had to find a new welding line, and plug it into a machine for amperage near the job we had been assigned. This was the most difficult part of the job because the lines were so heavy. But the chaos, disintegration of the work ethic, and disorganization of production would have made even Karl Marx a little nervous. At the end of each working day, lines were dropped where each worker stood. Heaps of lines got tangled in knots that literally took hours to undo, wrapped around debris, hanging down holes, and trapped under pieces of bulkhead. This caused a battle between welders because there were never enough lines to go around. People fought to be first to get a line since it could mean searching half a workday or longer for one.

This waste of labor time and money was astronomical, but apparently General Dynamics could absorb the loss, and since management didn't care, neither did anyone else. "Don't do anything you don't have to" became the motto. Standing around doing nothing was not my style, so for weeks, each morning I cried while stumbling over piles of junk, pulling until my arms could hardly move, getting a line half way to a job, and giving up with exhaustion. Most people gave the company at best half a day's work, and then found a hiding place to smoke a joint or sleep. As long as we were somewhere on or near the job, most foremen were cool, but a trip across the yard to the bathroom was suspect and timed to the minute. Women were watched carefully since we all crowded into the bathroom for fifteen minutes at the morning and afternoon breaks. It was the only place we had to give ourselves comfort, support, and protection from the constant confrontations, invasions, and harassment. We would arrive depressed, and, in the winter, stiff with cold, each with a story to tell, taking turns listening with empathy and sisterhood.

"I never thought drinking mud could taste so good," commented a petite welder, her blue lips sucking in the machine-made hot chocolate.

"My fingers are so stiff I can't even hold my cup long enough to taste it," another woman moaned, running hot water over her hands.

Some winter days I huddled on the asbestos covered steam pipes, too numb to complain or care about my safety. These "shithouse" meetings, as we called them, became the most glorious time of my day. I used to count down as I anxiously watched out for the meanest foremen, the real "ball busters," as the men called them. They would nail us for having to piss by handing us a pink slip, the equivalent of a demerit, and then scramble down the ladders and planks off the boats to their safe, warm shacks. Three slips meant suspension or even firing. But the punishment was applied unfairly, depending on the foreman's likes and dislikes; often it was a matter of skin color or sex.

Unhappily for me, winters came earlier to the Quincy waterfront than to Boston. I had to wear so much clothing that in the spring when I began taking off layers, everyone thought I'd lost 25 pounds. I began the first layer with a leotard, then came tights, a pair of long underwear, a thin pair of socks, a heavier wool pair, a long-sleeved shirt, a pair of pants, two sweaters, a down vest, a jumpsuit on top, with a pair of woolen lined boots, a scarf, an ugly canvas brown coat with a knit hat that I put under my hard hat, and down mittens. I could hardly walk, never mind climb, but it was that or freeze. As I stared through the dark glass window in my shield into the arc of my welding rod, the bright light of melting steel drew me inward. I didn't want to stop welding for fear I would begin to feel the pain shooting up my legs and torso. I got increasingly stiffer and less tolerant of the cold steel we had to stand on hour after hour.

Sometimes I wandered blindly off my job, just to keep moving. If I were stopped, I made up any excuse: my machine was down, I was out of welding rods, or looking for my foreman. Sometimes I climbed down beneath the tankers, and found groups of men and dogs huddled around burning trashcans or setting planks of wood on fire. The atmosphere of shadows, frozen beards with icicles, and crouched figures hovering and stomping was so primitive that I sometimes forgot it was a shipyard. The burners who ordinarily cut steel became the salvation of all the "yardbirds," with their torches capable of heating a whole bulkhead in a few minutes. The hot steel instantly relieved us with waves of warmth, making us grateful in a way I could never have understood before. Some workers stayed warm by destroying an entire welding machine, pulling out the coiled wires and attaching them to a stinger of a welding rod to generate heat. The only people who could work efficiently in winter were workers who didn't stand still, stage builders, carpenters, or others whose physical movements kept them warm.

During these moments of survival and sabotage, I felt like giving up, curling up in a dark hole quietly to die, or throwing off my hard hat and screaming till they carried me out of the yard on a stretcher with a welding rod between my teeth. The deepest depression came when I realized I was no different from these men I'd planned to lead into a revolution. I had no solution to this horror but to endure.

General Dynamics was a world unto itself, where staging broke, and injuries, even death, happened. There were no routine safety inspections. Each step I took I tested the staging for fear it was loose. I witnessed falling planks: once one landed inches from me as I welded. During my first year and a half, it was rumored that three people were killed, their bodies crushed and mangled, necks broken from falls onto steel 20-30 feet below. Frequently, the ambulance siren pierced the air, like seagulls crying out "accident, accident." If General Dynamics could declare a worker dead on the other side of the shipyard fence, it was not liable for benefits. We were told that rarely did anyone actually die in the yard. One morning we heard the shocking news that an entire crane had fallen into a basin, leaving the operator in three pieces.

Most of the equipment was broken, old and rusted from the inside, and rather than make repairs, GD gave the deteriorated cranes and other machines a second coat of paint, or hid them temporarily, to fool the Occupational Safety and Health Administration (OSHA) inspectors. OSHA had to notify the company before arrival. We were then instructed to pick up garbage and welding rods. The yard was swept and tidied, trash cans painted or new ones put out in visible spots, and all welding in the shops ordered stopped. When the inspector came, all she or he saw was an orderly, spotless, safe shipyard: the biggest, cleanest show on earth. One afternoon a woman inspector walked into our daily shithouse meeting while we were talking about what a farce the inspection was. We surrounded her, pouring out our complaints:

"Shirley's six months pregnant and she's still climbing ladders and pulling lines. She should be on the plats."

"Judy has carpal tunnel syndrome in her wrist and can't hold her welding rod any more."

"My voice has been hoarse and sore all winter because of smoke fumes."

We told her the truth, but nothing changed. The Nixon Administration's anti-worker policies had already destroyed OSHA's ability to enforce the law.

"This wouldn't happen in worker-run states, like Cuba or China," I angrily argued to Dee, who now sympathized with my politics. They'd report the shipyard and the inspectors! And they'd all be sent to jail!"

Red-headed Dee, who had heard this from every socialist cadre in the yard by then, threw me a yeah-dream-on look. "It's OK babe," she said in her sexy, hoarse voice. "What goes around, comes around."

"Right, in another hundred years!" I shot back.

One hundred years was too long for even the most dedicated cadre. I wanted to see what the "new socialist" man and woman looked like now. Socialist Cuba was the paradise closest to the shipyard, just ninety miles off the Florida coast.

Havana, Cuba, 1978

Across the table drinking coffee with lots of Cuban sugar sat two members of the Palestinian Liberation Organization (PLO). I had escaped from the shipyard for a week to experience a "real" socialist revolution. The Palestinians spoke quietly of their fight for a homeland as I shook my earrings expecting to wake up from a dream. My shipyard credentials apparently qualified me to attend the International Youth Festival with a Boston contingent. Prior to 1978, the

Soviet Union and the eastern bloc countries sponsored these festivals as a meeting ground for young Communist Party recruits and "fellow travelers." Cuba was the first third world country with adequate resources and infrastructure to host this cultural extravaganza.

Being a "red" meant I had to keep my plans secret from my fellow workers and the management at GD. Explaining why I chose Cuba as a vacation was enough to keep me quiet. Getting fired frightened me more than being harassed by the FBI. However, I had announced my trip to everyone else I knew. Secretly, I imagined myself returning to the shipyard with glowing reports to deliver to progressive workers ready to hear the truth about socialism.

I was furious that we had to enter Cuba from Canada due to the US blockade imposed by the Kennedy Administration, but my spirits lifted when I saw the tiny revolutionary island, a red speck in the gigantic, Yankee imperialist ocean below. "*Cuba, que linda es Cuba*" ("Cuba, how beautiful Cuba is"), we sang with the adrenaline rush of prisoners being released from a lifetime sentence.

Landing in Havana felt hot, sexy, and clandestine. The absence of street beggars, so numerous in most of the underdeveloped world, alleviated my guilt enough that I politely declined to give my US-made sneakers to a young healthy-looking Cuban man who asked for them. With the sound of Latin music, the taste of fruit, rum, and the wild dancing, the revolution appeared successful. Everyone we met seemed optimistic about his or her individual and collective lives. Even the billboards were beautiful, with non-commercial, artistic, and educational messages that blended with the landscape. Through the bus window my camera snapped children holding hands under the large letters *POR LOS JOVENES Y EL FUTURO* (For Youth and the Future).

On our own, we traveled around Havana without Cuban guides, meeting people who seemed to be living with a sense of purpose and optimism. They welcomed us into their homes with food and drink, eager to discuss politics and their daily lives. Fluent in Spanish, my roommate translated positive statements about health, housing, jobs, and education in the new Cuba. Workers appeared to be valued. I evoked sympathetic nods as I broke in with a description of my life in the shipyard under capitalism.

The Cuban sunsets displayed the tallest buildings in Havana, outlined and lit up with images of huge fists, symbols of revolutionary victory. My sacrifices will be rewarded, I mused, imagining fists painted on the New York World Trade Center. (Instead, fast-forward, my firstborn daughter threw one of her two year old tantrums at the top of this building, and witnessed its destruction on 9/11.) Nightly we witnessed performances from around the world, my favorite being an Afro-Cuban jazz band. The lustful musicians followed us through the streets until we ducked into a doorway, hid for ten minutes, then ran screaming, "Viva la Revolution! Viva la Revolution!

On a humid, sweltering afternoon, my legs aching and my whole body almost cremated from the sun and bodies pressing from all directions, I crowded into the Plaza of the Revolution, where thousands of Cubans had gathered to hear Fidel Castro speak—for hours. At last, I was in the presence of this black-bearded, cigar smoking leader who had dared to defy US imperialism. The sound system was poor. But catching only a few Spanish words didn't matter. I wanted to stay on Cuban ground more than anything, and was prepared to fling myself at Fidel's feet to beg for citizenship in case he felt my adulation hundreds of yards away.

After a week, a few of us were invited to a cultural exchange on a Soviet naval liner in the harbor. When a Soviet rock band played a poor imitation of Western rock and roll, I felt shocked that their music was not original. But I developed a mad crush dancing with a handsome young naval officer who seemed to feel equally excited. He took a hammer and sickle pin from his jacket and slipped it into my hand. I rushed to the podium, singing "Union Maids," the most international working class American song I could remember, though none of the men understood a word of English. As a singer in a women's band, I had been eager to share our culture's protest songs. The tapping feet and applause vibrated a deep longing in my heart for Russian friendship. Tearfully, I was escorted off the ship back to Cuba, waving goodbye to the man I knew I'd never see again. I could not bear the thought of returning to the United States and to the dreary, gray shipyard. I felt homeless, like the people of the PLO. But I envied them. They had something to fight for, and all I wanted to do was elope with the first foreigner who would ask me. Only images of Lenin's stern face and Mao's Long March convinced me that my revolutionary duty was to make the revolution in North America. Cold, grey New England, in fact. Upon my return, I remained absolutely mute, afraid of more repression from fellow workers or dismissal by management. Not one of the 5,000 workers ever learned of my "illegal" visit.

At that time, I left Cuba to return to the shipyard, positive I had witnessed a social experiment that would create a "new man." But as far as I can tell, twenty-four years later, these evolved humans are still embryos like the rest of us, and Castro only became an older dictator after the Soviet Union dissolved and the Berlin Wall crumbled.

After visiting Cuba, I felt bonded to fellow workers who came from the West Indies, Latin America, Puerto Rico, and Cape Verde. Most of them did not speak English, and the majority were welders, because it was the largest, dirtiest department. We were evacuated periodically when another unit was lifted overhead on the crane. A working leader yelled down to us in time to get out of the hole, but only those who were lucky enough to hear or understand English left for safety. Very few people bothered to communicate with these men because it took patience and care. Once I noticed that none of them followed me out, so I ran from person to person, taking the stinger from their hands, forcing them to stop and motioning with gestures to come. I learned that racism caused accidents just as easily as negligence. My best friends in the yard were minorities and my carpool always included three or four big black or brown men who also lived in the inner city. This led to taunts from other workers: "Kendall lives in Jamaica Plain with the jungle bunnies," or "Kendall sucks black cock," or "Kendall is a commie." Racism divided people almost as simply as the Revolutionary Communist Party made it sound: "Racism is a tool used by the capitalists to divide the working class."

The trouble was, we all hated the company, and in our own way each cursed the "capitalists and their running dogs," but stood alone in our despair. It was only at contract time that the enemy looked the same to all of us. Months before the contract expiration date, I began talking to people about what they wanted. I climbed around with a piece of chalk, carefully watching for foremen, and writing demands on bulkheads and tankers: Strike for COLA (cost of living allowance), Dental Plan, Higher Wages, Sick Days, Two Weeks Vacation, More Holidays. This complemented the more popular "GD Sucks!" Expressing my will on the tankers lifted me from my daily ant-like existence.

"Why don't you write something?" I asked Billy as I crossed the T on Two Weeks Vacation, a few feet above his head.

"I'm quittin' for a better job" he lazily replied, the smoke from his last weld circling round his head, his blower dangling ineffectively nearby. "I don't want nothin' anyway." He paused. "But if I do end up stayin', I want more money."

"Well, write that, man," I urged, starting the M for "More" and handing him the chalk.

I wondered if he'd even graduated from high school, as he painstakingly printed O R E. Half way through the M on money, I saw a white hat with a get-out-of-my-way look, huffing his way toward us.

"Look out," I gestured to Billy. Ducking under our shields, we simultaneously struck an arc to avoid a pink slip or worse.

Never before had I felt so concerned with the interests of people around me. My arguing for a better pension plan when I was 25 years old, having worked in the yard just six months, struck most workers as odd. Young shipbuilders didn't care about much except higher wages, and attendance at union meetings was small in between contracts. But as the contract date drew near, the rank and file began to crawl out of the pits and into the union hall. Those who hadn't given up came prepared to yell and do battle with their leaders, most of whom had become lazy, corrupt, and comfortable. It was clear that defending management rather than workers was their priority. Meetings were run with an iron fist, with the union's own interpretation of Robert's Rules of Order or the union bureaucrats' rules created on the spot.

I had been deeply touched by socialist historian Philip Foner's *History of the Fur and Leather Workers' Union*, a standard source for radical union activists. We didn't get chairs smashed over our heads by union thugs, as Foner described happening to leather workers, but anyone brave enough to keep pushing a point our union leaders didn't agree with was eventually shut up.

Young union activists eager to address working conditions and safety issues waved their arms at the older, overweight, white officers at the podium. Each leftist group, including mine, had its own caucus. Tensions and anger exploded as old timers and representatives from each organization fought to be recognized by the chairman, who was more interested in crowd control than in developing unity among the membership. It felt strangely exciting and out of control, like a Students for a Democratic Society meeting from the past. As I glanced around the union hall I was struck by the absence of blacks and other minorities. Only one woman was aggressive enough to be acknowledged. Boldly, I decided to risk individualism. Hadn't my comrades Linda and Bob agreed that we should address racism? Trembling, I raised my hand just as the gavel struck the podium. "Meeting dismissed." Rumbling complaints erupted everywhere. Angry and disgusted, the majority of men fled to the bar across the street where their grievances would be heard. Alcohol won again, numbing the pain and anguish, allowing people to forget. I decided it was not religion that was the opiate of the people, as Marx had stated; it was alcohol for the World War II generation and drugs for the younger Vietnam-era workers. I was the only sober person on my crews, and one of the few who did not daily pollute herself on the job.

The last crew I worked on before the actual contract expiration was Hank's. He was a young, handsome foreman who had not yet become demoralized or hardened and seemed to like and respect me. On his crew I met Ivy, a young African American woman longing for freedom from her traditional marriage, which included two children. A sharecropper's daughter from the South, she and her husband had relocated to Massachusetts where he went to work at General Motors. General Dynamics and her contact with political activists in Jamaica Plain where she and I lived were catalysts for Ivy's transformation. Because leftists in the yard pretended not to know each other, and my comrades Linda and Bob were a married couple, I had to rely on other workers for emotional support. Norman, my communist boyfriend, had left me months earlier, leaving me wide open to affairs with men, and to be truthful, women in the yard—Tommy, the sexy, after hours Irish cab driver from Somerville, six foot Kwami, the muscled ship fitter from Senegal, and Mike, the sweet one who's heart I broke, from Quincy. Then came Ivy. She began pursuing me with irresistible cheerful energy, greeting me at the time clock with her silky, chocolate face and eyes. Work bonded us quickly. Both of us were restless, curious women looking for contrast and excitement, and we were open to the unthinkable.

"Hey girl," her bright voice called down from the top of the deck. "Whatcha doin'?"

I stopped welding, peering upward from a comfortable job in a space where Hank had hidden me. It was large enough for two people but small enough that my droplight brightened all the bulkheads. Being alone in a small tank, our contact would be private, and I gladly put down my welding rod as she descended the long ladder.

"Nice bead," she observed, running one hand over the surface of my welding and offering me candy from her back pocket with the other. Yesterday, the kinky story of how she braided her public hair for her husband really jarred my latent Mormon-Puritan sensibility. What would I hear today?

"It's almost over, Ivy," I looked at my watch, relieved it was later than I thought. "Hank hasn't been down yet so I lost track of time."

Smiling and reaching for my hand, she asked, "Are you coming over tonight?"

Her husband worked second shift so my visits to their home were a secret. Not that we had done anything bad yet.

We both jumped as Hank came down to our level, playfully saying: "Hey what's going on?" I flipped the welding shield over my face to avoid answering. Everyday on this job assignment, he appeared at least once. When I was sure he wasn't there just to check up on my work, I normally looked forward to his visit. Putting her hard hat back on, Ivy knew she was lucky it was Hank and not her foreman. She left, but before the whistle blew, Hank made clear what he wanted. Dropping into the tank inches from my shield he said,

"Kendall, why don't you move to Quincy? You wouldn't have such a long commute, and you could be my mistress." Before hoisting himself out of view he looked back with a grin.

"I can't Hank," I smiled up at him, "I'm Ivy's girlfriend. Besides, you're a white hat."

When the contract expired many shouting matches later, the union leadership ignored the rank and file demands for safety and better benefits. Management offered an increase of a few pennies and rejected the union's counter proposal for a decent increase. All that remained was a struggle for higher wages. For days

I was furious and then so depressed I could barely drag myself out of bed each morning. Nevertheless, I joined my comrades and the progressive workers in support of a vote to strike. We held a rally outside the main gate, near Joe's Lunch. I agreed to sing labor songs, with sound equipment I rented and brought in my car, making me finally feel important and recognized by the other leftists. The morning of the rally, singing at the top of my lungs, I drove onto the entrance ramp of the Quincy Highway. Suddenly my car veered over the median onto the down ramp. I turned the steering wheel sharply right, holding my breath. My old Dodge Plymouth jumped back over the divide as if nothing had happened, and I continued singing, "We're gonna roll, we're gonna roll, we're gonna roll the union on," my foot steady on the gas pedal all the way to the main gate.

At last I was wearing two hats, union organizer and member of New Harmony Sisterhood Band, Boston's now famous, feminist string band, singing outside the largest shipyard in New England while my friends, lovers, and co-workers swarmed out of the gates during lunch. It made me very nervous to perform right below management's office window, in full view of their cameras. But I wore a scarf, took off my glasses, closed my eyes, and held onto the microphone to keep from falling off the stage as I sang my favorite labor song, "Which Side Are You On?" Watching the familiar faces I saw at Joe's every morning, together with friendly leftists and thousands of others I'd never seen, felt like a dream come true. Knowing that most of the yardbirds had probably never heard songs about workers or about their feelings gave me energy that left me trembling during the speeches that followed.

The first day of the strike, 3,000 spirited workers came out to picket, filling us with hope and excitement. However, within hours, the union president had destroyed the spirit by frightening everyone away with the company's threat of an injunction. The National Labor Relations Board investigator stated that he was pleased at how quickly the union had cooperated in curbing the mass picketing. It was the beginning of the end.

The left simply was not strong enough to fight a multinational corporate giant that had billions of dollars. We struck for three months, but did not put a dent in General Dynamics' profits. We marched, chanted, caucused in the heat, and picketed round and round beneath the company's cameras designed to intimidate by taking reels and reels of film. Our picket shifts were five to six hours long, which we endured by chanting militantly at the "White Hats" as they crossed our lines into work:

"Listen Mr. White Hat, you really are a jerk, no use going in, you don't know how to work! The boats aren't finished, a single boat ain't done, and nobody works until our strike is won!"

Our picket lines were made up of young men and women leftists with no more than two years' seniority and old timers with thirty to forty years in the yard. Other young men had motorcycles to ride and girlfriends to find. Family men could not survive on the meager strike benefits from the union. Blacks and minority workers were so alienated by the union's racism they stayed away. So it was the commies and the original union builders, shoulder to shoulder, inspired by ideology and a dream of democracy, walking with pride, who watched the union weaken and the number of scabs increase.

General Dynamics went to the inner city in Roxbury to recruit unemployed minorities desperate for work, a classic strikebreaking strategy that succeeded. It was tragic for us to watch one of the few black foremen drive in everyday with a van full of minority workers, in full view of the white workers who had to watch them take their jobs, breaking the strike, and destroying the union. We were paralyzed seeing how racism worked for the company's interests. We were stunned that the scabs did not understand the game. Couldn't they see we were all part of the same working class? Didn't they know that once the strike was over they would be laid off? We pleaded with those who came on foot to the main gate, trying to reason with them, but many more crossed than turned away. Money talked to those who had been out of work for years and now had a chance to make $7 an hour. The bitter reality destroyed years of preaching about organizing, unity, and strength in numbers. We couldn't reach most of the union membership, and the leadership had given up the first day of the strike. Our president sat on the curb with a bottle of booze the entire three months.

Chasing scab cars took our minds off the defeat briefly, but the truth hurt—worse than our sunburned arms, tired feet and backs, and hoarse voices. Learning more bitter lessons wasn't easy. The great proletariat had left me cold in the sweltering heat waves of the shipyard.

After the strike, I wanted to leave the shipyard, believing I would not survive another winter. But the steering committee of the Boston Party Building Organization asked me to remain at General Dynamics, although it was killing me to walk through the gate each morning. I endured for six more months, but then, at the end of a long day, I threw down my hard hat and walked out the gate for the last time, never again to see another person from Quincy or GD. I never contacted Hank, management never called me, and I abruptly severed my relationship with Ivy and other friends.

Like my confused grandmother, the dandelion puff who forgot everything in her frantic walks around the neighborhood, I wanted it all gone. Now.

My comrades encouraged me to train as a machinist at General Electric for another year. After that, the bomb dropped. But this time it was from my trusted comrades in the struggle. I received the following letter from the Boston Party Building Organization:

> *March, 1979*
>
> *Dear Comrade:*
>
> *The steering committee has reviewed your strengths and weaknesses, and scrutinized your practice under the principles of Marxist-Leninist-Mao Tse Tung thought. After reviewing your case, we have decided that you have failed to carry out the main line.*
>
> *Every member of BPO must work at all times, to keep our basic line in mind, to continuously raise our level of consciousness of the two-line struggle. You have failed to carry out struggle-criticism-transformation in the appropriate manner.*
>
> *With further investigation and study and reliance on the masses you will learn from your past mistakes and avoid future ones.*
>
> *You are no longer a cadre in BPO.*
>
> *The Steering Committee*

"What!" I yelled. "Seven years of sacrifice for this? Why those bastards are no better than the Russian politburo!"

The letter in my right hand began to shake. I paced round and round kicking the coffee table, rattling last night's snack dishes under a half empty coke bottle. My friends. I had been fired by my friends. Lenin's poster-smile now looked evil. Swiftly I grabbed the coke bottle and hurled it with all my might at his forehead. *Wham! Thud*, to the floor spinning like a top.

This was the ultimate betrayal.

Two years later, the new communist movement destroyed itself from internal contradictions. Five years later I could see the shipyard cranes twenty miles away on the horizon from my home in Mission Hill. Whenever I faced what felt like insurmountable hardships of any kind, I told myself, "You can do it, you survived General Dynamics."

With a long look back, I now understand that without the extremity of the dogmatic Marxist-Leninist movement and my belief in its strategy for revolution, I would not have witnessed shipbuilding and the human dynamic between workers and bosses. Sweating and struggling with the working class gave me a profound appreciation for labor and its untold story.

Notes

Twenty years later, in 1998, I found my tan colored hard-hat with a faded, red women's symbol in my barn inside a box next to a bale of hay. A spider ran across my New Harmony Sisterhood notebook, torn and ragged, but still protecting the lyrics to all our songs collected over seven years. Turning the rumpled pages matted with bits of hay, I found "Yardbird," a song I composed and played with New Harmony after the strike. Softly I began to sing the first verse:

Yardbird Blues

Here we go the start of another drive down to the Quincy shipyard
And we're heavin a sigh as we walk toward the street
On the way to punch in that time card.
Jimmy's complain' 'bout the heat and the smoke, welding down below in the tanks
Kathy her hand hurts from running the gun couldn't care if the whole damn boat sank.

Chorus:

Oh we're feelin' the pain
Of the big man's money game
And that's where you'd better put the blame
If you intend to make a change.

Kendall Hale, New Harmony Sisterhood, 1977

By 1979 the rank and file elected some of the new communist and militant workers as union stewards and continued to wage campaigns focused on racial discrimination and better working conditions. In 1982, the welders managed to isolate the right wing and elected a radical president who spent three years fighting with the older conservative officers of the union. Only young workers who could take financial risks ever participated in the campaigns for justice. Unsuccessful on the world market, the Liquid Natural Gas Tankers were discontinued by General Dynamics in 1980, and layoffs left 1,400 of the original 5,000 workers in the yard. By the mid-1980's all the radicals had "burned out" from a combination of union corruption and a workforce with no experience of how to fight the bosses. In 2004 the owners tore down the giant crane and closed the shipyard, leaving us yardbirds to the seagulls.

Founded in 1880, the General Dynamics Corporation is now the parent of several high-tech operating units involved in defense, aerospace, and advanced materials. The bulk of its revenue is derived from activity in the defense industry.

NEW HARMONY SISTERHOOD BAND

What seemed like a little thing to do—play music in a feminist band—now has turned into one of the most exciting phenomena of our lives. We have watched as women's culture has grown from a few attempts to today's present mushrooming of books, songs, movies, and plays. There is real emotional satisfaction in making women's music, but that is not all there is. It is important for me to realize that we are not simply entertainers, but that we are creating the strength for a movement that has the greatest potential for change this country has seen in decades. I am firmly convinced (yes, I have read political and economic theory, Mr. Leftist) that women's culture is revolutionary, and, best of all, it is accessible to large numbers of women.

—Marcia Deihl, New Harmony Sisterhood Band
(All Our Lives, A Woman's Songbook, Diana Press, 1976)

During two years that I worked as a welder in the Quincy shipyard, from 1976 to 1978, I performed with the New Harmony Sisterhood Band. I was living in two separate worlds, one on the performance stage, the other staging construction at General Dynamics. Often my voice was too hoarse from breathing welding fumes to sing, once causing us to postpone a recording session. At times I wondered if throat cancer would be my punishment instead of carpal tunnel syndrome, which plagued some welders. The band members, as well as my family, would have rejoiced at my leaving this "hell hole," but I was in the grip of duty to Marxism-Leninism and the revolution came first.

For some sixties youth, music itself *was* the revolution. Others listened to the charged messages of folk-rock singers and then took to the streets in protest. As for me, when I was an infant, my mother sang songs written by Mormon pioneers crossing the plains in covered wagons:

Put your shoulder to the wheel, push along.
Do your duty with a heart full of song.
We all have work, let no one shirk.
Put your shoulder to the wheel.

On every family car trip, we harmonized America's favorite folksongs, including many by Pete Seeger and Woodie Guthrie. My childhood connection to music continued with the civil rights struggles of the 1950s and 1960s. In 1962, Mom sang along with Negro spirituals on a record of Civil War songs. *We Shall Overcome* was a daily prayer in our household. At sixteen, I played Bob Dylan and Joan Baez on a guitar, with the only beatnik in town. After the Beatles, music was like food: without it I felt dead.

In the early 1970s, I heard both the Chicago and New Haven Women's Liberation Rock Bands. They blew my mind. Now I knew what I wanted to do–combine feminism with my childhood folk singing and classical violin training. At the time, the three seemed incompatible. But then, I began listening to Holly Near and Chris Williamson, both powerful feminist musician/song-writers making the national scene. In 1973 while I studied left-wing politics at Cambridge-Goddard, an alternative graduate school, I heard women singing Custom Made Woman Blues and Don't Put Her Down, by Hazel Dickens and Alice Gerard, a country/bluegrass duo:

Well if she acts that way,
It's 'cause you've had your day,
Don't put her down,
You helped put her there.

Immediately I started jamming with these women from school. After practicing a couple of months, we sang for our first audience, at a women's party, and were cheered enthusiastically. We were amateur songwriters and musicians, but our voices matched a call from a growing sisterhood. It was the beginning of connection between the feelings, hopes, and dreams of the women's movement and what became the New Harmony Sisterhood Band.

In our early gigs, five of us fumbled with our instruments and voices, but our lack of technique was overridden by our message. The passionate wild energy between the band and our fans filled me with love for performance, in contrast to the scary violin recitals of my girlhood. At the time, we could not imagine how inspirational our performances would be or the tremendous support we would receive from hundreds of feminist women and men over the next seven years.

"Men don't have to define their songs as 'men's songs' because almost everything that exists in this culture was created by men," we announced to all our audiences.

After we played and raised funds for women's celebrations, women's centers, and women's studies programs, we were sought by activists from all over Boston. We played free for union drives, striking workers, liberation movements, and early nuclear power protests. In 1976, we recorded with Paredon Records, a record company under the cultural wing of the Marxist-Leninist newspaper, the Guardian, and two years later, we traveled south on a tour we created ourselves.

Five of us met weekly for two hours of outrageous, irreverent fun. In an eclectic folk/bluegrass style we sang angrily about being born female. It would go like this:

"It ain't me babe, noo, noo, noo, it ain't me babe," Deborah is imitating Bob Dylan in a nasal drawl, twanging her acoustic guitar.

"Down with cock rock!" pitches Katy, gyrating her hips.

Marcia howls beside her on a mandolin, "And I'm tired of fuckers fucking over me!" She curtseys. "And this ladies and gentlemen is a new musical genre. Live from a real lesbian living room in Boston!"

We all get hysterical as Marcia's mandolin leads us in chorus:

> *When I'm walking down the street and every man I meet says,*
> *'Baby ain't you sweet'*
> *I could scream.*
> *But although those guys are sick and think only of their prick,*
> *It ain't sweet I feel*
> *I just feel good and mean.*
> *They whistle for me like a dog and make noises like a hog,*
> *Heaven knows they sure got problems I agree.*
> *But their problems I can't solve*
> *'cause my sanity's involved,*
> *And I'm tired of fuckers fuckin' over me.*
>
> —Beverly Grant, 1971

I yell when it's my turn to present a new song, "Attention, attention." Tapping my violin bow on a music stand, I roll up my cuff to expose a bare leg and croon into the microphone verses I finished at two that morning:

Went on down to the Two O'Clock Lounge,
looking for a quick day's pay,
From packing meat on the assembly line—
Now it was me who was prey.
Can you dance baby, baby, sweet baby, Can you dance?"

Katy and Pat stare at me in disbelief: "true feminists" do not shave body hair. But I had just been laid off from a local meat packing plant after working only six weeks. My unemployment checks were running out, along with my small savings account. Believing it might be possible to make some easy money until I could refocus my organizing strategy, I'd shaved my legs and blindly walked into a "den of sin," as my grandmother once described all of Salt Lake City.

"Did you really go into that topless joint in the middle of downtown?" Deborah asks. "And by yourself?"

"Yes and yes," I groan, "Thick smoke under dim lights and creepy, Mafia-looking men scared the shit out of me. After some weirdo guy watched me walk across the stage in a bathing suit, I freaked out and ran! Working conditions seemed as bad as a factory."

Our New Harmony member Deborah Silverstein spoke for all of us in her 1974 song, "All Our Lives":

Well I've only this to say, I look forward to the day
When women won't have to fight for an equal chance all their lives
And the purpose of our songs is to move this fight along
Until there's room for more than just the struggle to survive.

The New Harmony Band became a family for all of us, with caring support, as well as pain, competition, egotism, and disagreement. The product became a unique blend of my classical fiddling, Deborah and Katy's lead and back up guitars, Marcia's mandolin, autoharp, and recorder, and Pat's base. With our music reverberating through our bodies, into the furniture, out the windows across tree limbs skyward over Cambridgeport, we were a true sisterhood, with a song in the heart of the Boston women's movement.

New Harmony was my link to the women's movement, but within the band we also experienced many of the ideological struggles and political line battles playing out in the left. Often we nearly came to blows over absurd shades of difference. Labels were everything. I represented my own version of feminist Marxism-Leninism, Deborah became the socialist feminist, Katie Tolles, a libertarian, Marcia a feminist anarchist, and Pat Ouellette a lesbian feminist anarchist.

Squeezed into Marcia's tiny living room, between her piano, gas heater, and TV set, we were surrounded by plastic toy animals, dolls, old high-heeled shoes, bizarre off-color comic strips, and black-humor postcards. This paraphernalia was hanging, sitting, peering, and pasted on the refrigerator, doors, walls, and end table. Together with Marcia's comedian personality and Deborah's horny dog, Timber, it brought relief to our emotional sessions of confessions and personal stories woven around class, race, nuclear power, and third world liberation issues. We debated the lyrics and message of each song.

We had come together to play women's music, but the question became, which women: middle class, working class, African American, Hispanic, gay? And which issues? Was it OK to sing a traditional women's song, or did it need to be feminist?

Before Pat joined, I was bisexual and wanted to bring lesbian songs to heterosexual women. Ironically, when the band broke up, I was the only straight member. In 1974, we sang "Unfinished Business," by I.M. Reluctant.

CHORUS

I've got some unfinished business, well I just want to say
I've got some unfinished business to take care of today.
Well I know what's on my mind, and I think that it's time
To tend the unfinished business that we left behind.

Well they say that it's not natural.
They try to make you scared
To be a homosexual with feelings to share
With a good friend who it's plain to see
Is of the same sex that you just happen to be ...

I was constantly preaching to my band sisters: "We've got to sing about the oppression of poor and minority women too, not just privileged, white feminists like ourselves." I wrote about capitalism and imperialism in songs about my jobs, union organizing, black women's battles, Puerto Rican freedom fighters and other issues new to the white middle class women's movement.

"Yeah, Kendall, but your lyrics sound like a political speech," complained Katy. "Cut the rhetoric!"

"But she's got the right idea. Gay women have been oppressed for centuries," exclaimed Deborah. "No matter what their skin color or social class was!"

Within a couple of years, we created and arranged a song list linking historical figures like labor organizer Elizabeth Gurley Flynn and pilot Amelia Earhart to the most burning social/political issues of our day.

Our Paredon record title "Ain't I A Woman?" was taken from Sojourner Truth's famous speech at a suffrage convention in 1851. New Harmony's mentor from the Cambridge-Goddard program, Lanayre Liggera, put the powerful speech to music and we sang it for years at almost every concert. In their catalog promoting women's music, Paredon said of our record:

> *From the title statement taken from a speech by Sojourner Truth through songs about the frame up of Ella Ellison, the Joann Little prison rape case, and pioneer woman pilot Amelia Earhart, to songs about women in working class struggles, the strip mining destruction of mountain America, and songs about the painful process of self-discovery and "coming out" for lesbian women, the words give voice to experiences particular to women but of concern and interest to all.*

At one point a *Guardian* interviewer asked me if I thought the left had been slow to appreciate cultural workers. I replied:

> *On the left people don't believe to a large extent that cultural work is political work, and they don't really see it as a priority. Most of the party-building groups do not really appreciate the importance of how people relate to culture. Mass media and the music industry do control and powerfully influence people's emotions and thinking. Also, because our band is all women and sings about women, we have encountered a lot of sexism. Most of these organizations are male-dominated and have a weak position around the woman question as a whole. We've had people really trash us for being bourgeois feminists: Women's music could not be working-class music, because it was feminist.*

Feminist was a dirty word then, as it is today. Many people, the left included, believed we were man-hating separatists. But women who loved themselves and their sisters were listening, and by the spring of 1979 our record had reached some feminists in Philadelphia. This led to other invitations to perform further away. We rented a van and headed south to Philadelphia, Virginia, North Carolina, and Kentucky. On our way to Norfolk we passed through Washington, DC, to join 70,000 demonstrators in front of the Capitol in the wake of the "Three Mile Island" incident. To convey our support for the protest, we sang "No Nukes for Me" at a Norfolk coffeehouse the following night.

"We barely survived a melt down," I breathed into the microphone.

"Shut 'em down! Shut 'em down," a voice bellowed from the audience.

I continued, "We sang this song in Plymouth, Massachusetts, at one of the biggest anti-nuke rallies ever held against the Plymouth Nuclear Power Plant! Join us now in the chorus!"

> *"No Nukes for me 'cause I want my world to be,*
> *Free from radiation poison falling down on me,*
> *Those reactors that they're building are a giant hangin' tree, hangin' tree,*
> *Don't you build your hangin' tree over me."*
>
> Pat and Tex LaMountain
> Clamshell Alliance Musicians

After our concert on May 8, 1979, the local *Ledger-Star,* wrote: "There are no leaders in the group. On stage, as they would have it in life, all are equal. They take turns speaking, and Pat Ouellette steps forward to tell names "so if you have any particular tomatoes to throw, you'll know where to aim them." The words are angry, yet there's a positive sound in their music, a hopeful note that-very slowly-things are improving."

When New Harmony broke up in 1980, it was a traumatic divorce. At a time when I was most distant from my family of origin, Deborah, Marcia, Katy and Pat had sustained me through a rocky seven years of multiple lovers, communes, jobs, and political organizations. Belonging to a pack of wild women who howled at the moon and everyone else gave me the voice I'd always wanted. Singing from our hearts, we told stories that few people had ever heard. But underground conflicts, combined with different personal agendas, forced us to split up. Marcia wanted to take her music in a new direction. Katy and Deborah wanted their own bands. Pat wanted to move to Western Massachusetts. It was the end, but I didn't want to let go.

The women of New Harmony individually incarnated into many musical expressions lasting well into crone hood. Visiting from Asheville, at a summer solstice party in Jamaica Plain in 2004, I backed into one of those sweet old crones, watering a blooming tiger lily with a bit of spilled wine.

"It's Marcia Deihl! I squealed at her through a mouthful of chips and salsa. "You haven't changed at all."

"No, I'm just forty pounds lighter with grey hair," She snorts back. "I used to binge after every concert."

Laughing, we embraced like lost soul mates. The next day we took the subway to Harvard Square, and sat down in Club Passim to remember where Joan Baez, Bob Dylan and our band had performed.

"Do you know I was born in Asheville, North Carolina?" Marcia asked eating diet food brought from home in plastic containers.

"Unbelievable! I shook my head crunching huge mouthfuls of pesto pizza.

"We also drove through it on our southern tour." She leafed through her band album to a photo of us arm in arm beside a rental van.

"We did? I must have been asleep in the back of that big white ford, behind the window with the Super Woman cartoon."

"With your red beret covering your face," Marcia chortled, choking on her aduki beans.

"Well if the band toured today, Asheville would have a huge star marked on the map with red letters: Appalachian Shangri-La, home to scores of talented acoustic musicians: Stop Here!"

"Oh yeah?"

"Yeah," I grinned. "Maybe it's time to come home, Marcia. "

A CD of New Harmony Sisterhood's 1976 record "Ain't I A Woman?" is available at www.worldmusicstore.com or www.smithsonianglobalsound.org. You can listen to the 1981 New Harmony Sisterhood Band Reunion concert at www.radicalpassions.com

LOOKING FOR MAO

Communist Meltdown

It was the last night of 1979. My musical sisterhood had dissolved and I sat alone still shivering from the walk to my apartment from a New Year's Eve party up the block. Attempting to read more political theory, my mind wandered through the previous decade, paralyzed at the idea of 1980. American communists had truly believed that democratic centralism worked; yet in every organization we formed, it produced hierarchy, blind acceptance, and pathological behavior. Where had we gone wrong? I still had my doubts and wondered if I had picked the wrong friends or the wrong organization.

Since 1973, factory work had separated me from academics, new leftists, counter culture freaks, and feminists. No one went there except people exploring Marxist Leninist politics, because no other theory directed middle class people to the assembly line. Like high school, my values were different from those around me. I had witnessed too much pain and suffering, spirits broken by overtime, speed up, and low wages. The streets one mile from my job overflowed with sports cars, marijuana and conversations about parties on Martha's Vineyard. The shock of factory life, next to the fancy leather boutiques and furniture stores filled with the world's elite angered me. I got less and less tolerant of the self centered *petite bourgeois* revolutionaries who didn't even seem to know about the working class. I had taken a risk, dared to cast aside my formal training, so why couldn't they? What was stopping them? Fear, privilege, or hatred of people less educated? My overwhelming urge to spit at people in Harvard Square finally drove me from the Cambridge social life.

My job as a machinist at General Electric felt as raw as the steel I held in my hands: parts milled one tenth of an inch too short for the aircraft engine. It didn't fit. After seven years of industrial jobs, I knew I could no longer survive as a factory worker. I could blame sexism, my middle class background, bad behavior and sectarianism in the left, working class oppression-it didn't matter. I just didn't belong. Cold air leaking from the window above the couch drew my attention outside to the road, now covered in a foot of snow. Maybe Leningrad looked like this, I thought. Still convinced that the trouble had started with the theoreticians in the Soviet Union, I opened the book, hoping this author had found the missing piece of the puzzle in Stalin's theory. Sighing, I could still feel my father's attraction to the powerful promise and vision Marx portrayed in the <u>Communist Manifesto</u>: the withering away of the state and the end of all oppression. Chairman Mao looked hard at me above the mantle. Maybe the truth lay buried in China where I would retrieve it for the American left. I imagined returning to Boston with a clear head and renewed dedication. Unable to face the thought that socialism might be a fantasy, I began dreaming about a trip to China. With savings from my two years working as a welder I could just afford the $3,600 fee.

Suddenly the phone rang. A male voice asked for Gene. He sounded familiar and I knew it was Steve Norris, that odd but handsome man with the gold starred tooth I had met during a union drive in Dorchester.

"What are you doing alone on New Year's Eve?"

"Reading political theory and dreaming of going to China", I said.

"What?…. What did you say?" he asked. He was a West Point dropout turned hippie radical, so I knew he understood.

It was Steve blown in from a camping trip. He is the crazy one, I thought. How many more times I would think this over the next 25 years! Imagine, sleeping outside in a New England snow storm and enjoying it! Listening to his deep, warm voice made me curious, and momentarily, I wished he had been calling for me.

In a short time, Steve did call again and this time it was for me. He was a gentle biker, both a father and mother archetype, who sped me to Chinatown on the back of his motorcycle at 11pm after my second shift job, or cooked stir fried tofu at his old dusty house with a sketch of the wood burning/passive solar house he dreamed of building hung on the kitchen wall.

"Where are you doing to build that?" I gestured to the sketch with my tofu loaded fork. I was hot for Steve, and somehow I knew I wanted to live in that house with him.

"I'm planning to build it on some land on the Back of the Hill, I bought from the city for $1300." he answered loading another log into the wood burning stove he had installed without his landlord's approval. "I was the only bidder," he laughed. "After I left factory organizing, a neighbor asked if I'd repair the gutters of her home. Another neighbor had some rotten front steps. More or less by accident I was in business in my own neighborhood. I've been living in run down 100 year old houses for years, and now I want to use my skills on something of my own."

When Steve's naked body pressed against mine on the futon next to the crackling wood fire, the heat of his builder's muscles soaked up the pessimist in me, smoothed my jagged critic. His buoyant energy sent me sailing so high I couldn't see all the dirty towels and little bitsy hairs that covered his bathroom floor and sink. It punctured the ugly, shameful disappointment wadded up in my heart. Despite my mother's strong disapproval, several months later with a boiling passion, I moved in with him. No one, least of all me, could believe that a feminist who scorned the nuclear family and the institution of marriage, was following a man.

Mom sent us a wooden salad bowl in honor of the occasion, but thankfully she never saw the apartment that became our home days before my journey east to China in the summer of 1980. I was going to look for a successful revolution.

Looking for Mao

I had landed on the other side of the world, to see the end of a dynasty and the results of a socialist society. By my standards, Mao Tse-Tung had "done the right thing." He led the Long March, built a new political party, and overthrew the dreaded feudal empire of Chiang Kai-Shek. In 1980 I believed Mao and the Red Guard had replaced the Chinese elite with a classless society, a society of agricultural communes and factory collectives, women's equality, and children's palaces. "Let a hundred flowers blossom, Let a hundred schools of thought contend," captured my imagination as did the romantic posters of workers and peasants building a socialist China.

This mysterious country had intrigued me from the moment my father handed me a copy of Mao's famous red book. Later, the University of Wisconsin graduate students' glowing report of a new society only deepened my enthusiasm. *Long Live Chairman Mao!* beckoned to me from thousands of miles away in a land run by dedicated, honest leaders who had mastered the wisdom of dialectical materialism.

I found it humorous that the Chinese gave free trips to members of Maoist ultra left groups, while I was flying with the US-China Friendship Association to the "most glorious land under heaven" on a weekly disability check from General Electric. A month earlier I pulled a muscle in my back landing myself in bed just five days before my trip to China. Luckily, after one visit to a chiropractor I was strong enough to travel to the 'socialist paradise" while collecting disability benefits from my capitalist corporate enemy. Paradoxically, both the Chinese and General Electric assisted my escape from the industrial working class.

Our group of fifteen Americans quickly polarized into two camps; an older, established capitalist minded group of teachers, and a younger, socialist leaning, self righteous group of leftists. I made a point to stay as far away from the fat, middle aged, bourgeois couple from New York, whose main interest was in purchasing expensive art. They in turn, viewed me as a quaint combination of naiveté and brain washed. By the end of the trip the camps were sitting at opposite ends of the tourist bus. Mao would have loved it.

A friend from the Boston party building movement, a Chinese-American, gave me a tape recorder to take to her cousin who otherwise could never have purchased one. Like so many Chinese, he was trying to learn English as fast as possible in hopes of getting a better job. Although we never communicated directly, after his commute by train from the countryside, he found me in Beijing on the steps of the Temple of Heaven, a huge building with a blue roof and six red pillars. The cousin, a man wearing a clean, white shirt with short, dark hair, and black glasses boldly approached me. I noticed he wore a watch with a black wristband. After a quick handshake, he asked me, "Are you meeting with the Central Committee?" Startled at this inquiry, I was convinced I had misunderstood him. Dressed in blue jeans and sandals, I asked myself, do I look like someone who would meet with the equivalent of the American Congress? Apparently at that time almost all foreigners in Beijing were political delegates. Through our conversation of sign language and choppy words, we established that I was a lowly tourist.

Within the next fifteen minutes I learned that he hated the Gang of Four, the Cultural Revolution had destroyed many people, and he wished he could live more with his wife and baby.

"Where *do* you live?"

"Next to factory," he answered. I remembered an earlier time in American history when workers lived in towns owned by cotton and steel mills.

"Can't they live with you?"

"No much room," he said sadly.

Dismayed that I could do nothing to remedy his problems I handed him the tape recorder from his cousin in Boston. "So sorry. This isn't much. I hope it helps," I sighed with a puzzled expression. He nodded and smiled. I did not tell him that his privileged, well educated cousin in Boston worked for socialist revolution in the United States. He would not have understood that in any language.

Disturbed by his depressing answers, I blamed my confusion at his statements on the language barrier. It couldn't be all that bad, I hoped. Outside the Beijing Hotel where we were staying was a huge granite sign with a red background and gold characters. "Serve the People," our guide translated. Serving the people was a slogan I believed in with all my heart. It resonated with my childhood of Girl

Scouts, World War II, and the Civil Rights movement. But as the days passed I became more perplexed when I could not find one copy of the Quotations from Chairman Mao anywhere, not even in the bookstores. Why? Both Marx and Engel's' books appeared inside the hotel, but all that remained of Mao's collected writings was a book of his poetry. I found it puzzling that the works of one of the greatest political strategist's was absent in his own country. After a week I decided: Mao was missing.

In 1980 relatively few Westerners had visited China and even fewer Americans. For decades, the Chinese had not welcomed foreigners and referred to the United States as a Paper Tiger until after President Nixon's visit in 1972. White skinned people in colorful clothing with lots of electronic equipment were still alien, especially in the rural areas outside Beijing. Our bus could have been from the moon. Hundreds of excited people swarmed around our tourist bus just to look at us, pressing hard against the doors making it impossible at times to get off. At first I feared hostility or anger but quickly realized they were simply curious. "We're like the Beatles,' I whispered to my bus mate staring through the windows into the eyeballs of a boy on top of a man's shoulders. This was what superstar jet setters and royalty lived with everyday, I thought, afraid to admit part of me liked all the attention.

A crowd followed us from the bus to the center of town. Looking over my shoulder I saw a group of people following twenty feet behind. Each time we stopped the sound of marching, sandaled feet quieted, only to begin again as we continued browsing through markets and stores. Before long it became irritating to have fifty people waiting outside the door gawking, pointing and asking questions in Chinese expecting an answer. Unfortunately none of us spoke a word of their language. Three of us on impulse decided to dart into a wave of bicyclists commuting to work, hoping to lose the spectators. Cars belonged only to elite communist party members, so the streets belong to pedestrians and two wheelers. A man with a black and red plaid couch balanced miraculously on the back of his bike, swerved to miss hitting me. Another woman biker with chickens in a bamboo carrier strapped behind her seat whooshed past, frightening us across the dirt road next to a tea seller stand. Operated by two white haired women dressed in blue shirts and brown pants, one served tea to a man with a live chicken perched on his shoulder. Beside them a working woman in a pink shirt squatted on a stool in front of a sewing machine. Young female fruit sellers in loose fitting black tops lined the crowded sidewalks, their pink and red swaddled babies strapped to their backs. A bald headed man in sandals sat on the ground repairing shoes. Overhead I noticed dried fish swaying in the breeze outside apartment kitchen windows, dangling from strings attached to coat hangers hooked over clotheslines.

I could afford to purchase what I thought were beautiful objects because my US factory wages made me a millionaire in China-a red silk jacket for my mother, a hand painted thermos, a block print, a lotus flower painting, a silk wall hanging, posters, post cards and stamps. I felt ashamed passing the young men on foot pulling rickshaws filled with coal. Construction workers without hard hats laying brick in shorts and sandals rattled me. Delighted by a wooden stand with tiny 3x5 inch books, I bent over a young boy seated in the dust reading a cartoon. He smiled and a crowd began gathering. Suddenly I remembered the jar of bubbles and the wire slinky at the bottom of my backpack. Blowing rainbow bubbles, the boy followed me beneath a silvery spray of bursts attracting more and more people. Moving to a set of stairs, I placed the slinky at the top, and like magic, it walked down the stairs one at a time drawing *ohs* and *ahs* from the onlookers. One brave peasant snuck up to the slinky, poked, and jumped back, his wide spaced teeth glowed through his grin. Sharing these simple toys filled the deeply wrinkled adult faces and the little boy with amazement and joy far beyond words. No one asked questions. We were just human beings laughing at a silly thing on a warm July evening.

The countryside looked exactly as I imagined. Fields and fields of rice, with water buffalo pulling primitive farm machinery, red soil being mixed and formed into bricks, mostly for housing. The poverty looked different than poverty in the States. At home, rural America is piled up with old cars, TV's and refrigerators rusting away in front of barns or in ditches. Here there was no excess anything, only dilapidated wooden farm tools that look picturesque to my eyes, much like our pioneer days. It was shocking to see peasants ankle deep in water, smile from the muddy summer heat and wave at us well feed, well dressed Americans, jumping off an air conditioned bus taking photographs of them. Our greatest hardship was squatting over toilets that were cement holes in the floor with foot rests on either side. The elite treatment continued that evening as we were served ginger flavored lotus roots from the beautiful lotus flowers with pink blossoms we saw growing all over the farmland. Some English teachers joined us and two of the women spoke excellent English. We discussed their families, children, their own childhoods, when in a spontaneous outburst the older of the two women began describing the Cultural Revolution. Bitterly, she began, "My childhood was so happy … and then my father was accused of being a 'capitalist roader' because he was a professor. He had to wear a sign around his neck. Eventually he was sent to work in a factory. The Red Guards harassed me because I was his daughter. They hated anybody who was educated. Mao told them to punish us." For a moment the air in the room hung empty. "I was saved from this "re-education" and a life of hard physical labor by our new Chairman Hua." Even I, who always had an answer for everything, held my breath. "You Americans are rich," she continued.

Humbled, I ate more lotus root. "There are many people in America who suffer from poverty, unemployment and discrimination. Upset, I proceeded to describe the broken windows, and crime in my own neighborhood. "Who do you think is the main enemy of the world's people?" I questioned, expecting them to say the United States.

"Soviet Imperialism," they all answered together. I had nothing to say.

We had arrived at Mao Tse-Tung's tomb. This was it. I was about to see my idol for the first time. His embalmed body lay under glass, and I shivered with excitement but noticed that our Chinese tour guide seemed subdued. Each time I questioned her about Mao Tse-Tung thought or his life, her answers were vague or the subject changed. My instinct was to race up and down the line of grey/blue figures behind me, laughing or crying, explaining that I was an American woman who loved Chairman Mao. "You are so lucky that you can still see him," I wanted to say. The closer the line moved to the tomb, the calmer I felt. And there was the face, the face I had worn as a button, hung on my walls, glowed at in books. There he was. The skin under his jaw sagged slightly. Even the large mole on his chin remained. I exhaled deeply.

With a dull expression the guide stated, "They may have to remove him. It has been four years, but the temperature has not worked as perfectly as it did with Lenin's corpse." Overwhelmed I gazed at his dark jacket the fingers at the ends of his sleeves. I longer to lift him through the glass, turn him upright and shake his peasant hero hand. As I dug for my camera, the guide waved us forward, and I remembered: no pictures. The line surged forward. A young woman behind me pressed against my back. My turn was up. Angrily I wondered if I might be one of the last Westerners to view this famous leader. The political climate has changed here and so has the party line. Did the temperature in Mao's tomb really have anything to do with it? Perhaps the Central Committee really wanted to bury his body *and his thought*.

As the tour progressed, the only clarity I found was how unclear China was in comparison to my expectations. Twisting my hair around my pencil on the Beatles bus, anxiously I waited for a new fact or a revelation to strike. "It is a land of extremes, opposite poles, you know, yin/yang," my bus partner said soothingly.

"But history does not reverse itself at a moments notice," I insisted. "My theory book explains that dialectics goes slowly two steps forward, one step back."

"Well, maybe they're hopping," she giggled. Too serious to laugh, I grimaced.

"Trouble is, I can't tell if the Chinese are in a backward or forward step now."

Excited by a visit to a factory I knew must be run by workers, a spokesperson told us that a Labor Council assigned young people right out of middle school to jobs where they remained for life. The thought of spending the rest of my days in an electronics plant or welded to the shipyard made me choke. This didn't sound like my idea of socialism, but then again, what was socialism in an underdeveloped nation? I questioned my diary. Most people in China are very poor, uneducated, and doing well if they have food, clothing and a roof overhead. Maybe socialism for this many people can only follow a tremendous accumulation of wealth. Maybe they must go through capitalism first? I could hardly think such a thought, and continued to write in tiny cursive:

> *Once again my idealism is knocked flat. It happened in Cuba, but somehow it is like a pancake here. I see two classes, one that does manual labor and speaks only Chinese, and the other professional, managerial, and party members who speak Chinese and English. To make matters worse, our guide in Nanning was racist, described the Mongolians as very ugly, with Korean features unsuitable for movies. How can people who call themselves communists be racist? At least the communists back home fight racism within their own ranks.*

I left the factory so depressed I tried pushing my mouth into a smile. And the Great Revolution? Where was it? Oh, how I wanted Mission Hill and Steve's loving arms. He could explain it. He was *so* smart. Maybe his degree from the Johns Hopkins School of Advanced International Studies would be good for something after all.

On the last day of our three week visit, the Beatles bus drove straight into surrealism. I picked a bike off the public rack and rode around the enormous government buildings and memorials in Tiananmen Square. I rang a little bell on the handle bars. Mao's great eyes watched me from a wall. What the hell was that? Whining and high pitched it was distinctly Chinese, but Jingle Bells started pouring out of the loudspeakers. My ears hurt. Ten yards in front of me, a lines of men in green uniforms marched in unison followed by women in white shirts and green pants. The guide said, "It is the People's Liberation Army." I was stunned. They weren't heroic like the monuments and statues or the mythic villagers I envisioned following Mao's banner. They were young and they were goose stepping to an American Christmas carol in July. When our guides told us all the statues of Marx and Lenin had been removed from the square and Mao's would soon follow, I felt like throwing myself face down on the pavement. Anguished, I moved away to hide my tears. So much for Red China I sobbed. Nine years later Tiananmen Square would turn red with the blood of its own children.

Flying home with more questions than answers I told my journal:

*All I know is that I am no longer sure who or what to believe, except
that almost nothing I have learned about the Chinese political system makes sense.Only one thing remains clear. China's priority is
modernization. Everyone agrees with that. And when it comes right
down to it, I am a spoiled American completely unprepared for the
conditions in a poor non-industrialized country with millions of
people living in poverty. It's embarrassing to admit that I miss good
plumbing and clean indoor toilets.*

North Carolina, 2006

My twenty three year old daughter, Moriah, walked into the kitchen with a load
of expensive organic groceries. A college graduate in the age of globalization she
was now an advisor. "Mom, you've got to see the new Wal-Mart movie, "High
Cost of Low Price". You'll never shop there again. All that stuff you bought for
your guest cabin, Mom." She shook her head, "From now on go to Target."

When I witnessed the working conditions of the Chinese employees on the
public library movie screen a month later, I understood why our prices are so
low. Row after row of former peasants, the grandchildren of those people I saw
in 1980, were crammed into regulation-free factories and factory dormitories—
poorly paid, poorly fed, over worked. Necessary for the selfish, Chinese elite who
want a shot at being top world player in forty years. Remembering that I had
filled my new guest cabin with Wal-Mart towels, sheets, kitchen supplies, and a
barbecue grill just to save money made me slump deeper into the metal library
chair. But I have to stay competitive like all Americans do, I thought, wishing
guiltily that I had purchased the new cabin deck furniture for my summer guests
before the show. Well, I can always hope that like the French farmer who drove
his tractor into MacDonald's, villagers in rural China will drive a herd of water
buffalo through Wal-Mart's consumer paradise.

It looks like China in Catch Up Mode might equal the American Empire in
forty years. All those bikes will be cars emitting $CO2$, no one will be able to
breathe, or drink clean water; cancer rates will be high, but as long as everyone has
an ipod who cares? Apparently the world is flat again. Re-engineered for corporate
globalization to make the whole world one big happy family of consumers. Wal-
Mart exploits its American employees too—busts unions, discriminates against
women. Marx was right after all. Welcome to the international proletariat.

Hannah Hall Jacobsen (right), Maternal Great Grandmother, her three children, Eunice (second from left), my Maternal Grandmother, her sister and brother, Logan, Utah, 1894.

Archie Quayle Hale & Otelia Baker Hale, Paternal Grandparents, Logan, Utah, 1917.

Alys Miles Hale and Myron Q Hale, Mother and Father, late 1940s.

Shanks Village, Rockland County, New York, 1952.

Kendall Hale, 1953.

Kendall, Mother and sisters, Columbus, Ohio 1961.

Miffland Street Block Party, Madison, Wisconsin, 1969.

Cuban flag, Mifflin Street Food Co-op, 1969.

Anti-Vietnam War demonstration, Portland, Oregon, 1972.

Union meeting, Kendall singing "Which Side Are You On?"
Cambion Strike, Cambridge, Massachussets, 1973.

New Harmony Sisterhood Band, Boston, Mass., 1975.

New Harmony Sisterhood tour, Kendall and Super Woman, 1979.

New Harmony Sisterhood on tour, 1979.

Mass. Childbearing Rights Alliance

INVITES YOU TO A
POLITICAL/CULTURAL EVENING ON

CHILDBEARING RIGHTS 1979

DISCUSSIONS ON RECENT DEVELOPMENTS IN THE MOVEMENT FOR:

*ABORTION RIGHTS

*FREEDOM FROM STERILIZATION ABUSE

*CHILDCARE

*WORKER'S REPRODUCTIVE RIGHTS

PRESENTATIONS BY:

MARIAN McDONALD	FOUNDING MEMBERS
PAULA GEORGES	OF
KENDALL HALE	MCRA

NEW HARMONY SISTERHOOD BAND

Sat. November 17th 7:30pm

CHURCH OF THE COVENANT
67 NEWBURY ST.
BOSTON

$3. OR DONATION FOR UNEMPLOYED
AT DOOR

CHILDCARE PROVIDED
CALL 776-6759

General Dynamics Shipyard, Quincy, MA, 1978.

Picket line, General Dynamics, 1978.

Kendall in Beijing, China, 1980.

Bike transporting a couch, China, 1980.

GETTING NORMAL

Motherhood, Marriage and Mission Hill, 1980

Steve hadn't told me that our new neighborhood was a prime target of crime from two housing projects, whose mismanagement by the Boston Housing Authority had led to widespread neglect and abandonment. Or that his apartment was burglarized once a year. Or that the manager of the corner store was murdered behind the counter. I later learned that a woman neighbor knocked on his door all bloody, a mugger's victim and that his roommate was wounded by a random bullet as he rode his bike past the project. In the mid seventies there were three or four fires a week set by gangsters who collected insurance, and by owners who burned their homes because their value fell below what they'd paid and what the buildings were insured for and by kids who burned buildings for fun.

Steve adored Mission Hill and what he did tell me was that the Irish settled here but were now outnumbered by Latinos, African Americans, Chinese, Poles, and Greeks, that activists were well organized, and that he played the geographer and the snake in a neighborhood production of The Little Prince. "No one in the community affected me more than the ragtag assortment of kids and grownups acting in the community theatre, "Streetfeet," he always said. A sixties survivor, Steve was a PhD political scientist who wore work boots and carried a hammer. He left behind a potential career in the military when he quit West Point, he left a wife and two sons, and a second career as a professor. Now he was the best educated carpenter in the world. And probably the happiest.

After months of studying the principles and practices of solar heating, Steve worked out a design he liked. In the spring of 1980, he received a loan for $30,000 from a bank who responded to his discrimination complaint with the Massachusetts Banking Commission. He had been turned down twice because the neighborhood was poor. Soon afterward, I went with Steve and his parents to the house site on the Back of the Hill with a pair of lopping shears and a chainsaw. He pointed out to his Dad and Mom that the three lots he owned faced south, had lots of trees and a beautiful stone wall. "And 30 feet above the street you can see the ocean to the east and the Blue Hills ten miles to the south," he added not mentioning the run down park or that the city owned our back yard and driveway. Thus began what the <u>Boston Globe</u> featured in a front-page Metro section story: "Roxbury man Builds His Dream for $35,000." My motorcycle knight with help from many friends and members of the community, managed to take a slice of a dying city neighborhood and bring it back alive again with an inexpensive but attractive house that had the most ancient and modern heating system—the sun.

"Look, Steve," I pointed to the sweetest little girl I had ever seen standing on the deck of a whale watching boat in Boston Harbor. About three and a half feet tall with dark brown shoulder length braids she enchanted me with the power of a princess. The humpback whales leaping from the ocean were large enough to swallow her whole. Their knobby black and white heads thrilled us over and over again rising and falling in the waves squirting water through blow holes, and waving their fins. "The whales are great, but I'd like one of her. Please."

Without hesitation he answered. "OK."

Things stayed pretty sweet between us until Steve fell into the black hole of my psyche. A void that ran through every cell in my being. How could he know? I was not wearing a tee shirt or a button advertising who I really was: Damaged Goods. Beware. Attacks Without Warning. Or: Unemployed Marxist-Leninist. Major Identity Crisis. Watch Out! A potent mix of grief and anger hung over me like invisible armor.

One afternoon in a corner of our dingy, tiny living room I sat diligently sorting slides for a presentation I was to give on my China trip.

"I'm off to Melrose to see my Dad," Steve said cheerfully holding his motor-cycle helmet and a bag of potato chips. "See you later tonight." He blew me a kiss.

"Wait!" I jumped up. "Don't go visit him *now.*"

Puzzled at my intensity, he said, "But he's expecting me."

"No, don't go."

"Why?"

My lips puckered. "I just don't want you to."

"Well, I want to see him. I'm going."

After he left, I exploded, fumed into his study, pushed everything off his desk onto the floor, glared at the typewriter, picked it up, shook it and heaved it across the room.

Lucky for me, Steve had lived through his own identity crisis, been in therapy and was a member of the Boston co-counseling community. But the truth was, he needed someone to save—and I was it. A car wreck on two wheels.

And I kept driving, right into Steve's dream, with lopper and chain saw. Building a passive solar house together on Fisher Avenue cemented his love affair with Mission Hill, with me and with interpersonal battles on the construction site. My shipyard welding skills were not useful, so for weeks I installed pink insulation wearing a white face mask, jealous of Steve and the other skilled carpenters, frustrated being the builder's lover. Fortunately during the house construction I got pregnant, which made me a happier ex-Marxist-Leninist, until the nausea and exhaustion.

For three months I slept ten to fifteen hours a day. With one glance my bed yanked me flat and became the center of my life, leaving me irritable when I got up. The nurse practitioner, friends, pregnancy books—all assured me it was natural, normal, and alright to feel tired but my conditioning yelled louder. "Get up, fight, wake up. Look at Steve. You need to be working harder." More attractive than life, my dreams led me inside my own dark, comforting womb. Nothing held my interest except food which I craved not out of loneliness, neediness or frustration, but simply to construct new life. Eating had always been a means to an end, so thinking carefully about which foods had iron, protein and amino acids felt burdensome. I read all the nausea tips in the health clinic pamphlets, like eating crackers or toast very slowly, rising from bed very slowly, but I vomited constantly, not matter what prevention method I tried. Our apartment felt smaller, dingier and dirtier each morning, and any odd smell or even a natural odor, like the gas burner, brought on queasiness forcing me to stare into black stains or pieces of last night's salad at the bottom of the sink. Then, up came breakfast.

Like magic, I felt wonderful in the second trimester of pregnancy. The rush of hormones helped me leave the revolution and New Harmony Sisterhood behind. Now I had a man, a new house with a rental unit, and a baby on the way. Six months later we moved in. Within weeks, I joined the neighborhood security watch so I could walk the streets in groups of five at night with a club on my shoulder, and began attending Back of the Hill meetings with Steve, who was best friends with Judy Howard, the president.

Judy was a 50 year old genius who collected and resold junk. Her house was filled with odd knick-knacks, used furniture and boxes of hats, jackets, ties and other strange clothing. Frequently Steve came home wearing it. Her house was surrounded on two sides by overgrown, vacant land owned by a local church. The side next to her driveway was also a vacant lot owned by the Boston Redevelopment Authority. The whole area was covered with blackberry bushes, saplings, and random trash, neglected for years except by kids who had built a tree house, now decaying. Judy was famous for occupying Mayor Kevin White's office in City Hall with neighbors and young children until he agreed to meet with her about low income housing, later known as Back of the Hill Apartments.

In preparation for my new baby I dug out a corner of the back yard for my future garden. Like the rest of the back of the hill, the top of the hill behind our new house was a meadow with a city park that looked more like a dump. Mothers took their children to the playground covered with beer bottles, shattered glass and cigarette butts. Paint peeled off the jungle gym and the decades-old ducks and chickens sitting on giant springs. The trash cans had all been stolen so paper and plastic blew around in the tall grass overlooking the city, Boston harbor, and south to the Quincy shipyard. Luckily, it was before AIDS and widespread condom use. Sometimes a tethered pony grazed at one end while drug dealers hung at the other. On weekends I swept rainwater from under the swings and glass from the end of the slide with our second tenant, a white mother of three black children with two different African fathers.

The first tenant in our new house was a diehard Marxist Leninist who soon moved to California after frozen chicken was stolen out of the refrigerator as she slept. We then decided to get two German shepherds who ran loose on the hill but faithfully returned to frighten off intruders until one bit a child and the other disappeared. It took me weeks of setting off the security alarm by accident entering the back door before I routinely flipped the switch. It sounded like a school bell but ten times louder. So loud, the elderly nursing home residents across the street always knew when I got home. Steve installed it after a robber stole the gold pendant watch with tiny birds on the cover my grandmother gave me and some tools from his box. Once after that I saw a shadowy figure through the backdoor window trying to hide behind a tree. The trouble was, he was wider than the trunk. I opened the door.

"I see you, you bastard thief," I screamed as loud as I could. "Get out of here fast before I call the police!" Two seconds later he vanished.

My new job as a unit secretary at Mass General Hospital bored me to death, but gave me the health benefits I needed. As my belly grew rounder, the idea of a natural home birth intrigued me. My midwife would be Shafia, an African American Muslim woman who wore long flowing dresses and a turban. She successfully delivered my friend's baby at home so why not mine? I was a pregnant radical feminist who viewed most institutions including hospitals as invasive and controlling. It didn't help matters much that I now lived in a community of people with a history of being over run by them. I shared their suspicions. Years earlier, our feisty neighbors had successfully organized to stop encroachment by Leahy

Clinic and the Ruggles Street Baptist Church. The two institutions had bought up an eight-block area, evicting tenants from 50 triple-decker buildings—each with three apartments—in order to build a hospital and a church. The new facilities were never built and the ravished ten acres was now a tire filled, overgrown mess on Back of the Hill. The bodies of two young Latino men were found there by someone walking their dog.

Since I believed in self determination, I wanted to be in charge of our baby's birth. Totally. We attended birth classes, practiced Lamaze breathing, and read birth books with the idea that Steve would be present to catch the baby. "Will you be on my birth team?" I asked six people explaining that I needed friends to clean house, cook food, keep the wood burning stove lit, and manage the exit and entry of everyone assisting in the birthing bedroom. I read a book on midwifery and as the due date grew closer began making lists of instructions written in red ink to hang on my bedroom wall for my team.

Early in Labor:

1. Page Shafia, pick her up or pay for her taxi
2. Call the hospital to announce labor
3. Prepare one car for emergency hospital visit
4. Shovel snow
5. Set up space heater and humidifier
6. Feed cat and dogs

During Labor:

1. Help me breath, smile and hold, counsel and massage
2. Make comfrey tea for compresses
3. Put on soothing music
4. Load film
5. Get the sterile shoe string for the cord
6. Unplug large clock at birth

After Birth:

1. Put placenta in bowl, bury in garden
2. Remove soiled sheets and plastic
3. Cook, dance, sing and drink

Weeks before my due date a local TV station called. "Could we film your home birth for a news story?" Even with shadowed faces my instinct was, no. What if something went wrong?

Eighteen hours of labor made working in the shipyard seem like a beginners course in pain. Once the cramping started it was like all the menstrual periods I ever had from age thirteen rolled into one. Soaking in a bathtub of hot water didn't make any difference. My teammates rubbed my shoulders, my feet—rocked me from side to side, lifted me forward, backward, pressed hard on my lower spine. One brought ice, another herbal tea. Steve told jokes until I ordered him to stop laughing. When my midwife arrived I was exhausted. "Shafia, it hurts. It hurts so much. There must be something wrong!" I moaned. She took all my vital signs, checked for cervical dilation, and held my hand. "Breathe, breathe through the contractions," she said, as her lips formed an O shape. Squatting felt worse, so I lay on my back wishing for drugs. Four hours later the driveway from our house through the park was covered with a foot of snow. "I want to go to the hospital," I decided. Both Steve and Shafia were bewildered. "Take me to the hospital!" Outside, the team mobilized behind Steve's truck as the wheels spun deeper into the snow, pushing and shoving as he waved hand signals. A tiny passionate red star glowed over my head from the center of a beautiful diamond shaped wall Steve had built for me. I felt like a betrayer when I heard someone tell the hospital we were coming. "If it were legal for me to give you a mild pain killer I would," Shafia comforted me as I moaned asking again and again why it was so horribly painful. Urgent voices echoed: "Lee, can we take your van? Steve's truck won't budge!" "Help me get Kendall into some clothes."

Steve held me as Lee's old VW van bumped and slid over the muddy ice covered road through the park toward Brigham and Women's hospital ten minutes away. The staff determined nothing was wrong and gave me a drug that helped slightly. When the nurse came to shave my pubic hair I refused, reminding her that I did not want an episiotomy. "It was supposed to be natural childbirth, 100%." They cut me anyway, and wheeled me into a delivery room on a hard metal table full of blinding flood lights. "Stop pushing," a nurse ordered. "The doctor's not here!" I looked for Shafia. "She can't come in here", Steve whispered squeezing my hand. But my baby was in control now. Contractions propelled her down the birth canal—there was no turning back.

And so our daughter Moriah joined us.

A baby girl was the best gift the whale Goddess could have arranged, and here she was. My happiness took on another dimension. Nurturing new life converted every bit of my body's loving energy into breast feeding which was a wholeness larger than the universe, expanding my tenderness to the stars and back. No goal or task accomplished ever felt so deep. Steve built Moriah a wooden cradle and our baby lit flames of joy under the Christmas tree in 1981.

As could have been predicted, eight weeks later a neurotic need to do 'something important' (feminists couldn't stay at home) drove me to enroll in a photography course, plan for graduate school and search for daycare providers. Soon to follow, monthly meetings with two of my best friends, both working moms, were better than a seminar with Dr Spock. The next spring and summer I planted my first garden seeds, and planned our marriage ceremony, proud to do everything backwards. Our wedding invitation read: *Moriah Norris-Hale Invites You to the Wedding of Her Parents.* On August 21, 1982, our friend Ed sat on the roof of a shed playing an electric accordion as our friends, families and guests walked up the long cement stairs from Fisher Ave to our backyard wedding. My former female lover baked a cake with 'Getting Normal' written on top, and true to our hippie roots, all the food was potluck. The suburban looking lawn we celebrated on, a present from my parents, had been rolled down the week before. We wrote our own vows, my talented opera singer sister sang, as did former members of New Harmony Sisterhood. Loving, supportive words flowed from the lips of everyone during our participatory speak out. Except my mother, who graced us with the following comment, "This is the first thing Kendall has ever done that did not totally terrify me."

My father stood proudly holding Moriah, relieved I was finally married, even if to an ex-political scientist, and grateful for the appearance of stability. For the next 10 years Dad told me over and over, "You and Steve are the smartest, most creative people I know"

"We are," I would ask in amazement. "Why?"

"Because you figured out how to beat the system. You don't pay heat bills and by God, you don't have a mortgage."

"And one other thing," I added to amuse him, "We use these funny spiral bulbs in our lamps that use less energy which lowers our electric bill. Do you want to know what they're called?"

"Why not."

"Compact fluorescents"

"Hmmmmm. Send me one, I'll take a look."

In 1985, the Back of the Hill organization was an odd combination of fugitives, victims, two yuppies, and one Christian. The blacks and Hispanics were mostly victims of poverty. The white people were recent fugitives from the middle class. Some of the people with white skins were old timers too stubborn to leave. We never could figure out why a single Christian woman built a gigantic house adjacent to us, but it probably had something to do with land the Ruggles Street Baptist Church sold her. We worked together because we had to, and the organization's meetings were worse than any anarchist could have ever dreamed up. The staff person was Roger, a tiny Jewish man who later became a comic writer. His student intern took notes, but often simply gazed at the ceiling with a *get me out of here look*. Roger took orders from president Judy whose voice was so shrill one needed a microphone to be heard over her, but it didn't much matter—she wouldn't follow Roger's agenda anyway. The meetings really never had a beginning or end, but from what I remember the first half hour was spent trashing John who lived in a run down triple decker house he was always planning to finish but never did. I was relieved when he did show up because everyone shut up which meant we might get home by 10pm. The yuppie thought he could make money by building a crazy three tiered house with steps climbing skyward that looked like it belonged in Thailand rather than the inner city of Boston. Three hundred pound Chris came to meetings because they were downhill from his house. His breath shortened even walking on the level and his black skin sparkled with sweat in the middle of winter. The Irish sisters had lived together on back of the hill since the time of the buy out and massive eviction, teaching in the public schools. Both had hair the color of an Irish Setter, pale skin and lots of freckles, and one of their voices was loud enough to occasionally get the president's attention. My husband was proud he was a West Point drop out, and I thought we would live here forever, just like I thought China was a socialist paradise. Which brings me to Nate, the really gorgeous grey panther who spent all day every day at social justice meetings before stopping off to complain with us. Somehow in the midst of continuous pandemonium important decisions were made and carried out. I think it was because we all *were* missionaries on a mission in Mission Hill.

If you go to Google Earth the internet will show you the building for low income elderly and disabled. It won't show you the sign Steve made in front with the orange sunrise behind the letters "Back of the Hill Apartments." People live there now because loud mouthed Judy and her co-conspirators forced the mayor to build it, and learned how to manage it. You can also see affordable housing built by the Brick Layers Union where the empty vacant lots used to be. Our wacky group ultimately made a decision to make that happen, and also prevented the octopus like New England Baptist from taking all the land it wanted. But, you cannot see the nurses' apartments next to the hospital at the top of the hill behind our solar house. That's because the hospital bull dozed them early one morning in the summer of 1984 and put up a parking lot.

At 6:15am Judy called. "Steve, they're tearing down the apartments."

"Is that you, Judy? What are you talking about? Who's tearing down what?"

"The hospital—they've got bulldozers up there on the hill behind your house. Didn't the noise wake you up? They're knocking down the brick apartments. We've been trying to save those apartments so families could live in them, and they're destroying them as we speak. We've got to get up there and stop them. Get out of bed and drive me up there."

We barely understood what she was talking about, but then Steve remembered Judy had been working hard to save nurses quarters previously owned by another hospital before New England Baptist bought them. The Baptist Hospital had plans to turn the area into a parking lot.

"Ok Judy, I'll pick you up in five minutes," I heard him say. We heard the dull throated moan of heavy equipment operating not too far away.

When we got to the hospital ten minutes later, there were two enormous flat-bladed bulldozers plowing through brick walls, seemingly in a hurry to do as much damage as fast as they could. They'd already laid waste to about a quarter of the 25 or so single story apartments by knocking big holes in the sides of each of them.

"We've got to get in there and stop those 'dozers. Just park here in the road and let's get over there."

Hospital security guards blocked our way. We saw their uniforms and badges and felt intimidated. Judy, in contrast, flew out of Steve's truck in a fury, past the chief of security right to the front of the bulldozer.

"You don't have demolition permits, and you don't have the authorization to plow the asbestos that's in the basements into the ground. I'm going to sit in front of this 'dozer until it stops and the police get here. And then I am going to tell everyone else who will listen how the hospital breaks the law and poisons the neighborhood by plowing up asbestos."

Steve stood between Judy and the security guards who looked like they might try to carry her off. Judy, never in very good health and dressed in an old coat to ward off the morning chill, looked even more fragile than usual. Within minutes a squad car arrived, siren blaring and lights flashing. The middle aged cop, who looked as haggard as Judy, seemed as confused as everyone else to see a frazzled grandmother in house clothes sitting in front of a bulldozer.

Within half an hour, two inspectors from the Building Department appeared and said demolition and construction would have to cease until the matter of permits and asbestos was resolved. Later that day, the mayor showed up to inspect the carnage. And Judy appeared on the nightly news as a heroine sitting in a mud hole in front of a huge stalled bulldozer.

Members of the Back of the Hill decided to stage a funeral for the demolished nurses quarters. Dressed in shorts and sandals, I was making a video for my masters thesis and filmed the procession of mourners marching behind a black casket to a grassy spot near the hospital. People dressed casually, since no one had been killed over this, except Judy's son who wore a tux with a black, silk top hat and carried a bouquet of flowers. Most residents could not afford treatment at this hospital because it did not accept Medicaid. We were pissed off, but believed that the orders to negotiate issued by a state agency funding the hospital would lead to a victory for the neighborhood. We wanted the hospital to commit to limiting its growth so that no more houses would be destroyed and to develop off-hill parking to relieve traffic congestion on the neighborhood's narrow streets. The hospital's goal was to renew construction, committing to as few limitations as possible. I don't think many of the administrators heard Joni Mitchell singing about People's Park, *They paved paradise, put up a parking lot, ooooolaalaa,* from our battery operated tape player below their office windows.

Take Back the Hill, a documentary produced by the author is available on her website www.radicalpassions.com

MAMA CLARA'S GARDEN

Journal: Esteli, Nicaragua, 1985

> *I've felt a deep depression about the living conditions here: the filth, the unsanitary conditions, the dirty toilets, the parasites, and the mud in our room and all over our daughter. She is so frightened by the large crickets on the toilet seat in the outhouse that we have a bucket in our bedroom that she uses. I'm almost better, but the bactrim has not eliminated her diarrhea, and now Steve has a large parasite in his stomach. Tiny lizards crawl up and down the walls of our room, making it smaller than ever; moths and mosquitoes buzz around a single light bulb hanging from our ceiling. I am grateful for the roses that bloom in Mama Clara's garden and the beers that a gentleman brought us for lunch today. I feel crazy forgetting why I came.*

Mission Hill, 1984

Steve and I sat one summer evening in our back yard while Moriah, raced around in her three-year-old world. It was the yard we had planted and been married in. It was the yard that had hosted numerous fund-raisers for political causes, and the yard we now played in with Moriah. That June evening the idea of the Vecino project was born. Under the stars of the inner city, I listened to Rachel, one of my most adventurous friends, describe the northern town of Esteli, Nicaragua where she had lived and worked. She was a true internationalist, born in India, raised by English missionaries, fluent in Spanish and well traveled in Central America. As she told the story of a people who reclaimed their humanity through years of successful organizing, party-building, and war I found myself edging closer to the front of my rusted lawn chair. Inhaling her stories stimulated an old longing for another chance at revolution.

"The Sandinistas were successful without a Marxist-Leninist party tied to the Soviet Union. They have a united front of mixed ideology," Rachel explained.

"Wow, maybe they had the right formula. The one none of the others could pull off," I said referring to China, Cuba, the Soviet Union and our failed American socialist revolution of the sixties. Instantly, I saw myself speaking Spanish in the mountains and using a hammer and a video camera. I can still be a part of a socialist success, I thought to myself, looking at Moriah, innocent and protected from the world of poverty, malnutrition and the political strife we spoke of. Yes, I wanted to stop the *Contra* war and the Yankee imperialists, but I was also now a devoted mother with responsibility. Below, the ambulance at the nursing home on Fisher Ave caught my ear. Someone's dying or dead, I thought. Am I ready to die? Above, I noticed a new moon, a sign of new beginnings and the same yellow sliver hanging over Esteli. I wondered how people there endured? Thousands of women in Nicaragua were mothers and revolutionaries, many leaving their children for months to join the rebels against the dictatorship. Fear of death, loss, and separation had not stopped them. It had been easy to consider dying for my convictions as a single person. But could I sacrifice now? And was I really risking my life? Or my child's? Fear jolted my body against the back of the lawn chair.

"You can take Moriah with you," Rachel's confident voice answered my internal dialogue. After all, Rachel had borne a son with a man who was a member of a revolutionary organization in El Salvador. "The women in the community will help take care of her. She'll learn Spanish and...." Her words faded, as I looked at Moriah hanging upside down on the monkey bars, her tangled dreadlocks dangling in the dust, a forerunner of what was to come.

My conflicts were never addressed, but a year later the three of us were living in Esteli where I swung between bravado and terror. I had lived in turmoil during the student movement in Madison, but chaos in poverty and war with a three-year-old tore to the core of my motherhood. Bringing our daughter and a fragile marriage to a war in Central America nearly ended in divorce. But half way through the project in August, 1985, Steve and I were featured on the front page of the *Boston Globe*. A picture of us building a health clinic for the Sandinistas was directly below a photograph of Nancy Reagan hugging President Reagan in a hospital, as he recovered from nose surgery. Years later, staring at that picture erases everything but the triumph, and I know I would do it all again.

For months before leaving for Esteli, I struggled with Steve's leading role, his flirtations, and his ability to calculate, collect and send building materials for the project via Canada with the help of underground activists. My anxiety and jealousy of the attention he received from new Vecino members including his obvious attraction to a local woman organizer made me ever more anxious. Motherhood and a recent master's degree in mass communication created even more uncertainty about Nicaragua. My rational side begged to stay in Mission Hill with Moriah, and my unfulfilled professional life screamed for attention. Yet my rebel dreams could not detach from a project so close to my heart: the anti-imperialist war. For months cuddled in bed before sleeping, Steve and I read about Sandino, a Nicaraguan leader who led his people against the US—backed dictator Somoza in the 1920's. Just as the Vietnam, Cuban, Chilean and Chinese revolutions had captured my imagination, so did the music, poetry, art, and ideology of the insurgents who dared to fight for a better future in Nicaragua. While the passion and righteousness of aiding this youthful revolution drove me deeper into the Vecino project, I felt our marriage destabilizing, the chemistry altering. "Nicaragua, Nicaraguita, …" As I write, remembering the long bus ride from Managua to the mountains of Esteli, words from this beautiful song flood my throat. I cry now as I cried then, the tears streamed from my eyes watching the crowd gather to greet us, realizing the enormity of our accomplishment.

I shed another skin in Nicaragua. All the slogans and all the rhetoric shattered as we passed through a looking glass of comfortable living full of good food, indoor plumbing, new cars, accessible healthcare, large homes, and skyscrapers into an impoverished country void of material benefits but abundant in spirit. I was simply outside the time, space and culture that shaped me as middle class North American woman.

Steve, Moriah and I lived with "Mama" Clara, Eusabio and their children in a house with dirt floors and no indoor plumbing. In 1980 while I traveled with the Chinese-American Friendship Association to China, I lived in luxurious conditions like a member of the Central Committee, but here we lived with and as peasants. Trying her best to accommodate our every need, Clara cooked for us, washed our clothes, and took care of Moriah while we worked on the clinic site. Steve and I shared a single bed, and ate rice and beans three times a day with some eggs, cheese, coffee and occasionally a little meat. If we had arrived during Moriah's breast-feeding year, life would have been relatively easy, but without milk or familiar food, she did not adjust well to her new environment. Our host family spoke no English and we knew very little Spanish. Our daughter had barely mastered her own language and here children spoke in strange sounds only vaguely remembered from Sesame Street. At least the roosters and farm animals living outside her bedroom looked like the ones at the petting zoo.

I felt guilty and sad leaving Moriah everyday to deal with these hardships, but Clara was very loving and I knew she was safe. Clara's daughters and a few neighborhood children came into our room at night and we played games in sign language pointing, motioning and laughing, all of us anxious to be liked and understood. Moriah's blonde hair in contrast to their black heads and darker complexions drew crowds of children on the street around her who reached out in curiosity, to touch and pinch her cheeks, until Steve began carrying her on his shoulders. Once in the safety of the children's playground she climbed down and drank the familiar tasting Coca Cola we bought her, served in plastic bags sold by venders on the street. It was appalling to me that Coke, this Yankee imperialist drink, was abundant here when milk wasn't. The US economic boycott ensured that most children woke up and drank coffee for breakfast.

My insecurity about and competition with Steve drove me to the highest level of construction I could achieve. Fear of being left out or viewed as insignificant forced me to chose between my child's happiness and my own self-esteem. Each morning after we had cold showers and some breakfast, Steve left for the construction site, and I followed. We worked from 7:00 a.m. to noon, broke for two hours, and then resumed till 3:30 or 4:30.

Journal: Esteli, June, 1985

The community is bringing food, juice drinks and water to the site every day and large numbers of Nicaraguan volunteers including women and children are working. The children are creating a problem because they are barefoot, using unfamiliar tools, and in danger of hurting themselves. Without the presence of North American women on the construction site, it is obvious that the Nicaraguan women would not be here. I've been working hard, carrying lumber, digging holes, bending wire, preparing agendas for the general meetings and participating in the organized Spanish classes. I carry my dictionary in my back pocket, and struggle very hard to speak. It is truly frustrating but most people are very helpful. Children love to help me talk because it is empowering for them. Everyone on the brigade now has diarrhea and stomach aches because of bacteria in the food and water.

Few of the Vecino women were carpenters by trade in contrast to the men, but many of us had worked at manual jobs and all of us spent some time learning how to handle tools. We appeared rugged in blue jeans, T shirts and work boots beside the cotton dresses and plastic sandals worn by the women in Esteli who left the site after the first day or two to resume work at home and in their neighborhoods. I had stopped wearing a bra in the early 1970's when it was cool for feminists to burn them, but I did it primarily because I was flat-chested enough that it felt more comfortable. The Vecino women argued that "watermelons" on the construction site would send the wrong message, so the Nicaraguan sun became even hotter as I put on a second layer of clothing. At first, some of the Nicaraguan men tried to take over jobs we did more slowly or were just learning, but eventually a comfortable working relationship developed between the sexes and the cultures.

One of my goals was to produce a slide show for the unconvinced North Americans in Boston so I photographed people everywhere I went. After work in the evenings we listened to personal stories of what living conditions in pre-revolutionary Nicaragua were like, told in Spanish by local members of the Committees for the Defense of the Revolution. Imagining I would produce a sound track, I tape-recorded the stories of the people who lived it, their accounts of a very high infant mortality rate, sick children, lack of medical care, no education, illiteracy, housing shortages, vivid in their memories and translated to English word-by-word, holding us spellbound for hours. Before the Sandinistas took power, organizing began house-by house, block by block secretly until defense zones were created against Somoza's National Guard. The tape recorder and camera became my best friends and my hope of validating the Nicaraguan's truth. Each of the families our brigade members lived with had witnessed murder, lost sons and daughters, had been tortured themselves or knew others who had died in prison.

This revolution had brought them the freedom to organize and to speak openly about their poverty and needs. Conditions were slowly changing since the Sandinista victory in 1979, but dignity and pride in their sacrifices strengthened them as we forged ahead, knowing the war had not been in vain. It was hard to believe that people were still dying everyday defending their revolution and its beautiful vision, against the *Contras*, a small band of American supported terrorists. On June 24, I was horrified to learn that a little boy was badly hurt by a *Contra* bomb in the center of town. The war raged on closer than any of us imagined, and I began to fear for Moriah's safety as well as my own.

The weeks ahead continued to be a series of highs and lows. Just as I thought stability and routine had settled in and my self worth mended, a pleasure trip turned into a living nightmare. One Saturday rather than work on the site, I decided to take Moriah on a hike with Ralph, another Vecino member, and his Nicaraguan family, outside the town limits to cool off and swim in a waterfall. Dusty and dirty from a week of working and weary of the cramped living quarters, we walked for two hours searching for this oasis of pleasure and relief. I was dependent on Ralph's Spanish and his relationship with the young boy leading us. Suddenly gunshot fire rang out from the not-too-far distance. Waves of nausea and fear I had never experienced panicked me and I froze, clutching Moriah unable to move or think. Convinced it must be the *Contras* staging an ambush, I refused to go any further. I then remembered meeting some Germans in the hotel in Managua who described an ambush on some of their members participating in a housing construction project. At the time I had made light of their story, since we were going to Esteli, one of the strongest pro-Sandinista areas with a reputation for its invincibility. To calm myself, I pictured Clara's husband, Eusebio grinning at the dinner table with his tales of battle against Somoza. His words repeated in my head. "Three times we beat the guard back. Three times!"

I begged Ralph not to go any further. He hesitated as the shooting continued, getting louder which to me meant closer. The Nicaraguan children exchanged words I strained to understand.

"What did they say?" I whispered watching them inch down the trail. "Ralph, I'm staying here. Come back as soon as you find out who it is!"

As the little party of four disappeared from sight in the direction of the water-fall and the shots, I jumped under a large, low bush. Trembling flat on my back, I pulled Moriah close to my heart as images of the two of us being discovered, raped, tortured and shot for aiding the Sandinistas flooded my consciousness. Moriah tried opening her mouth to speak and I instantly slapped my hand over her lips, shaking and crying, "Shhhh, shhhhh, we don't want the bad men to find us. Quiet, honey, quiet." We both lay in terror, wondering in the stillness of the echoing mountains. The gunshots had stopped. The following ten minutes stretched beyond eternity. I heard footsteps pounding on the path, getting closer to our hiding spot.

"Kendall?" the sound of Ralph's voice gave me a chance to breathe a deep sigh as I crawled out. "It is a group of Sandinista soldiers on duty shooting at a tree. Come out and swim with us."

Gasping, I loosened my grip on Moriah, who took her nails out of my neck. My legs shook as I stumbled toward the soldiers. Mumbling in broken Spanish, I attempted to tell them why I was shaking.

"*Contras,*" I stuttered. They laughed as if the notion was absurd, so I smiled meekly and waded into the water, feeling embarrassed. The icy current stung my feet. When Moriah and I got out, the soldiers were gone and it began to rain as it often did for brief periods in the mountains. Lost during the downpour, we felt like Hansel and Gretel following breadcrumbs as we wandered into a primitive house of farmers living on subsistence income. Without hesitation they took us all in. A peasant woman quickly brought us a meal of cheese, beans, soup, tortillas, coffee and cookies. Still rattled, I held Moriah on my lap, giving thanks to these generous people and for the first time, to God, before I swallowed the food.

Soon after the waterfall adventure we learned that the *Contras* were staging a major attack on Esteli. Our trip had taken us to soldiers of protection, yet it could have been otherwise. Realizing that I was not paranoid, I decided I was not prepared to die for the Nicaraguan revolution or risk my daughter's life. Confessing even to myself that I wanted to go home felt shameful. No longer the strong wife of the Vecino leader, I felt I had become the most frightened person on the brigade.

My parents had raised me an atheist/agnostic in contrast to our Nicaraguan family who were deeply religious. Their simple house, like many in Esteli, displayed pictures of both Jesus and Che Guevara, symbolic of the fact that they felt no contradiction between Christianity and revolution, between spirit and the material world. One of our brigade members, a Catholic priest, was invited to hold mass in a neighborhood church near the clinic. Feeling lonely and weak, I sat through the service looking hard at the crucifix. For the first time, Jesus appeared as a human being. A peaceful man who believed in justice and loved the poor. If these wonderful people embraced him as their own, maybe I should reconsider. Here, he appeared as a revolutionary, and like them, poor and disenfranchised, he had been crucified for his beliefs by people with power and weapons. It seemed simple and true. Maybe I am a Christian with a small "c," I admitted. Our helping hands raised hope in El Calvario Barrio and now their belief in Jesus brought hope to me.

In early July, we had budgeted time for travel and leisure away from construction, which had slowed down due to a shortage of materials, internal disagreements over masonry techniques, and labor disruption caused by brigade members returning to the US. Our respite at the beach ended when tragedy struck Esteli.

The 15-year-old boy, Rommel Garcia, who had been injured earlier in the summer by a bomb blast at his home, died of head injuries. One of his family members worked for the Ministry of the Interior, the excuse used by the *Contras* to bomb their house.

Journal: Esteli, July, 1985

We went to a wake at his family's house. Many of us choked back tears, and I cried as we walked with almost 600 people down the street to the church. His family walked arm-in-arm behind a truck carrying his closed casket. All his schoolmates were there in blue uniforms holding wreaths and flowers. I imagined Moriah in the casket and sobbed uncontrollably. The mass lasted thirty minutes and then the procession went to the cemetery along with another fallen soldier and a tiny little casket bearing a newborn. I felt the presence of the many dead carried along this route. Gunshots were fired as the three caskets were lowered into the earth and I truly felt the meaning of the war—the senseless death of this young boy, following so many thousands before him. The Contra *war kills daily and death here is accepted as part of life. War has been going on for so long that, on the one hand, there is pain and sadness but on the other, a sense of pride that a loved one gave his/her life for the struggle.*

By late July, Moriah's health was poor and she had lost weight even as we adjusted to our new way of life. After she was diagnosed with tonsillitis, her third ailment since arriving, we decided to send her back to Boston to stay with a dear friend and wife of one of the brigade members. Before she left, Mamma Clara apologized for "our bad food" as if she were responsible for our decision to send her away.

I tried to sound cheerful as we put Moriah on the plane with the other North Americans in Managua. "Good-by sweetie, Annette will take good care of you and we will be home soon. You'll get lots of milk to drink." With both a deep sense of relief and terrible misgiving, I squeezed Moriah, kissed her and passed her on to Steve. Loss. Separation. I thought we came to Nicaragua to experience unity? This wasn't part of the contract, my critic voice screamed bitterly. At that moment I hated Steve, hated his flirting with Julie, and hated myself for choosing this miserable country with its poverty and war.

"You could be going home with her, you could be going home with her," the mother voice in my brain shouted louder, more critical each time. "But I can't leave Steve alone with Julie. She'll sleep naked with him every night." the jealous wife added. "I can't leave the clinic…. The revolution and my reputation," answered the warrior. Silently I watched as the plane disappeared into the clouds, leaving me behind with the heat, the unfinished clinic and Julie's winning smile.

"Your son. You haven't heard from your son in years?" I asked, horrified at the idea. At the breakfast table the morning after we returned from the airport in Managua, I scrutinized Clara's brown, clear face looking for signs of grief.

"He's been fighting with the liberation movement in El Salvador for five years. There is no safe way to communicate with him," Steve translated.

Gulping in air, I choked on the black coffee realizing she had no idea if he were dead or alive.

Clara and I had sat for hours after work at opposite ends of her dining room table attempting to communicate across the gulf of difference between our lives. My Spanish came directly from the dictionary I carried in my back pocket and was supplemented by hand signals, facial expressions and mime. I tried to describe tall buildings, subways, movie theaters, computers, Disney Land—anything to widen her eyes and smile, but after ten minutes her expression told me maybe I'd better get simple again. I asked for a Coke. At this moment she spoke rapidly as if we were her best friends. I nodded understanding half her words.

"Fidel Castro walked up and down the streets of the barrio after the triumph shaking hands with everyone he could, including me," she said smiling wearing a pink, cotton dress, one of two she owned. Then she revealed her most precious possessions. Out of her dresser draw she took three photographs. Lovingly she held snapshots of Che Guevara, Fidel Castro and a group picture of Thomas Borge, Castro, and several other guerrilla fighters standing together in Esteli. The black-and-white photographs held her devotion. They were the leaders who had fought for a vision of freedom she embraced. *Mama Clara Speaks*, I imagined her on the evening news as millions of Americans listened and saw her radiant eyes tell beautiful facts about the hairy, scary men they believed were evil.

After weeks of intestinal pain and diarrhea, my health improved and the clinic neared completion. I became accustomed to working peacefully on the roof as war planes flew over head. Reports of fighting in nearby Sebaco and La Trinidad and another funeral for three more *combatientes* didn't interfere with my commitment or desire to complete the project. Although I missed Moriah, we learned she was happy, drinking lots of milk, and gaining weight. One night with the war all around us, I sat peacefully listening to music on my tape recorder while Marie Elena, my Nicaraguan sister, crocheted. We had heard bombs earlier that afternoon, and I knew the *Contras* were trying to impress the United States by blowing up more bridges. Outside, a growing crowd of noisy people drowned out the music. Their shouts drew me to the window where Clara's younger daughter motioned me to follow as she ran behind them into the darkness. Nervous, but curious, I grabbed my camera with its flash attachment still not knowing what all the excitement was about and somewhat hesitant to investigate. At the crossroad, I could see the outline of a truck surrounded by people pointing and talking in the blackness. I heard the word *"Contra, Contra."* I turned on my own flashlight expecting to see a group of men in chains or at gunpoint. My eyes widened and I almost screamed as I saw a charred man with his arms blown off at the elbows and his face blackened and bloodied propped up by other dead burned bodies beneath him. Instinctively I jumped away with my camera dangling around my neck, disgusted and shocked at another American who was actually taking pictures. These were human beings, not just our enemy! Stunned, I returned to the house almost numb by what I had just seen.

"Why did they have to show us?" I asked Mama Clara, wanting her to say something that would make me still love the revolution.

She answered, "The Sandinistas want the people of Esteli to know they will not be defeated." My eyes searched her face.

"But ... but," my protest disappeared into the still kitchen air. I knew not to say anymore.

August 1ˢᵗ was the beginning of a city-wide mobilization and *vigilancia* to prepare for the possibility of a siege on Esteli by the *Contras*. We received word that Sandinista soldiers surrounded the city to protect us, and that night, armed citizens mobilized against the offensive with high morale, confidence and a fighting spirit reminiscent of the insurrection. There were no public signs of support for the *Contras*, which bolstered my belief in the people's ability to defend Esteli and the clinic, even though I thought seriously of hiding under my bed on the dirt floor. I wanted Moriah to have a mother and I could almost feel her presence in my heart calling me to Boston. Yet when the *Vecino* members decided to guard the clinic, the symbol of American supporters, I joined them. Together we paced back and forth in front of our brick walls watching for signs of an attack. Two months ago I could not have imagined this structure would become a fortress in the middle of the war. Three months ago I honestly believed the *Contra* war was over, or at least confined to the border areas of Nicaragua. I almost laughed in disbelief at myself. As the sky blackened we drank from a big pot of coffee for warmth and sang for comfort and strength. As men with guns sat inside the clinic, unarmed women and children gathered around late into the cold, tense night. At 2a.m. we broke up. Steve and I walked the muddy pothole-filled road back home, leaving the military victory to the Nicaraguans. I was never so happy to hear the roosters crowing the next morning. The *Contras* had been forced to retreat, and for the second time, I was grateful to be alive.

We continued our job which was to finish the clinic and talk to the American media. United Press International, Radio Pacifica and *In These Times* arrived a week later all eager to know what it had been like during the attack. Mike Wallace from "Sixty Minutes" swooped in at a rally in front of the fire department where 30-40 captured *Contra* prisoners and their weapons were paraded out before a crowd of hundreds waving FSLN banners. He put the microphone in my face asking, "Why are you here?" He wanted something trite, catchy, or sexy for a two-second sound bite. Feeling like sales merchandise I fumbled for words. At that moment I felt more Nicaraguan than American. Glaring at his TV camera I pointed to the hundreds of Sandinista supporters and to the little group of North Americans standing under a banner made from a bed sheet I'd pulled off our cot with red painted letters: USA FOR NICARAGUA.

"Could there be doubt left in anyone's mind that US foreign policy had made a terrible mistake?" I spit out.

He shot me a neutral, controlled glance and pushed his way past me for some-one else's quote. I yelled after him,

"We will not be bought, we will not be overcome," that's the quote you want, Mike."

By August 10 we were working half-days, saying our goodbyes, dreaming about future plans for Vecino and preparing for the trip home. A final cel-ebration was organized at the clinic site with a *mariachi* band, speeches, and dancing. My Nicaraguan family gave us hand-sown shirts with *Esteli Heroica* and *Nicaragua Libre* embroidered on one side. The thought of re-entry into shopping malls, grocery stores, fast food chains and the enormous wealth and abundance Americans take for granted left me feeling so rich that I gave them my silver earrings, my shoes, my dress, my sweater, Moriah's crayons, notebooks, pencils, and my favorite 'Peace In Central America' T shirt. Mama Clara cried as she car-ried my almost-empty suitcase on her head all the way to the near-finished clinic where many key members of the barrio stood waiting.

"When are you coming back? When are you coming back?" they asked us again and again as we made preparations for our last trip to Managua. We waved good-bye from the back of a truck, watching Clara, Sonia, and Paulina, the back-bone of our project and their community, and the revolution disappear into the memory of Esteli.

Journal: Managua, August 12, 1985

> I am very sick from food poisoning lying in a bed in Managua. The pain is terrible, my fever is very high. It is hard to understand that while helping these ordinary people, my own country tried to destroy them, and me. I want desperately to figure out how I can translate this experience into a revolutionary strategy at home. My thoughts are pulled to Steve and Julie, and to Moriah and now I see Rachel's smiling face—Rachel in the US. But most of all I want to under-stand and communicate how it affected us as north Americans. How this tiny country with its poverty, food shortages, and hardships gave me more strength, joy and self-esteem than almost anything in my life.

DEMONS AND THE GOLDEN RAINBOW

I grabbed a kitchen knife and threatened to kill myself. "It's all your fault. You love another woman," I screamed watching Steve pack his suitcase. He said nothing. "What are you doing, where are you going?" I pointed the knife at my chest. He plucked the handle out of my fingers, and put the knife in his backpack. Tugging at his jacket sleeve, I begged him not to leave. I pulled harder following him from room to room, tripping over rugs and furniture.

"Let go!" he yelled picking up the phone.

"No, stop. Don't you dare call the police." I knocked the receiver out of his hand. It landed a foot from Moriah. "Who will be my Daddy?" she cried looking up at Steve as he opened the back door. "I will always be your Daddy. And I'll see you tomorrow." He hugged her pink pajamad body close before he exited into the dark, cold yard.

Vecino's success led to the near destruction of our marriage. After a honeymoon reunification with Moriah, Steve's affair with Julie shattered it all.

Journal: Feb, 1986

> *My Dearest Moriah:*
>
> *My darling daughter, I can't begin to describe the terrible pain I've been going through this entire fall and winter. Your father fell in love with another women, which absolutely broke my heart. I'm not pretending the problems were one sided. I was jealous, angry and hard on Steve. He withdrew and stopped communicating so that our emotional and physical relationship deteriorated at a very rapid pace. He left and what went on that night was simply horrible! I am sorry you had to see and hear it. I wanted to comfort you but I didn't want Steve to touch you. I was hurting so much that I told you Steve didn't love me anymore.*

I cried just watching you cry because it was like watching myself.
You were saying "Don't go, Daddy, don't go" My heart was breaking,
my anguish was almost unbearable". My dear child, I don't know
how this will affect you, but I want you to know that I never wanted
this to happen, I wanted more than anything to create a wonder-
ful, warm family life with two happy parents and maybe another
brother or sister. I wanted more than anything to mirror and reflect
to you a marriage that was equal, respectful and affectionate. I am
so terribly sorry Moriah that I couldn't make this happen for you. I
gave it my best try and my heart is broken. I feel like a failure and a
terrible, terrible mother.

To make things worse, I had abandoned my new career for Vecino—followed my husband to Nicaragua just when I needed to focus on my own work. Life back in the "belly of the beast" as the slogan went, had dragged me to the lowest depths. At times I wished I had stayed in Central America where things were clear-cut. Lots of women lived there without husbands and jobs. Women did not expect fidelity, support or romantic love in that world of machismo men. Lacking income, a job, and now a husband, and after years of collective living, including co-counseling, I at long last turned to a professional. Without the help of Gwen, a skilled feminist therapist, my demons would have run me forever.

Steve and I lived apart with joint custody of Moriah. Both of us felt guilty and frightened and we took her to a child psychologist. At the same time we met weekly with a woman therapist and a male co-therapist. Their approach looked deeply into the history of both our families' behavioral and emotional "baggage." The more wounds we each found caused by our parents' ignorance and limited beliefs the more compelled we felt to undo our mistakes. This was our dance. I would get hysterical, helpless, and blame Steve. He would get sullen, cold and withdraw. Grudges hardened like stale taffy. For days we lived as enemies on the edges of our house.

Our bad habit of endless, exhausting arguments till 2am set our bed on fire. And not the romantic kind.

"You never hug me," Steve complained, taking off his T shirt.

"What! I hug you a lot. The problem is you never listen to me. I can't get excited without the right pressure. You know, I never had that problem with Richard."

"Thanks. No, the problem is you never talk when we make love, so I never know what's going on."

"Well I'm telling you what's going on. There are no sheets on this bed. You never change them so I have to pull them off. Here," I threw the sheets at him.

Learning to disagree without "killing" each other took forever. So it was back to what the therapists had taught us. Listening without defending. We had to practice for a *whole* year before we both felt heard without judgment or interpretation.

Toxic. Dysfunctional. Enmeshed. Triangulated. The words I have used to describe emotional dynamics in my family of origin could stretch from Boston to Salt Lake City where I was born. My parents had created an activist. What else was embedded in my psyche, when it came to emotional relationships?

"Kendall there isn't anything men can't do better than women except have babies," Mom scowled angrily at my father across the table. I watched my father's face as he groped for a response.

"Well you know, your mother is actually smarter than I am," he answered without disagreeing. Sigmund Freud's black and white portrait watched sternly from the living room.

As intellectuals they admired psychotherapy, but never sought help for their own crippled emotions. Typical of their generation, neither understood their own behavior or its consequences. Their love and affection for one another although present, co-existed with a steady verbal antagonism permeating every aspect of our household. It took until I was a teenager when my mother left for a month to take care of my grandmother that I noticed how much my father missed and depended on her.

"God I miss that woman. Do you?" Dad said after tasting his chocolate cake mix. I sniffled a yes from the opposite end of the table. "Let's throw this burned mess to the birds, Kendall,". He hurled the frosted cake to the peak of the garage roof. It rolled down the shingles to a stop in the gutter.

At thirteen, Dad's father, Archie Hale, died leaving his mother and six brothers and sisters with no money. Dad went to work doing odd jobs and later at the Hotel Utah, part of the boot strap story we heard at every gathering. Insecure, he felt behind academically because of the lost years in the service during World War II, and discontented for one reason or another with the universities he worked for. A 1950's father, he was typical in his male distance and work-aholism with occasional outbursts of uncontrolled anger and violence.

Mom was at the stove stirring meat sauce with a wooden spoon. Just back from the university, Dad stood with his second glass of wine dressed in his suit pants and tie. He kissed Mom's cheek and squeezed her breast. Angrily hunching her shoulders, she pushed him away. "Stop. Stop! Talk to me. Tell me what you did today."

My sisters and I took turns setting the dinner table where we learned three fundamental truths. There was no God, the United States was not always right, and political science was *the* worthy topic of conversation.

"Politics is the basis of everything," Dad would begin to lecture eating a huge plate of spaghetti.

"Not true! Not everything is political, Myron! There's art, music, literature," she snapped reaching for her copy of *Moby Dick.* "What do *you* know."

My mother competed by reading up on every other subject she could find, till at 83 she read one book a day "I think Alys read every word in the library," her caretaker told me the week after she died.

1987

Therapist Gwen, both traditional and experimental, attracted wounded political activists from our circles. Before long, she took Steve on as a client, and introduced us both to her version of spiritual healing—a combination of metaphysics and Tibetan Buddhism. Her healing quartz crystals made their way into our house along with Thangas (wall hangings for meditation) of the Medicine Buddha and Tara, the goddess of active compassion. As our personal library filled up with books on therapy, human potential and personal growth, our bedtime stories now included chapters from the *Tao of Physics.* Gradually the black hole in my psyche stretched beyond materialism to the outer edges of human consciousness, deepened by participating in Gwen's group therapy retreats and other local meditation groups.

Then, Gwen took me to Maui.

Hawaii
Maui

I was floating alone in the outdoor pool overlooking the green of Maui's island valley. I felt radiant peace in every cell of my body. Only heaven could be more blissful than this, I thought. Don't forget, don't forget I whispered to myself.

After a week of intense psychodrama at a women's group at a high class retreat center, I was ready for wholeness. After days of grieving our dysfunctional childhoods and re-enacting episodes of family trauma, I was ready for the Harmonic Convergence. A planetary line up was all new to a recovering Marxist-Leninist curious but still cautious.

"Mount Haleakala is one of several sacred sites people from all over the world are visiting. Look at the shape of Maui. It is a woman's head, neck and breast.

It is the heart of the planet." Gwen's white hair, make up, and exotic blue dress reminded me that her newest brochure said Pleadian therapy on the inside flap with the seven sister stars outlined in violet. "I planned it so we could all be here for this event."

All eight of us sat cross legged in the glass paneled meditation pagoda chanting the Tara prayer. *Om Tara, Tu Tare, Ture, Sva Ha.* Twenty—one times our voices hummed with the purity of Buddhist devotion. "You, more than anyone, Kendall, resonate with this prayer," she later insisted. "Tara loves you, Kendall. Mother Earth is a living being. The Goddess of active compassion is helping the earth re-birth." Oh right, I thought, I am a vocalist who picks up new tunes quickly. Or was it because I had been a devotee in another lifetime? But the truth was, after playing with angel and tarot cards, and spooking ourselves with the runes, I just wanted to camp out with Mindy, another participant, and do some sightseeing. We had brought sleeping bags, a tent, and granola for a week, so if this pilgrimage to see the planets align was going to be fun, I had no objection, especially camping at the top of a volcano!

We had agreed to meet some of the other retreat participants and pray for world peace together on the top of Haleakala. Climbing from a valley of eucalyptus trees to igneous rock we watched the clouds sink below us, feeling euphoric as we graduated from therapy to outer space. At midnight we crawled out of the tent into a thick cloud of moisture.

"Mindy, do you think Gwen could be right? That we knew each other in another life?" I asked from the driver's seat of our parked rental car." Disappointed that it was too wet to create an altar on the ground we waited in the front seat.

She shrugged her shoulders. "Gwen's a Buddhist. I really don't know, but I'm getting out of this hot car if you won't let me open the window. She cracked the glass, swallowing the damp, black air.

"Where are they?" I groaned, feeling foolish in this unholy vehicle.

It was almost 2am. The planets were due to align any moment. No one had yet appeared.

"Maybe they decided to go down into the crater with the Kahunas." Mindy speculated. She hit the steering wheel. "Shoot, I'd much rather be with the local Indians." For a moment I regretted our decision. I closed the anger behind my eyes, sucked in a breath and chanted as loud as I could, letting each tone fill the front seat and the alter of crystals arranged on the dash board. On occasion I had held a crystal in both hands and noticed how the energy magnified, creating a dizzy sensation in my brain. Once it got so intense I came close to fainting.

Ten more minutes to go. We both opened the doors and stood behind the car.

"Nancy, Maran," our voices echoed into the dense fog. If our friends were out there, either they were deep in meditation or beyond the sound of our calls.

I managed to rise above the setting of our damp rental car, with a prayer for all the world's people, aimed at the recorder crystal, a special stone a friend who had sold it to me said would "remember" by absorbing the surrounding vibrations. "That was beautiful," whispered Mindy.

I smiled, pleased at my expression of new faith in the magic of astrology. "Let's go find them." It was 2:15AM. We headed in the direction of a parking lot reserved for Harmonic Convergence campers.

"This is really eerie, Mindy." I hesitated for a moment realizing we were completely alone, in a cloud, thousands of feet above sea level, on the island of Maui, at some hocus-pocus new age shin dig. What the hell was I doing?

Four feet away Mindy squinted down the beam of her flash light across the empty, hazy 'parking lot'. Where was everybody?

"It's all a hoax, I guess." Waving my arms, I did a breast stroke through the cloud cover. Now what? Before I could answer myself, my eyes widened. Against the far horizon appeared a luminous golden rainbow filling the night skyline. Swallowing hard I yelled.

"Look, my God! Look!" I pointed frantically at the impossible phenomenon before us. Startled and blinking, Mindy looked confused.

"It's gone," I whispered. A second later, a spiral of light jumped from a space directly in front of me above my head. Inhaling, I stepped back watching it hang in mid air. Again it vanished, only to re-appear to my left, a spiral of golden light. Instantly I reached out to touch the exquisite entity, but it melted back into the blackness. We stood speechless like astronauts on a moon walk.

The next morning we hiked half way down the dry, hot crater still dazzled by last night's mystery. Exhausted, I sat down to mediate again noticing only one or two moving dots far ahead down the trail. *Ohm Tara, Tu Tara* ... the prayer lilted from my lips. My next wish. I want a son. My voice sang for one.

Mindy traveled alone around Hawaii after I returned to Mission Hill. Two weeks later she called. Her voice was excited. "Kendall," she said. Guess what I found in a book of Kahuna myths?" *'Those Who see the Golden Rainbow Are Forever Blessed.'*

What a concept.

Forever Blessed.

LEGAL AND LIBERAL

1986

I steel myself for the subway ride to work. Stare straight ahead, swing my umbrella, walk fast. Gunfights, muggings and murders were routine in Boston. Females who looked lost, helpless or friendly were easy prey. Riding the orange line from Mission Hill to downtown Boston meant sitting with desperate looking people: a Latino drug addict nodded and slipped closer to the floor at every jump in the track. A thin, black boy with a face scar and no socks read the Help Wanted section. A wrinkled, white woman carried all her possessions in a bag. Sometimes I felt guilty and conspicuous wearing a new, red wool coat and carrying a lawyer-looking briefcase. At other times, simply thankful to escape verbal or physical assault from a male of any race or age. Teenagers traveled with thunderous boom boxes scattering mostly white commuters to other cars. During frequent subway breakdowns passengers were caged with graffiti and obscenity-filled lyrics. *Mother F ...-ing boom, boom, Mother F ... ing boom, boom.* Tension crackled like static electricity.

A psychiatrist friend said, "It's so inhuman not to ask these kids to turn down the volume."

"What do you mean?" I asked exasperated.

"You put them in a category of a machine. No face, no feelings, no intelligence."

"Yeah, but all it takes is one angry gun carrying kid with no self control, and bam!"

She didn't argue.

It never occurred to me to drive like the millions who wanted control over their environment. Parking prices in central Boston were formidable so I traveled for five years in the rumbling, stinking tunnels, fearful for my safety, bitter about how crowded, dirty and unreliable it was. Getting off the orange line in the dark winter evenings, I half-walked, half-ran for two treacherous blocks past the Bromely Health housing project, home to hundreds of people on public assistance.

"Hey baby," from a sputtering drunk. "What's up, mama," from a young pot head carrying a paint can. Closer to the commercial district of Mission Hill, the smell of freshly baked goods from Mike's doughnuts felt calming until I climbed the steep sidewalk past the sour smell of un-emptied trash cans to the top of the hill behind our house. Panic. My eyes swept the field looking for potential enemies. My fist clenched the keys like a weapon as I raced through the broken glass in the playground to our front door.

1986-1992

Back from Nicaragua, it was time for a regular pay check. I finished my documentary about the Back of the Hill, discovered openings at public access TV stations were scarce, (even with a Master's degree) and took a job at Greater Boston Legal Services. For five years I served as a Medicaid/Healthcare and Disability paralegal. My clients were poor, physically and mentally ill, disabled, and often homeless. Many abused alcohol or drugs. Most were women on welfare with young children struggling to find doctors and dentists who would accept Medicaid in their practices. Most of my clients needed medical benefits illegally denied by welfare workers who could not read the regulations, or not covered by the program. Hundreds of the working poor who called me daily were not poor enough for Medicaid and not earning enough to buy health insurance. Few had jobs with health coverage. All of them were poor because they lacked education, had few marketable skills, no daycare or health insurance, and no employment that could or would provide these benefits they so desperately needed. In comparison to people in the Third World, they were rich. Yet I realized in some ways their lives had more hardship than those of poor Nicaraguans I had lived and worked with, simply because living in the midst of American abundance, continually barraged by media images of that abundance, accentuated their feelings of deprivation. None of their lives gleamed like the television families with gleaming cars, gleaming houses and swimming pools.

I represented people from all over Boston who had been denied their disability benefits by the Social Security Administration; people with auto-immune disorders, chronic injuries and pain that met the legal definitions and standards, but needed advocates to prove their entitlement to a judge. For years I had worked in factories with poor, but able bodied people. Now my life purpose was devoted to an underclass of people disabled and helpless largely due to poverty and the lack of adequate social services. There was no safety net to catch them. I frequently felt like I was the last life line of my clients, their last slender straw of hope before they plummeted into the abyss. Our staff of lawyers, paralegals, and secretaries spent long, strenuous hours fuelled by coffee and outrage, day after day, year after year pursing reforms in housing, welfare, social security and immigration law. In an era of cutbacks and Republican conservatism, my case load steadily increased to the point where we became a production line controlled by how generous or greedy the corporate politicians were. Cuts in social programs would be announced, and we knew with certainty that within weeks or months and even greater swell of need would light up our phones. But we kept fighting. The central office near the State House gave us access to senators and representatives whom we lobbied relentlessly for the passage of bills and legislation on behalf of our clients.

My $ 25,000 a year salary was less than what I earned as a welder in the shipyard, but the job had good benefits and our unit was managed by women lawyers with young children who sympathized with the demands of young families on working mothers like me. Flex-time, maternity leave, and time off was protected by our union contract and part of Legal Services administrative policy. However, even the best most supportive liberal environment could not help me deal well with the mental and emotional strain of fighting an uphill battle. I reflected in my journal:

> *... Today I passed another one of my clients standing homeless on the corner. My gut feels anger that he is drinking away the social security disability check I helped him win. Exactly my age, he sat in my office, a Vietnam Veteran trying to recover his life. I felt his pain, the anguish of a soldier shunned by his government and his countrymen. I raged at a system that would first destroy him and then fail to support him. But I wanted to shake him by the neck and smash his bottle on the sidewalk. It felt even worse that he didn't seem to recognize me.*

I won almost all my individual cases but that success in turn became a problem. The cases kept increasing until the manila folders in my file cabinet grew from the desktop to the ceiling. I worked steadily for eight hours in an office with no windows beneath a framed picture of *Christina's World* by Andrew Wyeth, often skipping lunch to catch up. Christina is a cripple in a pink dress lying in grassy pasture at the bottom of a hill gazing up at a house she will never walk to. Her powerful presence motivated my inner victim—the one devoted to the people I helped. Each person I assisted felt like a minor repair in a damn bursting from negligence: I patched up the army of wounded and sent them back to battle with welfare workers, and social security representatives whose job was to mind the store not the people's needs. Laughter at the receptionist's desk, or a co-worker's birthday party drew me from my office, until the victims called me back.

One day a young thin woman with Crohn's disease was sitting with me. The bones on her pencil thin legs and knobby fingers poked alarmingly through the skin with little connective tissue or muscle. One sneeze could blow her off the chair I thought.

"I cannot eat. I have chronic diarrhea. My doctor says there are drugs but I can't afford them," she said.

The day before, an injured woman came in who was so weak she could no longer pick up a gallon of milk. "After the car accident my neck wouldn't turn," she said. "Then my shoulder froze. I went to physical therapy—it didn't help much."

Tomorrow will be a woman with gum disease. "Medicaid wants to pull the tooth," she complained, "but my dentist said he could save it with a root canal."

We were interrupted by a call from the homeless unit. My confused client, the one with the long white beard was here again asking for me. Mentally ill people reminded me of my sister, Jenifer, a schizophrenic whose illness eroded our family over a period of thirty years with endless frantic questioning: Was it genetic? Was it Mom and Dad? The environment? Crushed by a desperateness to heal her, we grappled in a relentless cycle of attacks, blame and anger that saturated our house in West Lafayette until all of our hearts wilted under a damp gloom. Sometimes my client's craziness brought out my compassionate stability, other times it simply blew me away. Like the person I was scheduled to meet with next week, a transsexual who needed an operation. A man who wanted to be a woman.

After five years I was drowning in my own case load. The only answer is to become a lawyer so I can do class action suits, I told the ceiling as I lay face up on the examining table waiting for my doctor to return with the biopsy results. At a routine check up, my internist found an irregular mole. The stiff green paper gown scratched around the neck and arms, but it felt good to have permission to lie in one place for a change, waiting and not doing. When the doctor walked into the tiny tiled room, his face was grave.

"You have melanoma," he told me. He wasn't much older than me. "We need to take it off immediately."

"That tiny mole on my back is cancer? I jumped up, looking at it over my shoulder in the mirror. Aggressive skin cancer? My body had betrayed me again.

"It could have been caused by childhood sunburns," he replied, scribbling something on a form. "Take this and see the front desk to schedule the procedure."

"Or because you have been carrying the weight of the world on your shoulders," suggested Gwen a week later. But the little brown spot of raised skin caused no pain, or fatigue. Once it was gone it was gone. I dismissed law school, and went back to battle for universal health coverage.

It's OK to be Liberal

Massachusetts had a chance to be one of the few states in the country with a single payer health care system providing medical benefits for everyone regardless of income, health or job status. And I was going to be a part of making it happen.

Health Care for All was a grassroots campaign working with the Dukakis administration to pass universal health coverage legislation. I knew it was the only solution for my clients as well as the millions of working and middle class people in Massachusetts without insurance. Proud to be a liberal, I felt empowered that the goal of the governor and Legal Services were the same. It was my responsibility to help my clients write testimony, read it to legislators at hearings, and attend rallies at the capitol building. If they could not represent themselves, I spoke on their behalf. But the liberals couldn't stop the insurance companies, banks and power brokers from creating a financial crisis that killed this progressive initiative. The legislation passed but the conservatives made sure there was no money to fund it.

TERYN AND THE BLUE FAIRY

In Mission Hill, our dream of community control over neighborhood development had come a long way. Much further than control over factory life. But when a teenager was shot on the playground of Moriah's elementary school and another child was shot across the street in an argument over a hat, we got scared. Then one night in early June, 1988, our last tenant made a money tree with large plastic dollar bills, lit candles to a money god and almost burned the house down five days before Teryn was born. That was it. Time to move. Two years later we held a good-by ceremony with a Vermont shaman who blew a conch shell to the four directions from the top of the house as we offered thanks and prayers of hope.

It was a late Tuesday afternoon in 1990 when I walked into my daycare provider's house to pick up Teryn after my subway ride home from Legal Services. Steve and I had reconciled four years ago and our new home was in Brookline, a neighborhood on the Green Line. It had green parks without broken glass, dead bodies or homeless people collecting bottles, green lawns with flower beds and huge green trees, houses without grates on the windows and people with gobs of green money pushing shopping carts full of new things. Gold at the end of the rainbow.

In Brookline, Steve startled everyone at community meetings when he walked in from house renovation with paint-spattered pants, work boots and a sweaty T-shirt. Everyday, I passed the street where John F. Kennedy grew up, I read best-seller titles in the window of Paperback Booksmith, and bought warm sesame and garlic bagels by the bagful at Kuples Delicatessen on Sundays. Living among the upper middle class was pretty astonishing. I felt like Alice, fallen with my husband and kids through a looking glass, into a wonderland of abundance and safety. No children had been shot on the elementary school playground. No one's property had been torched on our block, and my car had yet to be vandalized. Today, I felt especially safe and peaceful. I'd be with Teryn soon, and Moriah was walking home from school on a sidewalk with her new friend. Rebecca, Teryn's daycare mother lived two blocks from our new house. Maybe we'd make chocolate chip cookies when we got home.

I got to Rebecca's brick apartment building and she answered my knock on the door almost instantly. "Kendall," she asked her arms, crossed over her chest, "do you know why Teryn has such big bruises on his arms and legs?

Was she implying I was a bad mother? Defensive, I quickly answered, "Well, we've noticed them, but they seem to heal fast. He has such fair skin and blonde hair, I've been assuming that he just bruises easily."

"I reported you to DSS today for possible abuse," Rebecca replied. "You've got to take him to his pediatrician before he can come back." She looked at me half-horrified and half-defiant. I could hear the babble of children playing in the back room.

Abuse? Me? My precious son? Stunned, I swiveled past her, stepping over a trail of toys to get to the phone I knew was in the kitchen. Grabbing it, I called Steve. I was half-crying at this point. "Steve, Rebecca thinks we're abusing Teryn!"

"Why?" he asked calmly.

"You know, the bruises he has sometimes-well, ..." My voice began quivering.

"It's ok, Kendall." Steve's voice grounded me.

"Never mind, I'll see you at home." Teryn ran to me holding a yellow truck, his blue eyes laughing. "Hi, roly-poly acorn boy." I hugged him tightly. Almost desperately. Shattered, I helped him put on his jacket and we left, Rebecca closing the door behind us firmly, decisively, like a judge. Pushing his stroller felt harder than usual. I was feeling a new kind of pain—that of the unjustly accused.

Five days later on my day off, a stranger rang our doorbell. He stood there on the doorstep, a slight man in a short-sleeve shirt with a blue tie, holding a clip board. A social worker sent from DSS to see if we were beating our son. I told him through the screen door that I had taken Teryn to his doctor and we were waiting for her advice. He smiled, jotted down some notes and left. At least he didn't break the door down. Reminding myself that the daycare provider and the social worker were doing their jobs helped me feel less criminal. A little less. But what was wrong with our son?

Referred to Massachusetts General Hospital a week later by his pediatrician, Steve and I sat on a couch watching the hands on a big discolored wall clock, listening to our son scream as a specialist injected a needle into his bone marrow to take a sample for a biopsy.

"We need to rule out leukemia," the doctor had explained. Almost dizzy with fear, Steve and I held hands, barely breathing.

I thought of how I watched Teryn's beautiful face asleep at night, stroked his fine white-blonde hair—then of the photos I'd seen, of pale, bald children in hospital wards. Of needles, and tubes and poison carefully administered, drop by drop, to kill rioting cells. Was that Teryn calling my name? I clenched my jaws tight, tighter. Hadn't I already paid my karmic dues with him?

December 1987

The toilet paper was bright red. I'm pregnant, why am I bleeding? I stood up. More blood trickled down the inside of my leg toward my black boot. Gasping, I sat back down and layered paper into a sanitary style napkin hoping to stop the flow. My hands trembled as I buttoned up my winter coat. *But I'm healthy … there is nothing wrong with me.* Crying I left the women's room in Government Center to look for a phone. Quickly I dialed Legal Services and asked for my unit manager. "Lydia, I'm bleeding. I don't know what to do. Is this a miscarriage?"

"Don't come back to work. Go to urgent care," she directed me.

Petrified I took the green line subway squeezing my legs together tightly in the seat, rolling and unrolling my fists inside my mittens. When I arrived at the clinic the receptionist told me to go to the hospital. "But I might lose my baby," I begged. "Can I get a shuttle bus? She shook her head. Too upset to argue I sped out the front door into the frosty cold and walked many long blocks to emergency care, tortured by each step, realizing I should be lying down but too confused to call a taxi or ambulance.

A nurse rolled me into a room. "The bleeding has stopped. The fetus is fine." Steve arrived from his job site looking calm.

"I know you don't really want this baby. But I do!" I sobbed squeezing his large carpenter's hand. Flustered, the nurse dashed from the room.

Moments later the doctor returned. "Teryn has an autoimmune disorder called ITP, idiopathic thrombocytopenia purpura. His body is attacking itself by destroying his platelets. He bruises because his platelet count is too low to clot his blood. There is a danger of internal bleeding should he fall." The enemy had a name. But the irony was that this proof, that I was not an abusive mother, was also a potential danger to Teryn.

Western medicine has no cure for ITP. Children either grow out of it within six months or it is labeled a chronic case. So every few months we put Teryn's pajamas in his overnight bag, the one with the Ninja Turtles on the flap. (Ninjas, where are you? I need you to rescue my son.) We would take Teryn to the hospital for a day and a night, where he received an intravenous feed of gamma globulin that boosted his platelet count enough to prevent bruising. He wore a fearsome bike helmet outside on the playground to prevent internal bleeding in case he accidentally injured his head. On leave from Legal Services, I found myself constantly watching him, hovering, then racing to catch him at the bottom of the slide or under the jungle gym. A low platelet count did not slow him down, so by late afternoon I was exhausted trying to keep his helmet on. If I can stay close enough, I can put my body between my child and permanent brain damage I told myself. But the treatments were effective for only six to eight weeks. Teryn's platelet count inevitably dropped again, and the bruises returned. This pattern continued for six months.

The next step was one oral steroid treatment that boosted his platelet count, but failed to cure him. More could be risky. His pediatrician warned us that removing his spleen might be the only effective intervention. I could not accept that outcome. Without a spleen, Teryn's immune system would be compromised. Now, Teryn's wound became my wound and my life purpose became finding a cure. So I began searching for an alternative way to heal our son.

I started with acupuncture, a healing tradition Steve and I had successfully used for minor ailments such as poor circulation, bursitis, chronic fatigue. Our acupuncturist, an experienced Chinese gentleman with a efficient, traditional manner did not treat children under five. Those in the yellow pages did not either, until I called Shirley, a young American with a brand new practice. Since she had no experience using needles on a squirming two-year-old, she burned moxa, a Chinese herb, over the acupressure points to stimulate his meridians, the lines of energy that follow pathways through the body. With her encouragement, Steve and I continued using moxa at home once a day but stopped when we accidentally burned Teryn's skin as he rolled and jumped around on the bed. She then suggested giving him organic carrot juice, so I purchased an automatic juicer and a pound of carrots from the health food store. After one taste, Teryn threw the cup of juice on the floor, a strong message about a dietary approach.

What else could we do? I learned of a medical doctor who was also trained in homeopathy—remedies specially prepared to release the healing energy of a substance. I made an appointment instantly.

"Like attracts like?" I asked trying to understand the theory of homeopathy.

"That's right," he answered, "the law of similars and the power of the infinitesimal dose. What a substance can cause it can also cure. But honestly," he admitted peering into a large computer screen, "I've never treated this disorder."

One look at my desperate expression prompted him to add, "I'll do my best. Nothing I give him will do any harm." We left with a remedy he gave me and he promised to do more research. Teryn's face told me that the little white, tasteless pills that looked like candy were superior to carrot juice. But the bruises persisted and his platelet count eventually fell. Another failure. Homeopathy wasn't working. The doctor and I agreed that he needed something else. Steve agreed. But what? The homeopath had no ideas.

Incurable physical illness was not part of my own history or experience. I cried myself to sleep at night and I cried with Teryn, weary of all the hospital visits and the pain of the gamma globulin infusions. Even worse, there were no support groups for children with chronic ITP. Wondering where else to turn, I spent hours in the bookstore thumbing through books in the New Age section. At last I spotted a book with beautiful hands of light on the cover, hands that looked like they healed. Could they heal my son? Fascinated, I spent the next several weeks reading about the concept of energetic healing and examining drawings of bands of colored light above and around the human body—the human energy field or aura. Scared, desperate, I called the author of the book.

"Barbara doesn't heal people anymore. She only teaches now." Before I could protest, she added, "But I can give you a referral if you'd like."

Teryn loved the story of Pinocchio and the Blue Fairy, so that's what we named the hands-on-healer from Montana who could see auras, the light surrounding the physical body. The Blue Fairy was far from the New Age. The first time we met her, she wore cowgirl boots, a long denim skirt, and carried an extra large cup of Dunkin Doughnuts coffee. At his first glance, Teryn dove under the treatment table ignoring our pleas and bribes to cooperate. Thinking this was my last chance to save my son, I demanded that he come out. Teryn didn't budge. On the brink of hysteria, I relaxed when I saw how unruffled the healer was.

"Would you like to hear about my pet pig? The one who wears shoes in the house? the Blue Fairy asked sweetly. This got Teryn's attention. After coaxing him from under her treatment table, talking about the pig who lived in her house, The Blue Fairy slowly moved her hands six to twelve inches in the air around the edges of Teryn's body. Head, shoulders. Torso, legs. We watched, while she moved her hands and talked about what she saw.

"His aura looks bright, and I don't see anything in it that indicates he won't get better," she said. "Feed him plenty of red meat to build his blood, continue with his medical treatments, and over time he will need them less frequently."

Relieved, we chose to believe her. Maybe it was because we had exhausted all known resources? Maybe her confidence was what we needed to develop faith and more patience in the process? Possibly, her healing hands really did something mysterious and positive? Regardless, one important outcome was that we continued to communicate to Teryn daily that we loved him and that he would heal himself. And we did feed him a few hamburgers. Eventually his platelet count stayed higher for longer, eliminating the need for treatment which gave us the confidence to move to Asheville, North Carolina to pursue co-housing with Steve's old college friends. Duke Medical Center and an open minded pediatrician (a woman who put essential oil of lavender in her office) were back up to a woman practitioner with a clinic in a big purple house who specialized in pediatric acupuncture.

"You're four years old! What a big boy. OK Teryn, it's not going to hurt anymore than this." The acupuncturist smiled and gave him a little pinch before inserting a tiny needle into his leg. Then two more. After each treatment I took him for a McDonald's Happy Meal, a big motivator for a kid served tofu and veggies. Within months his new pediatrician announced, "Teryn's count is within the normal range. He is a very healthy child."

Overjoyed, I remembered the Golden Rainbow, said a prayer of gratitude to Tara and the Ninjas and drove straight to MacDonald's for one last big Mac. A year later he completely recovered, just as the Blue Fairy predicted.

Our first neighborhood, Mission Hill, Boston, Mass., 1980.

Steve and Kendall building their solar house, Back of the Hill, 1981.

Our passive solar house, Back of the Hill, 1982.

Steven Norris at his dream house. GLOBE PHOTO BY TED DULLY

Building his dream house in Roxbury for $35,000

By Paul Langner
Globe Staff

Steven Norris is building his dream house.

He has nestled it into a hillside amid great oak trees, lilacs, roses, and blackberry bushes. On a clear day he can see the ocean and the Blue Hills of Milton from the attic room that he knows will be his favorite retreat.

His backyard abuts a small, unused park and behind that are the grounds of a hospital. There will be ample privacy when he moves in.

In winter the low sun will shine through the bare branches of the trees and heat up the thick concrete walls and ground floor to store heat for the night.

In summer, the foliage will absorb the merciless rays of the sun, giving him tons of free air conditioning.

In what leafy suburb has he

found such a spot for a house: where did he get his 14,000 square feet of land for $1,300, or about 9.3 cents a square foot?

In Boston's Roxbury section, 25 feet below the summit of Mission Hill.

Norris, a 37-year-old carpenter, is doing a rare thing today by building a brand new, two-family home in Boston. So rare is his project that the city's Building Department, the Real Property Department, the Water and Sewer Commission, and the Boston Redevelopment Authority did not know what to make of it when he began working on it 2¼ years ago.

These agencies, Norris says he learned, have no difficulty mobilizing the bureaucratic machinery to get a skyscraper going, but when he came along with his private home, they were baffled.

NORRIS, Page 30

Steve Norris, Back of the Hill,
<u>Boston Globe</u>, March, 1981.

Little house on the frontier
Urban pioneers build a home on Mission Hill
by Renee Loth

Boston Phoenix 3/23/1982

The people of Mission Hill are a living testament to the notion that adversity builds camaraderie. For 20 years, this once-populous neighborhood between Jamaica Plain and Roxbury suffered through a land squeeze that threatened to choke off residential life in the area. Churches, hospitals, and universities — all exempt from property taxes — expanded their buildings on the Hill with seeming abandon in the 1960s and destroyed at least 150 homes and apartments in the process. The experience taught the residents who remained the necessity of organized resistance. Today, there are more community groups in Mission Hill than ever, fighting crime, pollution, the threat of further institutional expansion, and, always, indifference, the worst affliction of modern city life.

Attracted perhaps by the fighting spirit of Mission Hill natives, or perhaps just by some of the best views and open space left in Boston, a new breed of urban pioneer is settling into Mission Hill. They come for the opportunity to build alternative dream houses — solar-

powered, co-operatively owned — and, perhaps, alternative households. They represent a different kind of gentrification, and on Mission Hill they are welcome.

Steve Norris, 39, built his passive-solar 12-room duplex of spruce, pine, fir, and "whatever I could scrounge" on three lots he purchased from the city for $1300 in 1979. On sunny winter days when the temperature hovers around 20 degrees, six people and two dogs can be kept comfortably warm without expending a single kilowatt; cubic foot, gallon, or log. The house sits on Fisher Avenue, high on a ridge overlooking the Heath Street MBTA stop. It has 225 square feet of windowspace and an unobstructed southern exposure. With walls "superinsulated" with plastic and fiberglass and a floor and north wall of concrete, the Norris house is almost entirely energy self-sufficient. "In the spring and fall," he says proudly, "we can heat the house just by baking potatoes."

Norris lives with Kendall Hale, their three-month-old daughter, Maria Norris Hale; their
Continued on page 24

Brigham Village demolition,
Kendall, <u>Boston Phoenix</u>,
May 22, 1984.

Alys Hale protesting President Ronald Reagan's cuts to public school lunch program, 1981.

Affordable Housing demonstration, Boston, 1980s.

Wedding, Mission Hill, 1982.
From left to right: John Norris, Myron Hale, Moriah Norris-Hale, Jenifer Hale, Steve Norris, Elizabeth Hale, Kendall Hale, Alys Hale.

Vecino Builder's Brigade, Boston, 1985.

Paulina Alonzo, Mamma Clara: Community organizers/
Sandinista Revolutionaries, Esteli, Nicaragua, 1985.

Steve, Moriah hiding, and children of El Calvario Barrio, 1985

Health of the People, Vecino banner, Kendall and Moriah,
Esteli, Nicaragua, 1985

Hernandez Family, our hosts, Esteli, 1985.

Nicaraguan workers building the
health clinic, Esteli, 1985.

US volunteers toil
for Nicaragua's goals

By Pamela Constable
Globe Staff

ESTELI, Nicaragua — Ever since 1979, when the country's Somoza regime was overthrown and replaced by an experiment in Third World socialism, thousands of idealistic Americans have been drawn to Nicaragua to participate in the Sandinista revolution.

Some, motivated by sympathy and curiosity, have seemed to spend more time chatting in Managua coffee houses or protesting outside embassies than performing any tangible service for the nation. Among bemused Nicaraguans, they have become known as "sandalistas," from their image as casual political groupies.

There is nothing "sandalista," however, about Steve Norris, Fred Royce or Doug Murray.

Norris, a 42-year-old building contractor and community organizer from Boston, is one of 25 Massachusetts volunteers who are spending this summer with hammers, saws, bricks and mortar, building a neighborhood health clinic in the poor provincial city of Esteli, 75 miles north of the capital.

Royce, 32, an industrial engineer from Jacksonville, Fla., runs an agricultural training center in the village of El Cacao, where illiterate farmers learn how to drive tractors, re-

Boston residents Steve Norris and Kendall Hale work on a health clinic in Esteli, Nicaragua.
PHOTO BY SUSAN SPANN

NICARAGUA, Page 10

Vecino, Boston Globe, July 15, 1985.

Health Clinic foundation, Esteli, Nicaragua, 1985.

Eduardo Selva Health Clinic, Esteli, 1985.

SURE STARS SHINING

In a cloud of mist so thick it clung to the sides of my canoe, I heard only the paddle cutting in and out through the water, dipping down and back, down and back moving slowly to the edge of an unknown mystery with safe, firm boundaries. My body pulsed with the hormones of my last pregnancy, my breasts full of mother's milk. I was content to see no further than a foot beyond the tip of my vessel swirling in a crystal of peace.

In the summers of 1988, '89 and '91 Steve and I took a month's vacation to spend in a hunting cabin our friend Rachel knew about in the Northeast Kingdom. She had blessed us with Esteli, Nicaragua so why not the backwoods of Vermont? That first summer, Moriah was six, Teryn a month old, but I trusted Steve's outdoor skills, experience and eagerness to live away from the urban center and, fact was, we didn't have money to go anywhere else.

The cabin, located on Wheeler Pond three hours north of Boston, had no electricity, running water, indoor plumbing, or access by car. We brought our supplies in by canoe, including a futon and a trunk full of crayons, paints, puzzles, games, cards, we hoped would provide a month of exiting entertainment without TV. Every week we canoed and backpacked in food and bottled drinking water to a quiet refrigerator run on propane. Meals were cooked on the propane stove or outside on a campfire and we used a huge kettle of hot pond water to wash dishes. The outhouse became a reflective spot all times of day and night, until we set up a complimentary meditation tent on the grass below the cabin.

After late morning pancakes or oatmeal, we took turns swimming with Moriah to a raft in the middle of the pond to play water games for hours, or nurturing Teryn in the cabin, and hiked nearby logging roads together after lunch. Days would go by without seeing or talking to anyone but each other. Our family took on Native American Indian names, and slowly the sounds, smells and news of civilization vanished to the eerie cry of loons, beavers, herons and moose. Each night we cooked dinner listening to music on our battery powered tape player, lit propane lamps, sang, and read bedtime stories to Moriah by flashlight until the moose arrived for their supper of lily pads, a delicacy in the pond below our cabin windows. *Crunch, crunch, crunch* the kings of the enchanted forest feasted night after night while I nursed Teryn and Steve read poetry out loud. In the morning we each wrote down our dreams and shared them the following night after Steve studied the constellations. It was a time of deep emotional bonding, family joy and sure stars shining.

One late afternoon Steve took Teryn in his papoose carrier out to visit a nearby homestead where a farmer woman named Mrs. Whittaker sold zucchini bread, blueberry pies and vegetables at her roadside stand. Moriah and I were canoeing on the pond when a sudden storm blew across the water rocking us vigorously enough to speed up my strokes toward the cabin on the other side. I quickly hauled up the canoe, turned it over, grabbed Moriah's hand and hustled inside. We watched the rain drops outside the large glass window, expecting Steve and Teryn to appear any second. The rain got heavier and thicker forming a solid gray screen flashing yellow with lightening that struck nearby trees crackling intermittently with the sound of thunder. Where could they be? Stiff with fear I paced back and forth, pretending to Moriah that I was just chilled. But soon enough a huge rainbow appeared under the mid afternoon sun bringing back a cheery Steve with a sleeping baby boy snuggled to his chest.

"What did you do? Where did you go?" I asked as he handed me Mrs. Whittaker's baked goods and hugged Moriah.

"We just stood under a big tree with preacher Whittaker and watched." He smiled as if it happened every day of the week. No big deal.

The following summers we enjoyed the same routine but listened to National Public radio, took more trips out from Wheeler Pond to a fire tower, nearby lakes, festivals, local celebrations and the famous Bread and Puppet Theatre to meet friends up from Boston. The second summer Moriah caught her first fish, and the third summer went to summer camp nearby. By then Teryn was catching more frogs than anyone in Vermont.

Observing the constellations one August night, Steve asked, "Collapse? Did that NPR announcer just say collapse of the Soviet Union?"

We ran in from an astronomy lesson our friend Tony was giving on the front porch wondering if it could be true. A second visiting friend confirmed the announcement the following day. Did that mean the Cold War of fifty years was over? That night around a fire we spoke of hiding under our school desks in Civil Defense drills known as 'duck and cover,' the collapse of the Berlin Wall and Soviet General Secretary Mikhail Gorbachev's refusal to use military force to put down revolutions in Eastern Europe. The world was changing again, and so were we. Would the stars guide us?

The next night we turned to the oracle of the Viking Runes, an ancient Scandinavian system of self transformation. From previous experiments we knew that the twenty-five symbols acted as a 'mirror for the magic of our Knowing Selves,' a means of communication with the knowledge of our subconscious minds. The modern version of the runes is expressed on twenty-five one inch stones in a drawstring bag with a book of instructions. The full casting of that night is lost to me, but I do remember seeing the blank rune, The Unknowable, somewhere in the spread. It said:

Blank is the end, blank is the beginning.

'This is the Rune of total trust and should be taken as exciting evidence of your most immediate contact with your own true destiny ... Drawing the *Blank Rune* brings to the surface your deepest fears: Will I fail? Will I be abandoned? Will I be taken away? And yet your highest good, your truest possibilities and all your fertile dreams are held within that blankness ... Drawing it is a direct test of Faith. It represents the path of *karma*—the sum total of your actions and of their consequences. At the same time, this Rune teaches that the very debts of old karma shift and evolve as you shift and evolve ... Whenever you draw the *Blank Rune,* take heart: Know that the work of self-change is progressing in your life.'

NEW AGE IN THE BLUE RIDGE VORTEX

May 1998

For thirty years it's been the same nightmare. I wake up hot, shaking, panicked. A vision of a place I cannot find. I'm on the University of Wisconsin campus looking desperately for a class., I search building after building seeking a room number that doesn't exist and a professor who will help me complete my education so that I can finally get the honors I so deserve. I find the classroom but I'm late and the exam has already begun. Frightened, I can't answer the exam questions and turn in a blank sheet of paper.

Last night for the first time in thirty years my dream transformed. I'm at the student union where my radical career began. Changes like the 24 hour teller and the check-out scanner puzzle me. But I see my old friends sitting at the tables, now graying activists. I smile, feeling at ease. Then a beautiful scent fills the air, the scent of roses. My heart is joyful as I walk confidently to the conference room where a seminar on aromatherapy and essential oils is starting. As I walk through the door we gather and then exit out the back to my property in the mountains of North Carolina, to a field of lemon balm and phlox. The instructor gestures with excitement, thrilled by the fragrance and powerful healing properties of the red and pink flowers on my land. I wake up with a deep sense of peace and security: I have found my dream.

1992

Steve and I had been contemplating co-housing for years. The dream began ten years earlier at our annual New Year's Eve celebration at World Fellowship, a retreat center built in the 1930's in Conway, New Hampshire. A group of families with young children, singles and childless couples gathered for 3 or 4 days to enjoy the snow, sing, play games, and share our visions for the next year. One of those visions was to live the rest of our lives as we did during the holidays—sharing cooking, childcare, planning and organizing. We knew it had been done successfully in Europe and was beginning to appeal to a small number of Americans. Individual houses were built around a common house with a large kitchen/dining room. Co-residents shared other common facilities like a laundry, playroom, or work out room, and in some cases, a common garden. After years of dreaming, an invitation in 1991 to move south to share 150 acres with Steve's former Boston friends now living in Asheville, NC, felt like an answered prayer and another chance at our socialist dream. It took a year to rent our house in Brookline, pack the van, and head down south.

Co-Housing With Rich, New Age Polygamists

Celeste's mansion took me by surprise, because it really was one. Three stories of brick, six thousand square feet, embellished with white Grecian pillars, Celeste's home sat in the middle of her inherited 150 acres, next to an enormous five-car garage. Walking into her palace made me feel very small, much shorter than my five feet, six inches. Our one Boston millionaire friend chose to live a much less ostentatious lifestyle. In fact, for a long time I assumed he was living on his teacher's salary.

An only child, Celeste had red hair and lots of green, green money, inherited from her shopping center magnet father. I already knew Celeste had two husbands, Randy and Evan, and a child by each. That's not unusual for much-married Americans. But what was unusual was that they were all living together, in active polyandry. (Were my Mormon roots always going to pop up like this?) The ménage a trois were self-identified, hippie radicals living in the evil bourgeois setting I had dreamed of eradicating in my Massachusetts equivalent of the Red Guard only fifteen years before. Twelve years later, I had exchanged the class struggle for co-housing, a more modest project. Ironies abounded. Since we American revolutionaries had failed to kill off the bourgeoisie and their corrupt, filthy wealth, here was our chance to catch the trickle down from a shopping mall and help turn it into co-operative living in North Carolina. The political movements of the 60's and 70's had attracted some strange bedfellows, I joked to myself while I walked around the backyard admiring the fountain filled with giant goldfish.

Celeste's kitchen reminded me of every <u>Ladies Home Journal</u> my mother and I drooled over as we made do in our family's modest houses, until the last one in Indiana graduated us into the upper middle class. The mansion's kitchen dazzled me with its, spaciousness, the color co-coordinated tiled floor spanning an adjacent laundry room, kitchen nook, and phone center. The shelves were filled with all the glass ware, cookware, silverware, and electronic gadgets you imagined every rich person would have. And she did. Curtains with hand-painted bluebirds framed the kitchen windows. One fourth of the entire first floor was extra space, the rest a seldom-used formal entry.

Had we landed in a movie or on TV? No. I was standing inside the real thing. The gigantic second floor bathroom had a four person Jacuzzi, and Celeste's daughters Kristin and Melinda each had her own private bathroom. Celeste, head Queen Bee, slept in a master bedroom shared as she desired with each husband from smaller adjoining bedrooms. I preferred the one decorated with Grand Canyon wallpaper.

Their daughters had a trampoline and a club house large enough to sleep in with more living space than most people in trailers. Husband Randy had a tractor, bush hog and all the farm equipment he wanted for his gentleman farmer hobby. Two other rental units on the property were occupied by friends and students, and Celeste was building a third.

Steve, Teryn and I occupied a large open room at the top of the house next to the youngest daughter's whose bedroom had a built in slide. Moriah was given a corner of extra space on the first floor behind a screen, after Celeste questioned whether the eldest daughter, Melinda could share her oversized kid perfect bedroom.

Queen Celeste was the center of a matriarchal beehive enjoying the attention of all. Her husbands vied for her attention as did both the daughters. All five played a game of musical beds, the daughters simply imitating the adult behavior with no boundaries (a non sexual practice encouraged by the early co-counseling community) On any given night, seven-year-old Kristin might wake up in a different bed.

"Randy just sleeps wherever he wants," complained Evan, as if he had no control over the rules of polyandry.

"My ancestors were polygamous Mormons. Brigham Young had at least thirty wives, and didn't seem to have any problems," I joked. "Of course it was simpler when the bee went from flower to flower". Consecutive monogamy was simpler, I thought.

I wondered if Evan believed it was politically correct to live in a matriarchy. Perhaps this was his solution to all the patriarchal crimes of the last thousand years. For a moment, I felt pity for poor Celeste. She had two husbands but lived by the non-monogamous beliefs of the sixties, which meant any woman might end up in either husband's bed any given night of the week. I realized I might be one of them, in the queen's view.

"Good morning Kendall."

Celeste had a habit of looking at my waistline, thinner than her capacious one.

"I slept in Randy's bedroom last night," she said.

What was the hidden message in that? I shuddered to think that soon Steve and I might be drawn into the quagmire of free sex, an episode of my life I had already abandoned after several thousand dollars of psychotherapy. I needed an older sister, not a rival still searching for her identity after a failed PhD. dissertation.

I glared at two cats stepping in and out of breakfast bowls leaving milky paw prints all over the color-coordinated counters. Celeste's daughters lived on boxed cereals and they ate all day long, leaving a trail of half eaten Kix, Trix, and Cheerios across the shiny marble surface.

"I hope you slept better than I did," I said in my too-blunt way. "We've noticed Kristin likes to keep very late hours sliding from the third to the second floor and prances into our space whenever she likes."

Celeste's face turned as pink as the hand-painted bluebird's breast on the curtain behind her. Apparently, I was supposed to be grateful for the aristocratic accommodations and adjust to the notion of sharing the children's open-ended control of the mansion. She's lucky I didn't tell her that her younger daughter was one of the nastiest, spoiled children I had ever encountered, I fumed to myself. Yesterday morning in the Kitchen Beautiful, both Kristin and Melinda were screaming and pulling hard on Celeste's long red hair.

"She's my mother!"

"No, she's my mother!"

The girls hissed at the other, sobbing and clutching, with gobs of red hair in their little hands. Each had their own toys, bedroom, pets, and father, whom they both called by their first names, but there was only one mom. So they had to share. It was obvious to me why this created such dysfunction, but I was simply a guest and a potential co-houser. Does sexual experimentation always lead to such screwed up kids, I wondered?

Strangely, over the next month I had nightmares that Celeste's venom transformed me into a competitive female intruder. I fought back by weaving the strands of her red hair around her neck. We avoided each other, until I found a nasty note in my letter box. It read: I have decided not to do co-housing and want you to move out within the next few weeks. My self-hatred was at an all time high, for, according to Celeste, I was the reason our brief experiment was dead.

"I'm too frank and too insecure," I sobbed to Steve. "But why couldn't the five of us with the equivalent of three PhD's in counseling and mediation training empower ourselves to change?"

"You threaten her, is my guess," Steve surmised.

Desperately, I wanted Steve to fix the shattered dream of co-operative living, to persuade Celeste that I really was a kind, loveable woman with a good heart. That I was needy because I was ten on the Richter scale—afraid, rootless, without a job, all the obvious she could not and chose not to see. But Steve's strength was accommodation, not confrontation. And neither Randy nor Evan would call a house meeting. After all, they were riding on Queen Bee daddy's wealth, one working part-time as a computer consultant, the other for three dollars an hour in a marginal business.

Communal living meant imperial decisions, Celeste-style. After leaving our jobs, a great school system, health insurance, a house, and twenty years of community building, Celeste demanded we leave her estate. Two months after arriving in the ritzy loony bin, we were homeless.

It took weeks to locate a rental that permitted dogs, and the house we finally found in Haw Creek was empty except for carpeting in the bedroom. I was relieved to be in the sanity of a neighborhood where people lived 20 feet apart and parked their cars in driveways instead of five miles from the front gate.

However, being booted out of paradise into a house almost as shabby as those of my hippie youth challenged my material attachments. Steve's white construction van held only the four of us, our dog, our clothes, a mattress and camping equipment for a vacation we took out West before our arrival in Asheville. Since we planned to live in the mansion for the first year, all our furniture and household supplies remained in the Brookline house which we'd rented out. I had expected to live on bare floors and sleep in a hammock in Nicaragua, but Asheville had promised abundance and now we were using our camp stove and ice chest in place of a stove and refrigerator. Low, low, low.

An angel did appear one night at Woman Song, a Monday night women's chorus I discovered in the basement of the local Unitarian Church. A convergence of feminist witches much like New Harmony Sisterhood. During the break I pleaded our family case to the group at large, and within moments I heard a voice.

"A friend of mine got married and has extra furniture in storage," Meredith said. She smiled at me from across the circle.

"I'll take it!" I instantly responded, convinced my misery in Asheville had been noticed by someone from another dimension. I flashed back to the golden rainbow, Mindy's phone call from Hawaii, and the book of Kahuna myths. Meredith believed in telepathy, channeling, teleportation and a host of other mental gymnastics. (All weird, I'd mentally labeled them) But weeks later, I was sitting in Meredith's living room with her husband and other new age healers.

"Let's talk about energetic healing," Meredith said.

The Fourth Dimension
Jesus on the Swimming Pool, 1993

"I see resentment at the base of your spine," the healer said.

He stared at my coccyx bone from the front of the Holiday Inn conference room in Charlotte, North Carolina. About fifty of us, Meredith and I included, had been learning the energy release technique, a healing method developed by the clairvoyant leading our weekend workshop.

Short with curly black hair and a slightly pudgy belly, this man was a medical doctor who claimed he could manipulate energy with his hands. Volunteers rose from their seats in the gold and maroon meeting room with a huge chandelier and mirror at one end. The healer would read the distress in their auras, and through energy manipulation he changed something on their cellular level, healing their distress. So he claimed.

What was I doing here? Was the local legend of an energy vortex in the mountains that drew certain people to this area true? New Age seekers in Asheville had bombarded me with ideas of healing at the DNA level, to unleash torrents of past life garbage still programming every choice and thought we possessed. So I'd signed up for this session. The doctor's assistant, a female clairvoyant named Gina, saw etheric dolphins swimming above the chandelier, and she spoke to devas and nature spirits as we watched.

"Coming out my front door I bent over to pick a flaming red rose. Just as I did, a little elf jumped out of the bushes and shook his finger at me," Gina nodded toward the glass where she saw devas all over the lawn creeping slowly up to the windows. "Humankind drove them away when we stopped believing in the innate wisdom of nature." Her eyes were clear, her face relaxed.

"One day I was sitting outside at the edge of our swimming pool," Gina continued. "Then Jesus appeared". He went sloshing right across the top of the pool." I had been nodding off in the warm room, but I bolted upright. Jesus, pool-walking! Jesus.

I believed in the power of alternative medical remedies, having received many acupuncture treatments and suffering through the preparation and consumption of nasty but healing herbal brews and teas. At moments of life crisis and important decisions I went to astrologers and tarot readers, even psychics, especially after our move south. But this seemed over the edge, the pool's edge so to speak. No wonder the Baptists called us New Agers the spawn of the devil. How much did I pay for this workshop, how in God's name (Jesus) did I get here, and where was the nearest exit? I gazed around the room, looking for other doubters. But moments later we were bustled into a partner healing session, and I found myself paired with another woman.

"Come, look at her face," My partner called out.

She seemed transfixed by the session we had just completed. The other squiggling, writhing, moaning participants were now quiet on their blankets. "It's Mother Mary," she whispered as she looked at me, as if in the presence of the real mother of Jesus. I smiled lovingly trying hard to match the assignment, humbled by the holy presence I now embodied. So this is why I came to Asheville. To find my true identity. Now people will see who I really am: a saint.

The workshop assistant stepped up.

"Well, she does look at little like Mary, now doesn't she?" The assistant wrapped her arm around my partner and motioned the leader over. "Perhaps Mary temporarily shrouded her face," he suggested squinting at me. Obviously Mother Mary had taken off for other parts. Concerned for my partner, I concluded she was having a psychotic episode, but then I quickly reminded myself of the Golden Rainbow I saw on the Hawaiian Island of Maui. After that story, I admitted, many would have advocated for my institutionalization. Sainthood still sounded good.

By the following morning much to my chagrin, I sounded strangely like everyone else.

"Last night I dreamed I was almost taken by aliens," I told a middle aged classmate in glasses and a cardigan. He listened with serious attention. "But, I think I know why."

He's a lawyer, and his rational mind will talk me out of this, I hoped continuing. "It's because the woman I roomed with in Boston was actually abducted as a child, so she carries the energies of those beings. They were robotic-like with power enough to actually paralyze me. My arms were heavy as lead. When I tried lifting them, nothing happened." The attentive lawyer smiled calmly as if this were old news.

"So they came at me single file closer and closer. They wanted my essence. My energy. My soul. Then I visualized the cross on my forehead. Bright, glowing yellow. It worked! They faded, weaker, weaker. Gone"

"Maybe they were the Grays," he offered with a calm expression. "Quite opposite the Pleiadians."

"The Greys?" What else could I possibly say?

Some New Agers believed in the existence of these dark, insect-like aliens who acted like machines without emotions, seeking human qualities. I dismissed it as more Asheville fantasy. But on the other hand, he *is* a lawyer, I argued to myself. And on the other hand, it was laughable. For awhile, I was able to forget the confusion of our move to the mountains of Western North Carolina. I envisioned Steve reading the <u>Citizen Times</u> headline: "Alien Abduction Strikes at Spiritual Gathering in Charlotte."

My hotel roommate, Dawn, an Asheville native, worked as a hair dresser.

"I had a car accident that put me in a coma for months. Have you ever heard of a near death experience? Well, I had that, and I wasn't never the same again."

"How did you change?" I was intrigued.

"I could see stuff I never saw before. I could hear things I never heard before. I even remembered being abducted!"

"You're kidding," I tried not to laugh when she began nodding silently to someone not in the visible spectrum, at least not in mine, and referred to him as Zeron, a grey who apparently implanted her during abduction, enabling this unique form of communication. Her southern accent, combined with her science fiction behavior, tantalized me. I could not resist her offer to pay the motel bill. Unwittingly, I had moved in with Dawn and the aliens.

The next morning when the clairvoyant asked for volunteers my hand shot up fast. Exposing myself in front of people was never a problem. After performing with the New Harmony Sisterhood Band and acting out my childhood trauma in psychodramas, audiences just didn't intimidate me.

"Does anyone in the audience see or sense anything in Kendall's energy field?" the leader inquired of the thirty-odd people.

"Yes, I see a nun." someone shared.

"A nun. Does anyone else see her?" Several more yeses. The leader nodded. "That's what I see, and she doesn't look too happy."

"No, she seems upset actually," another audience member added. "I can also see a monk. A scrawny looking guy sitting in caves somewhere. Her soul star is twinkling above her head. They really want her to get it."

"Get what?" I asked smiling out at the faces.

"That you have your own inner Divine light," she answered. Dazed, I mumbled something about my dysfunctional family and sat down.

Before the conference was over I met the Lizard Woman.

"I always bring my lizards with me when I travel," she said reaching into her pocket and pulling out a little, green reptile with bulging eyes. "And I enjoy sleeping with them too."

I cringed, imagining it slithering up her leg and burrowing into her crotch. My Asheville friend, Meredith, must have noticed when my face turned the color of the lizard and offered this explanation, "She carries lizard body language, that's all. It's another race of humanoids. They have similar DNA but they look like reptiles."

"What?" I was totally bewildered. I stared at Lizard Woman, a perfectly normal looking blonde, for signs of scales, extra dry skin or a lumpy spine. "Excuse me."

Anxious to leave I passed another clairvoyant who reached out to hug me. He scanned me and kindly said, "I think you and your children were star seeded."

"Great! That must be why I've never fit in. I'm from another galaxy." I collected Meredith and we left the orbit of the Holiday Inn.

As the car left the Charlotte flatlands and climbed slowly back into the mountains, Meredith observed, "I can feel the energetic shift. Can you?" I was too frightened to notice. Marxism-Leninism seemed mild after this. Overthrowing the government was banal compared to space beings and past lives. Are my new Asheville friends and guides deprogramming the last remnants of materialism from my cells? Or have I been abducted for real? Steve will never be able handle this. Surely he'll want to go home to Boston now. I did.

A New Home

A passionflower appears in my garden bearing white fruit. I don't remember planting her and imagine it came from my neighbor's give away plants. Oddly, it is the same flower featured on my newest brochure for Menopause and Mid Life Radiance. She's exquisite.

From my deck, I survey our twenty acres of suburban homestead. Half an acre is a landscaped mélange of genetically bred flowers, ornamental bushes, plants and domesticated animals, visited by wild ones. Two of my cats are semi-wild, sheltering only in our garage during winter. From time to time I find the carcass of one of our free-range chickens or guinea hens, half-eaten by the possums, raccoons, owls and other predators that share our land. Wild turkeys and an occasional deer pass through. Birds, ducks, and herons swim and hunt tadpoles in our pond. The front yard shares space with native invader morning glories and Queen Ann's lace, beside cows grazing on open pasture. For me, Fairview is a halfway home, a meeting place between the ancient Smoky Mountains and the urbanized East, a place to watch wild flowers, grasses, weeds, insects, bees, birds, a place to dream of endless varieties, of more and more beauty for my own enjoyment growing together with the wild things. Every morning my heart is held where the green bowl of the goddess meets the blue mountain sky god. This daily vision is my staff and my hope.

The morning before I found Sharon Spring I had seriously considered returning north to be a lawyer. Two years ago, Steve and I had left stable jobs, friends, contacts and a wonderful neighborhood for a dream of a sustainable, communal life in the country. Now we were standing on property in Fairview a realtor had shown me the day before.

"I've never seen you like this, Kendall" Steve commented, feeling my awe, watching as I slid downward into the sloping meadow at the edge of the woods, my heart opening into the sunlight. I felt like my Mormon ancestors when they heard Brigham Young say, "This is the place," after their long trek across the great American Plains into the Rockies. My excitement about this piece of earth as a prospective home surged up the base of my spine, flushing out the last bad memories of the previous year in HawCreek after we first came to North Carolina and our initial experiment in co-housing failed. Memories like the man who ran over our eleven-year-old Moriah's dog, a fluffy white malt-a-poo we bought for her tenth birthday in Brookline. Jumping off the school bus to a still-strange neighborhood, she raced up the road only to find poor Skittles, her connection to Boston and her early childhood, left dead on the stone wall above the driveway. And tragically a month later, one of her best friends in Boston committed suicide by hanging herself from a rope in her bedroom.

"What a perfect place for a co-housing community," I murmured sitting in the grass facing the Blue Ridge mountains. I looked at the way the land gently sloped up to a natural rise covered in goldenrods. The sun was in the south now, and it fell on a meadow that would be the perfect place for a house. Our house.

"Steve, remember my life reading?"

"What are you talking about?"

"The one from California in 1988."

"No." He looked tired but curious.

"Well, the essence of the channeled reading was that my family and I would move southwest within the next few years. The end of the reading described a misty mountain vision that represented a staff of great support and comfort to me."

Our eyes took in the view. "That's it!" Our words echoed strangely. That's it ... that's it ... that's it-it-it-it.

Boston Goes Underwater

In the spring of 1995, Steve and I were having our first party on the twenty-four acres we had purchased in Fairview, which we'd christened Sharon Spring. Sharon is the name of our road, spring, the source of our drinking water. The neighboring half backs (New Yorkers who moved to Florida and then half way back to the mountains in Western North Carolina) were hiking up the driveway with a pot-luck dish and a roll of paper in hand. The other guests were spread out from the pond at the bottom of the pasture up to the Gates of Heaven, a swing Steve had hung between two trees that overlooked this treasured bowl of nature facing the Bear Wallow Mountain Range.

"Thanks for the food," I greeted Frances and Bart. "And what's that under your arm?" I motioned at the rolled up paper.

They smiled at each other. "Are you ready for this, Kendall?"

"Sure," I chirped without thinking. Having lived through the student revolution, the Vietnam war and Marxism Leninism, I felt prepared for anything. It was a map of the United States, but in the year 2012.

"You see, the earth will shift on its axis, and the poles will reverse." Frances said. "This will cause all kinds of tumultuous earthquakes, the melting of the polar ice caps, and climatic changes. The eastern seaboard will be under water."

Francis pointed to Boston, then New York City, her finger moving down the coastline. "The Mississippi River will widen," she said, "flooding over New Orleans. Of course, California will sink except for a few places like Mount Shasta." I felt dizzy, just imagining our solar house in Mission Hill bubbling under the Boston Harbor, along with Harvard University.

"But the good news is," Bart offered, "that Atlantis will rise again in the Atlantic Ocean off the coast of Florida, and Lemuria will reappear in the Pacific." I knew of the Atlantis myth. 'Lemuria? What was that?"

"The Hawaiian Islands were a part of this civilization. And the Kahunas are their descendants," Francis stated with authority. "Lots of people will die, but those who were meant to become light beings will remain. And Asheville is one of those chosen places. You will be safe here," she said.

Oh, so was the golden rainbow I saw in Maui a signal from Lemurian light beings? I almost asked Bart and Francis, but thought better. Their blissful smiles made me a little sick. Even homesick. For the rational, good liberals back East. People who made sense. Years earlier, my channeled reading from California had predicted we would move "southwest". From Boston that meant Taos, New Mexico or Flagstaff, Arizona.

Not Asheville, the city of New Age wannabes and red neck Baptists.

A Sleeping Pig

Steve and I gave up on the idea of co-housing. Instead, we manifested our own version of *Animal Farm* with goats, chickens, honeybees and cows, hoping for less conflict in the non human kingdom.

"Did you tell them how we live?" Kat questioned her husband before opening the door to their home. We were in the apple orchards of Hendersonville, south of Asheville.

"Sure," Ted answered. A gray and white billy goat bleated as it trotted onto the front porch, followed by a perky tan female.

We were still lonely enough to have invited ourselves to the rural home of Teryn's new daycare friend, Josh. Anxious to escape the billy goat before he ate my shoelaces, I stepped over the threshold into the living room. Still wondering how I ever got to this bizarre part of the world, I was determined to be informal and relaxed, to fit in.

Then I saw a pig sleeping on the living room couch. Her hooves were daintily crossed, and her teats trembled on her massive belly every time she breathed.

"Maybe I stayed too long at Celeste's mansion," I whispered to Steve, startled by the squawk of a parrot on the other side of the room.

"What is that?" I pointed at the pig, the biggest sow I had ever seen, including all the Ohio State Fairs of my childhood in Columbus.

"Heidi loves her place on the couch," Kat answered, tucking the afghan around the pig's ears. Across the room, Josh and Teryn were talking to the parrot. It sat in a huge cage where a bookcase would normally be.

"He sings God Bless America backwards and forwards," Ted laughed. Looking for a place to sit down, I envied that big, fat Heidi snoozing on the most comfortable seat in their tiny room. Bored with the parrot, the boys were already playing Nintendo in Josh's bedroom.

"We sell insurance to support our extended family," Kat explained, aiming a baby bottle into a blanket bundled in her arm. Before I could ask if it were a baby or another animal, a soft bleat sounded from Kat's chest.

"Not enough mother's milk for this one," she said, rocking the bundle. "So she lives in front of the fireplace over there. I feed her every few hours."

No wonder Kat is so thin, I thought. All these creatures are sapping her energy. Behind the house were a couple of horses, chickens, and a peacock. My mind's eye drifted back to our Nicaraguan family in Esteli, the memory of roosters echoing among clucking hens. Even in Central America I was given a chair, and chickens only roamed the dirt floor when Mamma Clara wasn't looking. I shot mental darts at the peaceful Heidi snoring on the couch. She'd make a lot of bacon and pork chops wouldn't she? The fitting-in part wasn't working too well for me.

"Stand beside her and guide her," the parrot's voice rang above the cacophony of the mini-zoo.

"She once attacked me," Ted said gesturing at the bird's mean-looking clawed feet. "Only Kat can control her." Ted went on telling a story of the night he and Kat hunted down a pirate raccoon raiding their chicken coop.

"Naked, I grabbed my rifle and chased it up a tree. Bam! One shot in the gut. It was the fattest raccoon we'd ever seen."

"Bam! Bam!. Gunshots and laughter from Josh's bedroom. "Gotcha! Gotcha!" shrieked Teryn.

Giggling nervously, I wondered why I wasn't with old friends in a comfortable Boston style triple-decker house, listening to familiar music, at ease with newscasters Chet and Natalie from Channel 5. Checking on Teryn, I considered joining them, (Bam! Bam!) when suddenly snorting sounds and a slight tremble told me Heidi needed to pee.

"Pigs are very intelligent, and easy to train," Ted assured us as the sow opened the front door. Relieved that she wasn't smart enough to use the toilet, I slid onto the sofa into a cushion warmed by their grotesque pet relative, thankful I had worn my oldest jeans.

"Through the night with the light from above."

The rattling noises in the cage and the parrot's flapping, turquoise wings sent litter-scented breezes over my face. Indeed, I did feel lighter. And the rising dough from Kate's bread machine made North Carolina almost smell graceful.

"Come taste this bread, Kendall," Steve stood munching in the kitchen door. Reluctant to give up my comfortable seat, I stepped quietly to the kitchen counter.

"Uhhhhhhhh!"

Next to the bread machine was an aquarium, home to a huge tarantula with big black, hairy arms. Looking for an escape, I headed back toward the living room. A huge Irish Setter now occupied my couch seat. Oh, for God's sake.

"Ammericaaa Bless God," squawked the parrot, reciting backward.

"Steve, I left my purse in the car ... I'll see you later," I hinted, noticing he was engaged in another animal tale with Kat. But Heidi was grunting on the other side of the screen door. And the front yard was full of curious animals. Animals with horns.

"Would you like three of my goats? You can take them for a trial period. I love teaching people about animals." Kat intercepted my escape. From the back bedroom, Teryn commanded, "Yes, Mom. Take them!"

Mail Order Chickens

"You'd better come get these baby chicks," the post office voice urgently suggested. I heard high pitched chirping in the phone.

"My chickens! I'll be right there. I'm five minutes away."

Back from the post office, excited to be raising my first birds on our Fairview farm, I ran down to the old chicken coop to make sure everything was ready. Steve had constructed a plywood box with an old screen door covering the top. A heat lamp suspended from a beam above rested on the screen in a bulb sized hole. It was an artificial mother hen. The water bottle sat ready on a newspaper floor, covered mostly with old copies of the Citizen Times, a fitting fate for a poor imitation of a good Eastern paper like the Boston Globe. "That's exactly where you belong," I gloated at a picture of Senator Jesse Helms, the antediluvian, ultra-right-wing senator from North Carolina, "Under shit!"

Nervous, I wondered if I had remembered to order the Quik Chick, the miracle powdered enzymes. You added it to water to feed chicks for the first few weeks of life, until they could eat store bought chicken crumbs from the local feed store.

Twenty-four babies had survived the plane flight from Iowa. The twenty fifth had been trampled to death on the bottom of their 12x12 cardboard carrier.

"Ohhhhh, I sighed feeling squeamish and sad. But the other 24 needed attention, so I gently lifted each one into its new home, leaving number 25 in her casket.

Organic food had become a passion of mine, even though we could only afford select items. I hated the hormone, anti-biotic fed birds that never left their cages, and we rarely ate chicken except on a night out. This seemed a wholesome, cheaper way to get eggs, ones with yolks that sat up—yellow, bright and fertile. Even tastier than our local health food store.

"Can't wait," I addressed the two dozen chicks, mixing a teaspoon of the Quik Chick powder into their pint water bottle. I tossed the package into a pile of dusty egg cartons I'd started saving for the glorious bounty of next fall. Worried they wouldn't find it, I dunked one chick's beak into the charged liquid. Like a new mother, I felt warmed as each one bobbed for nourishment before huddling back under the heat lamp. Relieved that the experiment seemed to be working, I took the chick-in-a casket down to the edge of the pond, feed for the trout I hoped were still there. "Good-by little one," I hummed pushing the casket until it sailed out into the water.

By morning, three more of the chicks were dead.

"I did everything right," I moaned at Steve while he stir-fried tofu for dinner.

"Are you sure?" he asked adding the garlic to his favorite soy dish. "You know you don't always pay attention to detail."

Pressing my finger into my brow, I closed my eyes. Detail. Detail. Reviewing the directions in the McMurray catalog over and over again, I brooded near my little puff balls, wondering what fate waited them. The next morning I slowly approached the coop, terrified at what I might find. I could see the lamp light, and hear their chirping. Pushing open the coop door, I held my breath. Four more dead.

"Ohhhhh, noooooo," I wailed. Then I noticed both water bottles were empty. Water, they're not getting enough water. That's it. I felt slightly better, as I placed the four little bodies into an egg carton. I gathered yesterday's egg casket of three with today's and headed toward our swimming pond.

"Mom, wait for me, what are you doing?" It was Teryn. His blonde head bobbed through the green upper pasture followed by our dog, Rudi. Darn, I forgot it was Saturday morning, feeling protective of my son's seven years.

"The chicks are sick for some reason," I said hiding the egg cartons behind my back and slipping them down to the grass. "Do you want to help me mix up some more Quik Chick," I asked, pointing to the silver package inside. He looked interested and began reading the directions. "Mix one teaspoon ... what's PER mean? Teryn wrinkled his eyebrows.

"Oh, that means you put one teaspoon in every ... Wait, what does it say? "In every quart." Suddenly, the death sentence jumped off the side of the package. I had been dehydrating these poor babies. The more they drank, the thirstier they got.

"Pay attention to detail," I said loudly.

"Why are these in here," he asked looking at the dried eyes and limp feathers under the egg carton lid.

"I didn't pay attention to the directions. I killed them by mistake."

"Oh Mom," he sounded frustrated with my failure. "Can I bury them?"

"Why don't we send them out to sea,? His eyes lit up and he ran to the pond's edge with both egg cartons, starting to push them under water.

"No, Wait! Just let them sail away, and sink by themselves. OK?" It seemed more dignified. He didn't answer. Our semi-feral tabby cat swished by my legs. "Shit! I left the screen off the top of the cage!" Leaping to my feet I tore up the pasture, leaving the seven chicks' funeral to Teryn's better judgment. I was quicker than the cat, and for years we enjoyed dozens of white, brown and blue eggs. I kept, sold and gave them away to friends and neighbors. And I learned a lesson: read the fine print, listen to your seven year old son.

Bees

Birds chatter at Sharon Spring all day long for my ears' delight, visiting both feeders as long as they contain sunflower seeds. There are days when I feel capable of spending the rest of my life in the middle of this pasture watching these winged creatures. Other times the intense green feels like a jungle and I almost appreciate the lawn mowers and weed whackers grinding away through the neighborhood. Today I want a huge machine to cut back the strangling grasses, honey suckle, and poke berry encroaching into my tamed portion of the field. Steve's old tractor is no match against the power of summer's growing tentacles wrapping the fences, spreading towards the driveway and under my newly placed mulch. I sense a lingering ancestral memory of the pioneers chopping through the Midwestern forests, but I also sigh with relief when the motors go dead again. I have poured a cup of tea, adding a spoonful of honey from the very last jar of Sharon Spring Farm's best. The bees all died last summer or swarmed to another hive. When I was stung by the honey bees I brought to our land, I lost courage, turning the bee keeping over to Steve.

"How about this? I'll grow the flowers for the bees. You capture their honey," I proposed. Without giving Steve a chance to answer, I ordered him a beekeeping suit, with big gloves, a helmet and a smoker designed to lull the bees into a stupor during the hive robbing. I never regretted my abandonment of this task, after watching Steve race inches in front of a swarm, past the barns, plunging head first into the pond. But Steve never complained about getting stung four or five times. He loved honey.

Goat Heaven

I was convinced that the next door neighbor had poisoned Brownie.

"You don't know that he did it," Steve challenged me. He had just buried our pet goat/lawnmower, in the swampy part of the barnyard pasture where the mountain spring widened on its way down to the catch pool above our pond. I was good at beginning life and less good at endings. Tall grass had shorted out the electric fencing weeks before, enabling our three goats to wander freely, browsing on the tastiest weeds, plants, tree bark and then the neighbor's garden. Contrary to most city slickers' beliefs, goats will not eat tin cans. Even with 20 acres of vegetarian gourmet pasture and woods, they will settle for nothing less than the most tender delicacy, in this case, Mr. Dalton's spring vegetable seedlings.

"I can't prove it, but he called once to let me know about the goat's first visit. I told him you were out of town and that I didn't know now to fix fences. One week later, he complained again and I assured him that we would take care of it.

He seemed pretty easy. After all, he came for a massage once. He even told me I had priceless hands."

"It is strange that one of them dropped dead with no symptoms and the other two are not sick," admitted Steve.

Kat of Heidi the pig fame had started us on goats. A fanatic, she even loved Billy goats, those smelly, aggressive male monsters. The three kids she sold us had all grown horns. Of course at the time, it was not obvious until their cute head bumps were too big to remove. The billy chased me up an apple tree after I tried to tether him to a fence post. Swearing from five feet up, I watched Brownie's horns smash the tree trunk whose bark was tattered from months of goat abuse.

"Teryn!" I called desperately. He was on the other side of the barbed wire fence watching me battle another cute farm animal. "Teryn, he's got me up a tree!"

"I know, Mom." He picked up his water gun aiming to shoot at the once-cute once-little Brownie.

"You'll never hit him from there," I shouted as a stream of water ran down the back of my neck. "Teryn! Hit the goat, not me." Another squirt hit the branch above. "Never mind, throw me a big stick and I'll try to whack him. Then I'll run and jump over the wooden fence."

Oblivious, Teryn was thrilled to be attacking a real enemy rather than a Nintendo X man. "Where are you going?" I screamed as he dashed through the barn. "Gotta get more water. I'll be right back."

"Jesus! If my Boston friends could see me now. No. This is not happening!" Furious, I tried kicking the goat's head. "You fucker", I fumed. "I hate the male species."

Last week one of the roosters had run up behind me and pecked a hole in my shirt.

I snapped off a dead branch, jumped four feet away from the tree, wildly swinging in all directions.

'I'm a Taurus you idiot. No bullshit!" I snorted fire at Brownie as I flung my legs over the rail. Shaking, I collapsed in the grass.

"I'm OK, Teryn, I got out," He looked disappointed but pelted Brownie with more water anyway.

So Brownie was now dead.

"You hated that goat, Kendall. Mr. Dalton did you a favor," my dear husband reminded me as he left to repair the fence.

Anti-Choice

For years, I raged at the sign downtown on the lawn of the Catholic Church in Asheville. Ten Million Unborn it advertised, with a row of crosses behind it on the lawn. A crazy thought seized me. Maybe Eric Rudolph and his friends in the Army of God, a shadowy group of anti-abortion extremists, were part of Osama Bin Laden's network? After all Muslim fundamentalists don't like women either. Their motto was: Keep them wrapped up from head to toe and stone them if they protest. Rudolph's was: Send anthrax to Planned Parenthood, murder doctors who perform abortions, even kill innocent civilians if necessary. I began to cry remembering the woman who died in the Atlanta bomb blast. The fact was, Rudolph was an adherent to the racist and anti-Semitic Christian Identity religion practiced in little congregations all over the country. Abortion clinics had been dealing with terrorist attacks on pregnant women for years and Planned Parenthood now knew more about anthrax poisoning than the FBI. It was 1995 in Atlanta at the summer Olympics where Moriah's passion for gymnastics led us within feet of the trash can blasted by a bomb a month later. Rudolph, a suspect of this and other abortion clinic bombings, could have been our neighbor. He was part of a 1990's anti-government, common law survivalist network with a keen interest in guns, who feared a "New World Order" of foreign interest. The dark side of New Age Western North Carolina.

"Mom, I can't believe you had an abortion! It could have been me," Moriah protested at thirteen in 1993. She was practicing gymnastics.

"Well, maybe it was you. Maybe you tried and succeeded the second time." I replied.

"Then where was I between 1977 and 1981?" she quickly asked.

"Probably a dolphin spirit," I answered playfully. "I believe I met you on a whale watch out in the Boston Harbor. On the ferry boat I noticed a little girl with brown braids standing in sea salt on the deck. I fell in love with her instantly and began wanting a girl-baby. I told your dad, "I want one just like her." And your guardian angel must have whispered, "It's time, Moriah's been riding those waves almost four years."

"Yeah, Mom. Sure," she said doing a back walkover. "But I am a good dolphin."

This morning Rudolph was all over the news. I decided to make pancakes and Moriah asked, "Do you think that Rudolph guy might be hiding in our woods, Mom?" Moriah had defended her pro-choice stance at a Reynolds Middle School class debate.

Living in the land of Baptists and Billy Graham was really different from Brookline and the Kennedy's. Whipping the pancake batter a little harder, I saw myself walking through our barn on the way to my morning trampoline work-out. Already glowing with Sharon Spring meadow fever, watching the spider web above the stall, I saw myself in fantasy, frozen by Eric Rudolph's outline crouching in the hay.

"We've heard about ya. You pro-choice Yankees better git on back where ya's come from."

Back to pancakes. "No, I'm sure he's in a cave only he and his terrorist network know about," I said, "far out in the mountains near the old growth forest." We joked for weeks over dinner wondering how long it would take the hundred or more FBI agents to find him, laughing at the local people who reported seeing him in a bar. Then deciding he was already in Mexico or dead from starvation. "But then again, Steve added from his seat in front of the dining room window, "maybe he and Danny Horning are hanging out in the Grand Canyon together. Getting ready to ambush some poor hikers." We all laughed remembering the escaped convict who showed up in the national park the very same week we did during our trip west before arriving in Asheville.

"We don't care what the Koran says or what the Bible says. Send out the anthrax. We will control our bodies. So says the Goddess!" I spewed at the computer, pounding my fist until the printer rattled dangerously near the table's edge. "Shit!"

I scanned down my long list of emails: The government of Nigeria is going to stone to death a woman who gave birth out of wed lock? Hatred swelled up. My Afghan Women email:

> *Women are roaming crazy in the streets, it said, they can't work, they can't speak, they can't go out of the house without a man. This is an abuse of human rights. Register your protest now. Click here.*

"Help. Help. Help us. Goddess, please! Swiveling around in my chair to face the tiny oval image propped up on the lavender candle, I pleaded again, "Mother Mary where are you?"

And what about abortion rights? Women in Afghanistan must abort babies. All women abort babies. How grateful I am to be an American woman. And thankful the clinic in Massachusetts where I terminated my pregnancy wasn't bombed by the right wing until after I moved south.

Healing Hands, 1997

"You have healing hands," a local healer told me. "I can see the energy around your fingers"

My career path in Asheville had been a series of low paid non-profit jobs that left me longing again for lost opportunities in Boston.

"Do you think the public will pay money for energetic healing? After all, it's not covered by insurance like chiropractic."

"No, but massage will be popular in another few years. It's big business in Florida and California. You could combine the two modalities," she suggested.

Massage school would give me a license to touch people, to transmit this healing life force that everybody in alternative medicine was talking about. Nine months later I graduated from the first massage school in Asheville to join the ranks of what would become a city of under-employed therapists, all competing for those with luxury money or a belief in preventative health. I quickly mastered a variety of techniques—acupressure, reiki, polarity, tui-na, all of which transformed stress, hoping to uncover a latent ability for medical intuition. Marketing myself as Healing Hands, I boldly hammered my first blue and white sign into the right of way along highway 74A. It disappeared in a couple of weeks. The second sign at the end of our driveway lasted several months before vandals spray painted one side. My third sign lasted for years on a very busy two lane road with no shoulder at the opposite end of our road: Massage * Hot Stone * Yoga with an arrow directing the public to my home based office.

Five years into my massage practice, I realized clairvoyance could not be learned. Intuitive hunches maybe, but talking angels, past life visions or colors in or around the body were not my privilege. My favorite quartz crystals sat at the base of the four massage table legs, amethyst stones on each end. Every so often a client told me about an internal pulsating green light they had seen as I massaged around their heart, or an apparition sitting in the corner on my fountain. There were sensitives who shared intimate information:

"My mother always comes to every bodywork session I have," Eloise smiled below me on the massage table. "And each time she brings a flower. Today it was a lily"

"I was guided by spirit to call you," a man once told me. "My guides tell me you are doing sacred work and it's exactly what I need."

"It was like God came right through your hands." Or,

"I could feel the family of light around me, especially Meher Baba."

Another client went spontaneously into a past life regression, writhing like a prisoner on a torture rack during the middle ages, his eyes rolling back in his head. My light wand (a flash light with a crystal and colored filters) moved over his spine following a distinct movement of energy rising from his tail bone out the top of his crown. A frazzled talky women with a self diagnosed endocrine imbalance announced from the table that black bowling balls were flying out of her brain. During an evening session while giving a foot massage, for a second my half-open eyes saw a violet cloaked figure at the head of the table.

The majority of people suffered from back, neck, and shoulder aches caused by hours at the computer. Many women complained of chronic fatigue syndrome, weight gain or fibromyalgia, a mysterious chronic, whole-body pain. Men collapsing from work stress, routinely fell asleep face down snoring or drooling through the face cradle. My fingers pressed acupressure points, rolled, pounded, squeezed skin and muscles that were flabby/hard, smooth/scarred, taut/wrinkled, but almost always white, a reflection of the community's racial make up. After years of practice, my hands knew every shape, size, and contour of the human anatomy, the curve of a shoulder blade, clavicle, rib and pelvis, the spinal column——a tree trunk of nerves wired to every organ, tissue and membrane where my fingers loved to dance—back and forth, up and down moving chi, lymph and blood. Restoring equilibrium and balance to the sounds of a splashing fountain, to the rhythm of drums, flutes or classical music. Even when I felt grouchy or sick and tired, I learned to focus intention from my heart through my hands, allowing transcendence of my personal pain. It was the first step on a very long path (lifetimes, perhaps) to becoming a master healer: a person capable of transmitting universal energy powerful enough to heal disease.

Each client inhaled the potent scent of essential oils mixed in coconut, canola or almond oil smothered lavishly over legs, arms, toes, ears—birch for sore muscles, eucalyptus for congestion, bergamot for euphoria, lavender for pain. While I channeled and circulated energy, together we exchanged and transmuted it like alchemy. Gliding strokes sedated, then transported them into a meditative zone—that place of utter surrender to the self.

"Is this the way we are supposed to feel?" a thirty-one year old man with a black and red shoulder tattoo asked me after his first massage, his pink face glowing like a sparkler.

"How *do* you feel?"

"Uhhhh. New. Brand new."

The only people who got off my massage table disgruntled was an occasional fellow who expected sexual favors.

Ring. Ring. "Hello. Is this healin' hands?" A male voice would ask. "Do you do full body massage?"

"I am a licensed massage therapist and I do medical massage." Pause. "Therapeutic massage."

"Well, I'm lookin' for full body."

After seven years I knew what to say. "There's only one body part I don't do, sir"

Ninety nine percent gratefully floated pain free out the door into their cars. Zapped by the force. No, I wasn't a medical intuitive, but I had mastered the art of healing relaxation. My conclusion: the fourth dimension workshop at the Holiday Inn had been an initiation to a piece of reality science had yet to study: subtle energies and energy medicine.

War Zones, 1997-2000

"Holy shit!" My Dodge Caravan swerved to the right, my eyes riveted on the new billboard. "He did it," I screamed. Blessed Be. WINNERS WANTED. Steve had finally made his mark on Fairview.

The SINNERS WANTED billboard simply made my blood boil. "Go to Hell!" I screamed out the window every time I past it. Which pathetic Baptist Church put that up, I choked almost daily, wishing I were back in Mission Hill where I could see the bill board Steve had sprayed painted on a midnight guerilla run when spray painting political slogans was a common activity among activists in Boston.

"Why would anyone want to join a church like that?" I repeatedly asked Steve.

"Kendall, you're just not guilty enough," he would laugh. "Your parents forgot to put original sin in your breakfast cereal."

We had joked about cutting it down. About setting it on fire. And changing the S to a W. Winners Wanted. Wow! That would be revolutionary and very sinful.

I congratulated Steve when I saw him.

"Me? It must have been the same kid who cut down that huge real estate bill-board last year."

He now worked fifty hours a week or more running two businesses to keep our family secure yet his political views and instinct for guerilla citizen action emerged whenever it could. Steve had an uncanny ability to sniff out corruption and greed, two of the worst sins in his book.

The swimming pond we had constructed at Sharon Spring was a sacred spot fed by an underground spring, so when the new cell phone tower's reflection from the ridge behind our house rippled into view, I felt rage at the company, and even more rage at the no-zoning sentiment in our county. As far as I was concerned, the chairman of the Buncombe County commissioners and his followers all deserved to have chemical plants, junkyards, and race tracks outside their bedroom windows.

All I wanted was our twenty acres of mountain beauty, clean air, and clean water just as the goddess created them. Every night the stars surrounded our dark neighborhood with infinite space. A passage to the universe. Our connection to the divine. My entire mood moved with the temperature, the clouds, each season, the sounds of the frogs and insects, the birds at our feeder and bath. Fairview was sublime beyond beautiful when we first arrived in 1993. A two lane road led a few automobiles into a leafy canopy with open fields of cows, horses and kudzu climbing like earthworms over everything in its path. Breathtaking mountain views relaxed my uprooted jangled nervous system, weary from the painful shocks of the early years in Asheville. Finding our piece of heaven made the move almost worth it.

But over the next decade, big out of state developers discovered Asheville and residential building permits leaped 48%. Thousands of middle class people moved into Buncombe County crowding into new subdivisions on ancient 360 million year old mountain slopes. The tax free rich, thanks to George Bush, surged into gated communities of Mc-Mansions the size of Queen Celeste's and bigger, many of them around the corner from Sharon Spring. The developers made millions, builders had steady work, and Steve's modular/foundation business brought our family income into the top 15%. And every last one of us became cell phone users.

Trailers were the only affordable housing left in the county, but today, we stood in solidarity with our neighbors as they squabbled with a local real estate/developer who intended to put a doublewide directly in front of a house they had sold them for its mountain views less than a year ago. A trailer would block our neighbors' view, and infuriated them to post signs on trees warning the realtors against such actions. I contributed several signs, posting my favorite one near their driveway: *Beware! Target Practice Ahead!* That should keep out potential buyers we decided grimly, wishing we had been smart enough to buy the lot at a reasonable price five years earlier.

Without land use planning our piece of heaven was dangerously near hell. Environmentalists reminded the public that Western North Carolina had the widest variety of flora and fauna than anywhere else in the world, that ¾ of the land had a slope greater than 30% (in 100 feet length there is a rise of 30 feet) and that sloppy, aggressive construction on these slopes caused soil and water erosion.

Our neighbors couldn't stop the trailer, but five years later the Fairview population doubled, land values and taxes escalated, and upscale development was far more profitable.

It was a Republican take over.

Strangely, many of the wealthiest ones landed in the palm of my hands at the Biltmore Estate. Massaging the rich at Vanderbilt's castle was not what I had in mind when I took my revolutionary vows in the sixties. From the massive gateway entrance it took another fifteen minute drive to reach the Inn at Biltmore where I sporadically worked as a sub contractor, rubbing oils over the stressed out bodies of America's top 1%. Until I had a newer car, I felt self conscious driving my old white Toyota covered with colorful bumper stickers: God Bless the People of All Nations, John Kerry for President and other local democratic candidates, through expansive cornfields, vineyards, bike trails and the wooded paradise of one of America's most famous estates. In the early years we were allowed to enter the front doors of the Inn with massage tables strapped on our backs, through the elaborate halls decorated with finely matched furniture, rugs, plants, orchids, chandeliers, twenty foot high windows, frequently soothed by live piano music before a ten foot high stone fireplace. Later we were re-routed through the employee's entrance where cooks, chefs, security guards, doormen, maids, cleaners, receptionists, cashiers and others punched a time clock 24 hours a day. Running late to my appointment, I scurried past groups of Haitian women folding bright white laundry, pushing carts, moving beds, mattresses, cribs and other linens in the hallways behind the walls, hustling with my own sheets stuffed in a red tote bag, dragging a large massage table. When I stopped wondering how much money each client had or how they had obtained it, giving a relaxing treatment didn't bother me much, especially if the tip was decent. What bothered me were the incessant images of war victims from the afternoon NPR report I listened to on the drive over. The right wing firewall. While my hands healed the toned firm body of an executive, somewhere just to the side of him, or under the table on the thick rug or behind the multicolored weaves of the curtain fabric lay a mutilated, blown apart human being in a pool of blood the color of his wife's toenails. That was a problem.

On the table under my palms, they were just like me or anyone else in the rat race who was tired, anxious or burned out. Naked of jewelry, dinner clothes, credit cards, make up, prestige and power their skin was skin. Rich skin, yes. Black, white, Asian. But just skin. The young Kendall wanted to jab an elbow into an eye socket, stick a finger into an ear drum, yank a toe, mash a collar bone, even brake a vertebra. The bourgeoisie still deserved the fate of Marie Antoinette, didn't they? Guilty by class membership. Deserving a car bomb on the way to the winery?

But I was all smiles at the end, handing them the Biltmore Estate bottled water, advising to drink a lot, take a yoga class, see a chiropractor after their vacation, slurping up the compliments, wishing them a safe journey. Take down was all chatters, while we stripped off sheets, turned off the CD player, washed oily hands, filled out paperwork. I squinted past the fountain into the empty room before closing the door. Someone had removed the war victims and their blood had been washed up. It was all good. And besides, I was on my way to a sushi dinner in downtown Asheville.

On the way out past the wine-sipping guests drunk on the classy Vanderbilt pastures, we stopped at the registration desk. I noticed one of my favorite concierges was gone.

"Oh, she was a single woman, you know. She couldn't make ends meet on her Biltmore paycheck. Said she was going to try real estate," explained my therapist colleague.

And that really was a problem.

Y2K

Bewildered, my eyes wandered out to the cow and calf grazing contentedly on the grass fifteen feet from our front porch as cows have grazed for millennia on earth. The young male would soon be on my dinner plate, his healthy meat replacing the grain-fed, anti-biotic filled monster agribusiness cows. According to some Y2K predictions, after all the computers malfunctioned at the stroke of midnight on December 31, 1999, the cow and calf might be stolen by a mob of hungry, crazed neighbors looking for food after their last visit to our local Food Lion, only to discover it had been ransacked by other Fairview citizens.

We had just returned home from a Fourth of July party at the Buncombe County Democratic Party fundraiser on Saylor's Ranch with new age political friends, Penny and Jacob. Chocolate and lemon meringue cakes were auctioned from $50 to $100 each to people packed in an open air lodge. Saylor had donated the use of his majestic cattle ranch with a man-made lake complete with food for the masses, ten minutes from our property in Fairview. I had driven by hundreds of times but never expected the privilege of an invitation, even as a Democrat. Obviously, I'd drifted a long way from Marxism.

"Well, I guess we could go find the hidden caverns over in Bat Cave," I grinned half seriously at Jacob who was quoting a description of the social pandemonium to come.

I cheerfully continued, "Don't worry. Think of all those bags of rice and canned food shelved in the underground kitchens of America."

"Seriously, what are you proposing we do?" snapped Jacob's wife, Penny, glaring at him from her reclined position on our couch. Days before she had been in the hospital emergency room with mysterious heart palpitations. We both wanted to believe her physical symptoms were caused by higher energy from the photon belt entering the earth's atmosphere, a popular belief at the time.

"Maybe your light body is expanding," I said handing her a cup of tea. But then again, menopausal women often have hot flashes, insomnia and heart flutters."

"So do older people," Penny grimaced, sipping the tea.

Jacob had left for a glass of water and now had Steve cornered in the kitchen with the details of a post Y2K catastrophe. Planet X, a runaway asteroid destined to hit earth in another year.

Sweating

Lance poured more water from the wooden ladle over the rock people, a pile of stones in a pit dug in the center of the sweat lodge. In a womb of blackness, twelve of us sat on a circle of towels moistened by wet grass, breathing deeply as the sparks glittered over the faint edges of the rocks we'd dug from the creek bed. A wave of heat surged into my face, and then more streams of water ran down my back and belly.

"Oh Wakan-Tanka, Oh Great Spirit be with us," Lance chanted in Lakota, "We are all related."

The Native Americans sweated. So did the Finns, and the Russians, and the Mormons. (Me. By heritage, anyway) Our first sweat lodge was led by a couple in Asheville trained in the Lakota Indian tradition. New Agers attended many sweats because land was available and fires were held almost everywhere except downtown. Rituals were a favorite pastime for me. I felt empowered and stronger in circles of focused people with good intentions.

Smoking the sacred pipe brought deep reverence for the Native Americans from each person who sat in the circle. I felt deeply alive honoring the four directions, the Great Spirit, and Mother Earth. Here I felt more spiritual than I did in most church services or other New Age ceremony.

Randi led the pipe ceremony for this lodge. She solemnly held the bowl of the pipe in both hands, and pointed the stem toward the sky, then toward the east, south, west, and north, and lastly to Mother Earth. She sat at one end of the thick woolen Indian blanket my mother had brought from Utah. The blanket was some eighty years old. I was my mother's daughter in this regard. My mother's fascination with American Indians powerfully influenced three-year-old Kendall when she created my first rain dance, handing me pots to bang on in my sandbox under billowing gray clouds. I was twelve when she took our family on a western journey to the kivas (underground ceremonial rooms) at Mesa Verde in Colorado.

Drums rattlers, tambourines, recorders and chimes lay in the center of the blanket, sprinkled with flower blossoms and herbs. Colored cloth lay ready to be made into prayer ties, one to each compass direction. Black for the west, thunder and the human shadow; white for the north, wind and clarity; red for the east, light and wisdom; yellow for the south, summer and growth. Each of us focused our intentions for self and others into the act of tying the cloth. We took time outside the lodge to listen in a circle, before clearing our auras with sage to prepare for entry. The prayer ties were then tossed into the fire and consumed on top of the stones.

An extremely thin man who had done dozens of sweats, Lance liked it hot. Too hot for some, who were breathing near ground level or pouring water from plastic bottles over their heads. Suddenly one person felt terribly claustrophobic with a memory of being trapped in a narrow tunnel behind another Boy Scout too terrified to move. He bolted through the sheets, blankets and black plastic hanging at the doorway. No one judged him for leaving, and now we had more leg room. In this sacred space, the smell of sage and sweet grass hung heavy in the hot moist air, toxins were released, pores opened, and skin cells washed away.

"North is the seat of wisdom and clarity," crooned Lance in a sing song voice. "Spirits, guides and ancestors, we welcome you. All my relations.… "Mi taku oya-sin." Each of us spoke a wish or prayer that needed the energy of the east. Our dog Rudi brushed against the plastic covering the lodge or turtle, itself a metaphor for mother earth. I prayed he wouldn't desecrate the alter this time. Crystals, shells, blossoms and personal talismans are arranged on a mound of earth in front of the fire attached to the lodge by a line of sprinkled corn meal representing the turtle's neck. The last ceremony Rudi urinated on the finished altar moments before we stripped off our clothing and crawled into the lodge. Most did not see it as a christening.

"I hope all the spiders, crickets and grasshoppers have left," chuckled Ginger. She loved to sweat but routinely had to leave by the end of the second or third direction. Her brother, a retired army officer sat on her left. It was his first sweat. Our prayers deepened in each direction as participant's imaginations grew with the expanded awareness of focused intention.

"I ask for support for my father who has severe arthritis and is in pain. May our love and healing reach him now." spoke the first voice out of the dark.

"I pray to the child within us all, and for the end to all abuse of children." spoke another.

"I am asking for release of all self deprecation. For the ways that I limit myself"

Prayers for peace in America, in Africa, in Bosnia, in Afghanistan. Each round lasted roughly twenty minutes as the intensity of songs, chants, and dripping sweat purified our internal organs, our skin, our worries, and fears. Knee to knee and heart to heart, each person balanced holding their place in the sacred circle until everyone simultaneously exhaled, "Open the door, I've got to get out!"

Jessie always went in naked, her full belly and breasts beaming the goddess to anyone who chose to look. In mixed sweats, men usually wore trunks, and most women went in dressed stripping naked when veiled in the womb's darkness. Native American men and women traditionally did not sweat together, but since we had passed the phase of "the Indians must have been all knowing" our ceremonies were distinctly modern American, with women intermingling and leading the men to their higher path. Honoring the mother seemed fundamental to the ceremony and our modern husbands and lovers were learning to be comfortable with their feminine side.

This particular ceremony was in the spring following the terrorist attacks of September 11th. All I wanted to do was pray for the victims here and in the Middle East. This sweat we began in the West, symbolic of the shadow, death and decay. I could see Osama Bin Laden floating above the rocks and the hissing water. His turban drooped slightly from all the moist heat.

"Let's surround Bin Laden with light and love," I requested. "Maybe he'll do something good."

It was very dark. The last round of dousing had just quieted, and the rock people breathed with us, heavy with heat. No one spoke. Maybe no one wants to send him light I wondered, paranoid because I could not see their faces. Was I violating his karma or the future of Afghanistan? My spiritual teachers always said if you asked for the highest good for all, nothing could go wrong. My right knee was aching and I could hear it crunching as I adjusted my crossed legs.

"Let's lift the dark veils from the Afghan women," Betty quietly spoke after another few minutes of hissing steam. I imagined a woman under a burka, her eyes peering through peep holes in her veil.

"Send her the strength to become a whole person. Someone began humming the Beatles melody "Blackbird flies … blackbird flies …" Twelve voices sang in unison for the liberation of our sisters in memory of John and George.

"I circle around, I circle around, the boundaries of the earth," began another chant. Soon we were all sweating, soaring and shedding our skin to the west.

I remembered the first sweat. Steve and I had asked that the souls of the farm family who had lived here in Fairview before us be healed from the suffering they had endured: the husband from Post Traumatic Stress Disorder from World War II, his son who died at thirty from Down's Syndrome, his daughter dying from cancer, and last and alone, his wife who had died of a broken heart. In the old tobacco barn we found a wooden table and chairs from their house, the "little white house" as we called it, and burned it in the ritual fire.

I loved the last round of prayers to the east where we could reach for enlightenment, that beautiful idea of sainthood, attainable after many lives, and many karmic rounds. Crawling on hands and knees, we each passed out the birth canal into the light of spring sunshine. Steve and Lydia ran yelping down to the pond, jumping from the dock and screaming as the cold water turned body heat into steam. Rudi was always outside the lodge to greet us, and sometimes a chicken or a cat, but never our children, who hid to avoid this weird adult behavior.

My hand painted goddess mandala looked up at me from the side of the barn. She held a crystal in one hand and a conch shell in the other. During my early years of unemployment at Sharon Spring I painted animal totems on round pieces of plywood that I nailed into a circle on the goat yard side of the tobacco barn. The goddess watched over the animals from the north end looking upward toward the sweat lodge and the wooded acres behind.

"Namaste," I bowed my head toward her before hiking up with the other slightly muddy, smoke-covered humans toward the kitchen for a sacred potluck dinner.

The Price of Wisdom, 2002

Our yard had been newly landscaped with flowering shrubs, butterfly bushes, and a variety of plants to appreciate. My garden was full of green vegetables, perennials, sunflowers, morning glories, comfrey, Echinacea, lilies, roses, wisteria, bee balm, rosemary, clematis-a spectacular show of nature's bounty and beauty. I grew more than we could eat, and now that Moriah was in college and Teryn hated anything but fast food, I gave much of it away. When the veggies were bitter or seeded, they became my organic chicken feed.

Every year I grew tomatoes, green peppers, beans, and squash, during the warmer season. By late June-July, most of the lettuces, greens, except Swiss chard, and radishes were gone. The asparagus had been eaten and my battle to keep back the grass had failed again. This year my blueberries bore their first fruit.

At times this garden was an Eden in the midst of my personal queendom, a daily renewal of serenity far from the great, roiling cities of my past, so much so that the neighbor's RV glittering white out of the green, stirred frustration in my breast. Each tree, plant, and flower that Steve and I successfully nourished spoke of the yard from which it was transplanted, or the person who gifted us at our housewarming, or the orchard we drove miles to find with children complaining in the back seat. Behind the house, four miniature apple trees displayed a few tiny apples, unlike the eight-year-old Wal-Mart granny smith in the middle pasture, a survivor that never fruited. In the lower pasture stood a slow growing weeping willow, a fast growing pussy willow; along the boundaries of Sharon Road and the driveway where right-wingers put Bush for President signs, where all the shouting, tree cutting, neighbor bashing, lawyer seeking cacophony dwelled among pines of different heights—shadows of personal tragedies, an abandoned double wide, barking dogs, sick dogs, dead dogs, run-away goats, a lame horse.

Our old, little white farmhouse where we used to live, was now shaded by the walnut and sweet gum trees we planted from three inch stems free from the local agriculture extension. Two of our Christmas trees were transplanted from the living room into the front yard. Before moving into our new passive solar modular house, finished by Steve and his crew, we lived in the old farmhouse for three years with no insulation, no air conditioning and no trees. To stay cool, we constructed a pond and went swimming almost every afternoon all summer. Our new modular, lit by new improved compact fluorescents you could actually read by, had overhead fans, lots of insulation, and a wood stove that heated most of the rooms all winter with some electric back up. The little white house was now occupied by tenants and memories—a fire, a broken lease, a broken family, late rent, no rent, weeds growing taller, stoned midnight parties, anger, accusations: your dog killed our chickens, your friend's dog bit Steve at the mail box.

This dry summer my babies were grown, my dog Rudi was dying, my pond was 2-1/2 feet down from drought. The trout were fished out by a trespasser and by blue herons stalking the edges. Frogs ruled the water now, and a scary snake slithered across the water, shading under the dock, as peaceful as my fearless swimming husband.

Teryn spent his youth here with other young boys, slinging mud, tipping over canoes, sliding down the zip line one and two at a time, dropping into ice cold water. Years of birthday photos and beautiful boys filled my album. Water balloons, and potato shooter projectiles *whizzed* past the barns, dropping near goats, rusting farm equipment, and over the trampoline where Moriah jumped her way through middle school.

Sometimes I could not bear the aloneness, the aloneness of jumping on the same trampoline in the huge pasture of blackberries and a field of squash, below the little white house where the chatter and laughter of my tenant's children lifted joyfully in the air above my exercise routine. My knee hurt for the first time. A stiffening. I sensed old age. My children did flips but I simply went up and down, with a slight twist rotating my vision: to the house and barn, to the new trailer hidden behind a green wall of pines, to the pond and the gazebo I helped Steve build where we sometimes did yoga, to the dock where diving used to be exhilarating, to the four acres we sold to other people when we believed we needed money, to the corner piece of land we considered putting an apartment building on, to Sharon Rd where Rudi was hit by a car-where I once jogged and now walk.

The wisdom of age came with a price. Steve's back hurt from compressed discs. Many of my friends have chronic pains. The Clinton years along with the energy of hope were history. Catastrophe felt closer than ever. Yes, it intensified after September 11th but death begins to sink into your consciousness at fifty. Friends have died or fight to keep from dying. My mother's mini-stroke paralyzed her leg, and was followed by breast cancer and skin cancer. Yesterday, researchers announced that hormone replacement therapy does increase a woman's risk of cancer and stroke. I warned mom about chemicals that caused illness and toxic waste, consuming the earth's body and ours, but she trusted drugs more than alternative therapies.

Today I learned that our faithful dog, had lymph cancer. Rudi swam with us for summers in our spring fed pond, breathed what I thought was fresh mountain air, played in sunshine, ran daily over our acreage. Had his cheap dry dog food caused it? The veterinarian assured me that cancer just happens. Had Rudi taken on his owner's potential diseases? Had the toxic building materials in the garage where he slept sickened him? These thoughts kept me awake.

The phone rang. A collect call from Teryn.

"So Mom, what am I taking next year? Did you get me into pre-cal? I marveled at how driven he was. "Mom, when you come to get me bring a Spanish Level One book so I can review before school starts." He is away studying math at Duke University, leaving me with no one to serve, no breakfast to make, no video to retrieve, no movie to drive to, no one to argue with over food. I sat often on his bed missing him. Looking around, I was embarrassed by his room. Where did this child come from, with his subterranean world, of phone, computer, scanner, TV, fan, electric guitar, Xbox, CD player, calculator, VCR? He came up for air only when he wanted something, generally food or money. To think that I shared a bedroom with my sister for seven years with a typewriter, a violin, and a Brownie camera. I sighed deeply. Teryn was aware only of what flashed across one of his screens, or what he typed into it. *You create your own reality* is a favorite new age slogan. His and mine were connected only by the water we both drank and bathed in. And most of the time he drank Gator Aid.

March for Choice

President Bush was determined to take away our right to choose. Roe V Wade was hanging by a thread in the Supreme Court. It was hard to believe that I thought the feminist revolution would be victorious by the time I reached middle age. Instead, I was attending NOW (National Organization of Women) meetings in downtown Asheville, speaking as an elder to young women who had never marched on Washington.

They listened with attention to my tales of past demonstrations in our nation's capitol. "My daughter Moriah and I will be marching together. But this is a young woman's battle," I said with a long face, "After all, I'm post-menopausal. Family planning is not really my issue anymore."

None of these young women had ever held a picket sign. Or raised a cry for freedom. My voice was convincing, painting a romantic view of cherry blossoms blowing past the Lincoln Monument onto a crowd of ... "Well it could be 500 thousand, or 400 or 200. This must be the third and final wave of our movement." I paused remembering the young Weathermen in Madison who riveted me into action thirty-five years ago. Ten of us sat in a corner grocery store inside a renovated neoclassical arcade, curious tourists circled round us and the folk art for sale. Only one of us was male. The Democratic presidential candidates were all male and claimed to be pro-choice. I was still dreaming of the end of patriarchy and the collapse of the Catholic Church or at least its metamorphoses. My mind wandered to Mary Magdalene. A recent best seller suggested she was the wife and partner of Jesus and possibly a high priestess of the Temple of Isis in Egypt. But I left that out of my speech, for now.

Landing in Asheville. A choice? Not what I expected, but over time I learned to live with paradox: something with seemingly contradictory qualities: *Asheville.* I drove a hybrid on the Reverend Billy Graham Freeway to a community at Green Life Grocery, the sacrilegious hot spot where I sat summer and winter in cold door drafts or air conditioning meant for frozen yogurt, offering relaxation chair massage to the frenzied organic eating public, a high tech zoo of cell phones users in neckties, spiked heels, briefcases—sandals, dreadlocks, and nose rings. "I'm also a yoga instructor and owner of this guest cabin, just 15 minutes from here," I explained to a curious shopper, pointing to the photo on my Sharon Spring Retreat and Guest Cabin rack card.

"Wow, you own that? How did you find that place?

"Well, it's … it's a long story. I feel very lucky, especially now that a major Eastern newspaper agrees we *are* the Paris of the South."

At the entrance to Green Life was a moratorium petition to stop ridge top and big box development. My friend, who happened to be a woman, was running for city council to help stop all that. She was accused of being a witch by the religious right who frowned on women who stood in circles casting spells to protect trees from developers.

To my back was a display of organic flowers grown in the old tobacco fields of Madison county, delivered weekly without pesticides or herbicides in a vehicle still run on gasoline. To my front was a 20 foot long mirror case of double image ecstasy dishes with names like chicken waldorf, mushroom lasagna, nutty trout and Thai-no beef salad. To my left, a female cashier with bright purple hair under a baseball cap rang up groceries next to Burt's Bees natural make up display, while a tall male dressed like Zorro took off his black cape to become a cafeteria server. He waved to a man wearing fashionable black framed glasses, a bun, and bedroom slippers. The hair colors, tattoos, and clothes (all made in China) of the Green Life parade as I called it, matched the mounds of red, yellow, orange, green organic produce to my right beyond the local baked breads and sugar free chocolate chip pumpkin muffins. Less fortunate customers ate their way through the store, filling up on yummy samples of cheese, dips or health drinks. A pair of cowboy boots stepped my way, drinking a large mocha latte, followed by purple clip on roller blades with flashing lights, munching a power bar. Soon the weekly high heel shoes slumped into the face cradle complaining about back pain, waving fifteen dollars for fifteen minutes.

I was certain that neither Reverend Billy Graham nor his son ever shopped here for food, spiritual guidance or massage. Wiping saliva off the empty turquoise face cradle of my massage chair with a brown paper towel, before my next customer, I ran to the counter for a cup of Peruvian fair trade coffee, right from the heart of Pachamama.

TURNING FIFTY IN PERU

PachaMama, 2002

My friend Temple spoke to the devas, asking that we be allowed to continue the Pachamama Ceremony. "Please stop the rain." Under a grove of trees, I was holding an umbrella over Bernadette's head and our altar of cotton, shells, grains, wine, chocolates, flowers, nuts, and fruit offerings to Pachamama. We sat at the top of the pasture behind my house mentally connecting the apus or mountain spirits to help stabilize different geographic areas of the earth.

"That was an immediate response," Temple assured us, "The leaves rustled right back." I don't want the rain to stop I thought, looking at the rust colored pasture. We were suffering now in Western North Carolina from a draught. Our tenants had no water. Our pond was half full. Remembering that in Andean culture the llama was associated with water, and the creation of springs and lakes, I visualized one enormous llama over Asheville.

Trained by a Peruvian shaman, Bernadette was required to lead a sacred Inca ceremony to mother earth every August according to tradition. She sat on the ground with her inner prayers, then called aloud to us one at a time. We knelt on the blanket before the offering, each piling on more delicacies. The gift pile grew taller and more beautiful with each layer. I enjoyed the alphabet soup exercise we shared, searching for tiny macaroni letters of our names, and spelling them into a plastic cup. Then you would pick out the initials of people whom you thought needed healing. All names were sprinkled into the offering pile, to be burned in the lower pasture fire pit, near our sweat lodge site.

The llama spirits must have heard my wish. Now we stood in raincoats. Bernadette and the gifts were under a tarp awning that my husband, Steve, had quickly constructed. My knee ached and bending was almost impossible even with the chiropractic adjustments. The hard rain softened, lightly fluttering off leaves above us. My detoxification diet for chronic indigestion prohibited sweets or carbohydrates, but I desperately wanted a taste of the tart. My will power broke over a few sips of wine. Drifting from a tape player in the grass, haunting Andean flute music carried me back to the portal (an invisible gateway) I had visited in Bolivia two years ago, near the Peruvian border. The rain stopped.

April, 2000
Asheville

I had been planning my trip to Peru for almost a year, intending to celebrate my fiftieth year, pleased my hormones no longer controlled me, thankful not to not have blood stained underwear. I was just beginning to enjoy my pre-adolescent androgynous state again. At forty-eight, menopause came earlier than I expected. Entering the wisdom years was no small occasion, so when I received a flyer titled Re-Activating the Ancient Temples in Bolivia and Peru, I called excited. "You are leaving almost a month to the day after my 50th birthday on April 26th," I breathed in one of my mysterious this-is-a sign voices. The local organizer was not a big shot guru but she did fit the category of new age freak—an astrologer who channeled out-of-body Akashic Records (a library of the universe). Besides, I really didn't want to be at Machu Picchu with 100 people following a famous guru.

Shortly after I made the phone call, my fiftieth birthday party evolved into a ceremonial playback theatre, a life review I created to make sense of a half century of seemingly unconnected random events that brought me to the doorstep of crone hood. It was a life in four acts, the maiden, the rebel, the wife/mother, and the overt spiritual seeker who embarks on a journey to Peru. I had been a seeker in Cuba, China, and Nicaragua up to now, and Peru would be the next destination. Sadly, neither my mother, father or sisters could attend, but my fellow enactors included Asheville friends plus two close friends from Boston. The four acts lasted four hours with a grand finale of me spinning under a tunnel of outstretched midwife hands that birthed me into the spring green sunshine of the adjacent yard. An old dress was torn up symbolizing the ending of a half century. *Half a century!* My astrologer friend interpreted my chart. Clearly I was ready for the portal in Peru.

May, 2000
Bolivia

As I stood at the portal, I began to experience my wondrous, beautiful entry into it. Yin energy pulled me straight into the "New Sunrise", the womb of the mother, the eternal city hidden within a Golden Disc. My visions were bigger than my imagination and clearly a gift from the plant spirit, A Chuma or San Pedro. A Chuma took me through multitudes of inter-dimensional cities all of which began or returned to a cave, a tunnel, or an opening into the earth, with stairways leading to magnificent temples and pyramids. The colors changed from gold, to shades of blues, greens, red, and faces of Egyptians, Aztecs, Mayans, and Incas. Rooms filled with statues, stone circles, cliffs and then the Eye of Horus, pulsated powerfully in the center of my head. Then the Easter Island statues appeared. I followed a tiny figure down a tunnel while faces of ancient races grew from the rocks. Below were masses of people beneath a space needle, a rocket-like vehicle cruising through a pyramid city. Suddenly I saw a modern skyscraper city surrounded by temples, then fierce ugly faces like ones I had seen at Chitchin Itza or in Tibetan art. Swirling volcanic-like waves shook my body. I touched the earth with my vibrating hands as if to hold her steady so she would not turn on her axis. The visions of this beautiful Queendom continued.

Now, the black bearded Peruvian shaman/anthropologist who was our leader asked each one of us to stand beside him in front of the 'portal', a natural imprint shaped like a Celtic cross in red rock out in the middle of a field. By this time, the local Indians were accustomed to tourist buses pulling up suddenly, emptying spiritual seekers into their dusty landscape and trudging together excitedly toward the same goal. The spirit plant, A Chuma, made me slightly queasy as the shaman warned, so I welcomed his spraying floral water into my face through his teeth on the bus ride. Now I heard him working with the dark, energy in another tourist's energy field, the sucking in and spitting out of nasty etheric plasma. Vomiting out karmic sludge! Ugh, what an awful way to clear people, I thought. I only half trusted the shaman, but it was enough to bring me up to the portal. There I climbed up onto the hard packed ground.

"Let your mind go," he told me. Stop trying to figure everything out. You are working too hard at making everything meaningful."

I began to hear drumming from the North and assumed it was a group of campesinos hiding behind the rocks playing for us. Then I heard pipes and voices singing, first loud, then softer. But the drumming remained steady. The wind blew strongly several times. "Who are the people playing music", I asked the shaman. He looked at me suspiciously, as if I were making it up.

Then he answered, "Those spirit voices used to be in bodies'.

"Are you sure singers and drummers aren't behind the rocks over there?" I pointed to my right, certain he was joking.

"No one is there," he assured me.

Tiahuanaca/Lake Titikaka

"The Viracochas, arrived on the plains of Bolivia and Peru about 14,000BC, around the time of the destruction of Lemuria and Atlantis," our young female American guide called back to us from the front of the bus. "Virachocha means shining being."

At the archeological site, a thin, brown skinned Aymara guide clearly proud of his heritage told us, "This entire region was heaved up from sea level 10,000 years ago, to form the altiplano, or high plateau where we are today, 13,000 feet above sea level." We stared at a barren mound disappointed that the pyramid was still buried.

"The Spanish destroyed the pyramid by stripping away all the gold from an earlier Aymara civilization. Later a natural disaster buried it all, leaving the plateau empty of human habitation for hundreds of years. Seven levels of consciousness are represented in the physical structures of this temple." He pointed to seven stairs and seven magnetic stones. He placed a compass next to the stone to prove his point. The needle riveted. "Unfortunately, at the present time our government has no money for the excavation"

Next he led our group of fifteen Americans to a wall near the Sun God and winged condor gate where the initiates of Aymara had passed, those who had earned the highest level of consciousness and could speak with the elements. Thanking the guide, an elder member of the spiritual seekers named Giselle, took over, explaining, "Some of our group members lived in California with the author, Hertak, when he floated out of body to be with the light beings who gave him the information told in the *Keys of Enoch*." Her white hair waved gently above her head and her eyes glistened as she held up a thick white book. "You see, an extraterrestrial being called Melchizadek built Tiahuanaca at sea level. It was the city of the Lords of Light." All seriousness, she proceeded to read us the relevant section about Bolivia and Tiahuanaca from this channeled text.

"Was Melchizadek the guy who knew the secrets of splitting and moving great stones with sound waves?" I asked a tinge sarcastically. "Are we activating the pyramid?"

"Yes to both," she whispered back. We ended with a prayer to the ancestor light beings. Luckily, I had been reading a book about the secrets of the Andes. My gray pony-tailed bus partner Fred had not, although he looked comfortable enough with all the cultish activity. I wasn't sure how I felt. We moved to a squared temple site below ground level to observe a series of ancient faces carved on four walls. A Cyclops stared back at me with three eyes. Other faces with strange looking expressions peered across the plaza.

"This site was built by the aliens who wanted a museum for the ethnic types of humanity that were tested before the time of Egypt," Mica said matter-of-factly, stepping down to the lower level. Clearly he was a true believer.

"Where does it say that?" my roommate Adrian asked skeptically.

"In the Keys." He glanced at his girlfriend, Lily. Wind blew a purple llama-wool cape around her legs.

Lily added confidently, "I know my body has a crystalline structure. At this moment I'm feeling an energy shift." She paused. "Now, I'm receiving information." Inhaling loudly, she breathed out, "All the records of this site are buried below in crystals."

When no further information ensued, I moved away to a bearded male statue standing alone in the center of the square with one hand on his heart, the other on his solar plexus. "What do you believe, Mak Ma, you white savior?" I whisper at his stony head, calling him by the name in my guide book. "Tell me," I commanded. "Are you holding the records?" I glanced over my shoulder nervous that an every-day tourist might be listening. I wasn't yet a true believer.

A man from the nearby museum handed us a sketch of a possible future renovated archeological site. The vagueness of it all exasperated me. Three llamas peered at us from over a hill as we climbed to the top of another dirt covered pyramid, surrounded by the modern poverty of women with babies selling trinkets. I was sure they were living with no electricity, no phones, no indoor plumbing, planting by hand and herding a few animals.

Here was something concrete. Did those women care about this pile of rubble and dirt? There are no public schools, and even tuition to the cheapest private schools is too much for these Indian children who begin working when they can walk. Will uncovering a mystery here bring them anything? My political self questioned my spiritual self. My eyes burned as I watched these Indians, who grow over 400 kinds of potatoes and live in adobe shelters with thatched roofs like their ancestors who must have been very different than the mysterious ones in the book. During my visit to China in 1980, I had watched a man from my bus window plowing with a water buffalo. Twenty years later on this high plain surrounded by snowy, jagged peaks, these Peruvians were doing the same. I was drawn back to the esoteric by the guide's voice. "Some say Mamacocha came here to bring in the feminine power of water. The feminine light rays enter the earth at Lake Titicaca."

"Who is Mamacocha?," Who *was* she? I corrected myself.

"A master in the sisterhood of healing priestesses." His words blurred in the commotion of the market place just outside the temple. The campesino women proudly held up their babies behind pottery, weavings, and other wares spread out on cloths. I purchased a tiny stuffed alpaca, wishing out loud that I could own a real one like the woman veterinarian in Asheville with an llama farm.

"They're just useless expensive pets for modern people with cars." Mark slurped as I counted coins for the craftswoman, admiring my new toy. Mark was 60 pounds overweight, a chain smoker, and at 11am was on his fifth coca-cola. His boyfriend was our leader's former husband, a lawyer with a mouth at least the size of Mark's waistline. They both rubbed me the wrong way.

Today our destiny by bus was Copacabana, a town on the shore of Lake Titicaca. Scrub brush, pine and eucalyptus trees clung to a very dry, arid soil molded around little stone walls to keep in animals and to heat the earth for vegetables.

"The lake story," our guide continued, "tells us the shape of the water resembles a puma, a human, and a fish. They say a puma jumped from the water to the sun during the big flood". A different version of Noah's Ark, I thought studying the map in my hand. I could imagine fish and pumas. I turned the map upside down staring hard. Other animal shapes jumped out of the borders. Across Lake Titikaka the mountains looked like Mt Everest and the Himalayan Range with jagged, frosted peaks in a deep, blue sky of white lotus-like clouds and sun. My eyes riveted to a second lake with mountain tops peaking out of the water. "Wow, look over there," I pointed excitedly.

"It is a mirage. Moisture on the lower mountains creates a watery-mist in the valley below," our bus driver explained to my disappointment.

Within a few hours we were headed across the lake in two motor boats with no life jackets. Our new native guide claimed, "There are cities under the water, 10 meters down lie the tops of citadels. Deep sea divers found huge walls at the bottom and toads longer than 3 feet."

My head snapped toward my companion. "Fred, do you believe any of this?" Everyone else seems so accepting." I turned to hear his answer. Fred was nodding out under the motorboat spray, his headband drooping over his eyebrows. No answer.

We stepped out onto the Island of the Sun where people have a life expectancy of 60 years. It was sobering, since I'd just turned fifty and chose to celebrate by being here. Children with rotten teeth, surrounded us, looking for candy. The American guide had told us no medical care was available and the infant mortality was high. The political me grew alert. Their work was back breaking and I felt mostly white and privileged, watching people harvesting their crops by hand, carrying enormous bundles of grain on their stooped backs like the burros running beside them. I noticed a few sheep and pigs. "The campesinos own their land, love Pachamamma and live with great dignity", the local guide pointed out. Ok, so they died a dignified and early death.

My body felt invigorated in the cool air, but several of the flatlanders were still suffering from altitude sickness, worried the hike might be over strenuous. "Chewing coca leaves helps restore balance," our leaders instructed us. Unconvinced, the group separated into sitters and hikers. At the front of the hikers I headed off to the tip of the island, my body filling with enormous energy, in view of snow capped mountains, rugged rocks and cultivated fields with sunlight radiating off rippling water. I felt buoyant, my feet practically flying over the dirt path, happy to leave behind the dead weight of the sitters. Far below the ruins, the waters of Lake Titikaka parted at the point of both shores. Our shaman passed his leadership role to a young local man who led a ceremony using a woven piece of cloth placed on a square stone surrounded by a circle of round stones. Speaking rapidly, with a stick he passionately drew a calendar shaped like a square cross in the dirt. I managed to hear, "The square cross is the foundation of Andean cosmology," but the wind blew away his words as fast as he spoke. I grimaced at his Nike hat, the international symbol of power and wealth that had invaded this Peruvian setting. Suddenly, he sprang bare footed up a rock formation above our heads that looked like a puma, to identify a bearded goddess. He sketched the outline with his fingers. The Nike hat looked smaller now. It no longer mattered that I couldn't hear. It mattered that it was his story and a legend of the Andean people.

Journal

> *Many of us are so attached to creature comforts that I can't help but compare this experience to the Vecino Builders Brigade, to the young, idealistic rebels with a cause! Spiritual journeying seems almost a joke in comparison. Perhaps it is the definition of 'spiritual' that is the problem. We don't have a common idea. For some, it is reading a channeled manuscript, for others it seems to be astrology. No one on this trip has a larger, realistic vision for humanity or even their own community. At its worst, their lives have become a series of self help workshops. I try not to focus on what I perceive as weaknesses and assume each person has something to teach me. But true to my political background, I prefer listening to the natives discuss their own lives, or learn Peruvian history. My social consciousness keeps my heart very open and vulnerable to the poverty and suffering around us, but no one on this spirit journey seems particularly interested or concerned about the material conditions. So I am forced to sit with the American New-Agers chattering on about all the continents they*

*have traveled, comparing food, hotels, etc. The group loud mouth is
so obnoxious he actually feels like poison to my system. I get up from
supper with a stomach ache.*

Our bus headed to Puno, an hour from the hotel, the largest town on Lake
Titikaka. I looked across the aisle at a snoring companion, almost everyone else was
asleep. Outside, campesino families harvested the fields together by hand. I saw an
occasional tractor and some homes with metal roofs. I used the time to question
our shaman/anthropologist about economics and politics as we continued our
bus ride from Bolivia to Peru. My restlessness kept me awake cursing Fujimora,
president of Peru, for not helping these poor people, still without running water
and electricity. The comfortable snoring made me angrier.

Past the Pepsi billboards on the open plains stretching below the mountains
where women wore bright red dresses, and men tended cattle, were hundreds and
hundreds of stone walls and structures marking plots of land. Graffiti for politicians Toledo and Fujimora was scrawled over rocks and walls, evoking memories
of the Spanish invasion. When the Spanish rode into Coricancha, the 'place of
gold,' it is said they pinched themselves to make sure they were not dreaming.
They proceeded to slaughter thirteen million people and steal all their national
treasures and gold. My heart spasmed with the memory of this holocaust.

*In the Golden Disc vision at the portal I was in a fantastic queendom, robbed by the
hatred and greed of the Spanish invasion. Each church I enter sends shivers down my
spine. All of them are constructed on top of the beautiful sacred Inca temples. Watching
the converted pray to the Catholic Christian god after the slaughter sickens me.*

We passed through beautiful mountains with large herds of llamas in a valley
full of eucalyptus trees. A tiny volcano grew at the edge of a spring with water
hot enough to boil an egg. At the temple of Wiracocha, our shaman delivered a
lecture about the Inca Empire, "it reached from Ecuador, Bolivia, Argentina, and
Peru. The standard of living was very high, in fact, the Spanish found seven years
worth of food storage. The Inca spoke to and with the elements. The temples and
sanctuaries were sacred because they were modeled after structures that existed in
visions at the cosmic level where things are perfectly ordered."

I noticed the superiority of the stone work below many of the Christian built
church foundations. Were they Inca or pre-Inca? My hands pressed against a rock
weighing 200 tons. They were beautifully fitted without mortar, so tight I had
trouble believing it was done by manual labor. Struggling to imagine how any
human being using simple technology could have moved it at all, I recalled my
elementary school textbook drawing of Egyptian slaves hauling stone blocks. The
next stone was air tight. My thumb nail would not even wedge between them.

Shaking my head, I heard the shaman, "… their mastery of energy and astronomy, went far beyond what we can imagine. I believe these stones were cut by the energy of light and raised by sound vibrations." Several heads nodded, smiling as if they had been present while it happened. Pressing my forehead against the magnificent stone I prayed for a vision of the truth, wishing for the assistance of the plant spirit, A Chuma.

Four members of our spiritual tour group returned to the United States because of family emergencies. The rest of us traveled through the Sacred Valley of the Incas, two hours from Cuzco, along a very narrow, dirt road following the Urubamba river that eventually flowed into the Amazon. *Here the last great Incan emperor and his families traveled from Cuzco to enjoy the bounty of this magical place,* the brochure read. Today, the bounty of the harvest season was at it's height. Fields of red colored quinoa plants called to my camera. Corn was drying everywhere in pens, on green lush, ground. Cows crossing the road forced our bus to a halt. An occasional bike or car passed by. Women washed clothes against river rocks below Mt. Pamawonka, looming behind green foothills and rocky-canyon-like peaks. We arrived at Willka-Ti'ka, a Quechuan word meaning sacred flower. This beautiful guest house built by local craftspeople, staffed by Qechua and owned by an American woman was a joy to enter. When I learned the owner was not here, I felt betrayed. Thirsting for the wisdom of a middle aged woman with her courage and power, I believed she might help balance the ragged, disjointed energy of our group. I was in awe of the garden she built, a total of six flower, vegetable, and herb paths in concentric circles, around a 500 year old Lucma tree. With my back against the bark I asked for some of its wisdom. Malki means both tree and ancestor in Quechua. "Malki, I called. Malki." I visualized nourishment and balance rising from its roots and descending from its branches filling my veins and meridians/energy pathways.

The morning market at Chicero near the guest house was one colorful collage. In the cool air and bright sunshine, I pondered what to buy, watching the individual craftsmen, clever and pushy, anxious to sell as fast and as much as possible. I could have stood for hours absorbing the nourishing energy of the colors, smells and sounds of people exchanging produce and beautiful creations. My body could barely contain the vitality and excitement of it all. Later, my joyful feeling blackened as I passed a Mass in progress at the Spanish church above the market place. Memories of bloodshed in the name of Jesus spewed forth. The Spanish only saw the devil in this holy place of the Incas. But the devil resided within themselves, I thought, as they reduced the population from 18 to 5 million. I wanted to hurry past the poor compesinos crowded within the church walls into the ancient past behind the village, to the gigantic, sacred Inca stones overlooking the valley of terraced hillsides. An old Inca trail was visible across the mountain, and instantly my feet were walking there, time-traveling back to this wondrous culture. Meditating to the Inca stone I asked for the ability to 'throw my energy", to become like Melchizadek, the Viracochas, and the light beings.

"Further down is a cave," our young boy guide pointed to the base of a gigantic rock, "A gringo entered there and never returned. No one ever found him. Now the entrance is covered." I felt an urge to pull back the stone, to disappear into ancient mystery, but no one in the huffing and puffing group was able to walk any further. "We must stay together,' the guide directed me back.

Chewing coca leaves I chose to sit alone on the bus.

June

As I listened to a bus mate who was a follower and devotee of Sai Baba, a spiritual master in India, our bus lurched up a very steep switchback to Machu Picchu. "Every time I fly," the devotee smiled, "I ask Sai Baba to put his hands under the plane. At his ashram in India, I saw the vibuti ash coming from the center of his palm." Sai Baba was known for materializing things from the air, from nothingness. The bus swayed dangerously close to the cliff's edge, choking and sputtering toward the ancient summit. Terrified, I took her hand.

"I've always wanted to visit India. Can we ask for his help now? The Quechua still believe human sacrifice is necessary to pay back the crimes of robbers who stole from Machu Picchu, you know."

"Of course," she rolled her eyes upward. "He is here." I held onto my amethyst healing stone and my seat just in case he wasn't.

The next day heavy rain trapped us inside the hotel. "A storm will not keep me from this ancient city," I announced. At 9am I began roaming the terraces alone. Dressed in yellow rain gear, I locked into the large, liquid eyes of a guardian llama. We stared for a long, long minute. The llama did not blink. I turned away, afraid to offend or scare this magnetic creature, awed by what felt like a Buddha gaze from a higher state of awareness than my own. Finding a spectacular ledge overlooking a terraced mountain sweeping hundreds of yards to the river below, I sat wide eyed following a bird's flight pattern, dizzy at the sharp drop off. More birds sailed up and down churning my stomach above the abyss. Afraid of fainting into the river below, I moved back to an open window facing Mt Waynapicchu, realizing the shaman and the group were leaving without me to a secret ceremonial site. No more than five minutes late, I waved my hands from the top desperately trying to get their attention.

"Shit!" By the time I scrambled down to the open grassy mall, the group had disappeared from sight, and I began cursing. "Damn you! Wait! Stop!" Frantic, I was determined to find them, poking my head into caverns, caves and thrones, absorbing the miraculous energy, listening and calling with no response. Tempted to enter one of the silent tunnels, I imagined myself plunging down deep or getting stuck between rocks, turning into a skeleton for a future anthropologist. Forty five minutes later, exhausted from climbing, I stopped all movement to listen. All I can hear is my own anger at being left behind, swelling fiercely, then blaming. Wasn't Laurel responsible to come back and check to see if I was there? Didn't anyone care about me enough to wait or call my name? Surely I would hear them? How far away could they be? Were they in an illegal place? Was I missing an important initiation? Impossible. Me, miss an important initiation!

My emptiness became so big and so dark I feared losing my equilibrium. I collapsed with my legs dangling over a ledge. Turning onto my belly to rest, I noticed it was an entrance into a dark, beautiful underground ceremonial cave with a serpent and a puma carved in stone at the opening. "The sacred animals of the Incas," I hooted. The cave had natural seats carved into its rock walls radiating with magnificent frequencies.

Adrenaline rushed through my veins and my heart began speaking. "It is the new millennium. I am re-birthing into the second half of life. I've rehashed the first half one too many times." I announced out loud. "You can't imagine how many rites and ceremonies I've been through since the mid 1980's," I explained to my imaginary audience.

"I try to stop judging the people around me, but it's hopeless. I have lost almost all interest in these freaked out travelers. I even dislike both the shaman and his assistant who seem disinterested in us as North Americans, and ..." My voice echoed off the rock from behind. Was all this tension with people just my own negativity reflected back at me? My own neediness, or approval seeking? Was it all a lesson about my dependency on Steve whose faults marriage forced me to accept? Or did this place enlarge all of our shadow sides? Determined to show them I could rebalance and calm myself, I forced the idea of happiness into the moment. Lightness poured over me, melting the panic. My inner smile turned into a huge grin. Of course. Surrender. **This is my life lesson**. Right in front of me. Fear of abandonment, and loss of control. I can re-capture my power by simply relaxing into the now—remembering the words of Echart Tolle, one of my favorite philosophers. Calmly, I began to write:

Oh Pachamama, your enveloping mists gently caress the mountains, our hearts, our souls as we honor the wise voices calling from your depths. Your song carries the sweetness, the terror of centuries upon centuries of human celebration, souls yearning for love, friendship and freedom, holding the possibility of perfection seen in the portal, behind the veil. Washing us clean, your vapors settle pushing deeper into a subconscious part of ourselves, working the disappointment, frustration, re-awakening our desire for freedom.

Footsteps at the cave entrance startled me. Suddenly a camera light flashed off the stone path. "Can I take a picture of you for a spiritual magazine? I am a French journalist," she assured me. "You look *so* peaceful." My teeth clamped on my nasty words. Instead,

"Sure. Why not?" I sat in lotus pose, eyes closed mustering all the inner peace and forgiveness I could find, sending blessings to everyone in our group, to the ancient ones and their persecutors, to my family and friends, ex-friends and the horrible journalist. More camera light filtered through my eyelids.

"Thanks." I heard the journalist step past me while I continued concentrating on an inner light flickering somewhere in my third eye. It brightened into the feel of the golden disc. I breathed deeply hoping to sustain the light.

Asheville

Bonita listened to my description of the portal in Bolivia as we ate dinner in Asheville.

"Yes, it sounds to me as if you were shown all the cultures on the planet that were gifted with the golden disc. You see, it was a liquid, gold temple of illumination, a gift from the galaxy, Pleaides. The Ancient Masters and Saints went back and forth throughout the world using the energy of the golden disc to sit in council. I think you were in a hologram. Time traveling."

"The shaman said he did not believe in inter-dimensional cities, and kept repeating that everything I saw was just my imagination," I complained. Bonita's grayish, long hair and turquoise ringed fingers added power to the moment, relief from the condescending Peruvian shaman.

"Well, she explained, "He is not a shaman in the tradition of the "Monastery of the Seven Rays." Leaning closer, she confirmed that a hotel owner in Peru discovered this portal. Almost whispering, "He had dreams of red rocks, and pink stones leading to a doorway. When we have ceremony there amazing things happen. Remember the semi-circles on either side of the door? Well, one has ascending energy and the other has descending energy." Bonita jumped deeper into new age mythology, her version. "Our galaxy is moving closer to the central sun, known as Althion. That's where the photon belt is coming from. And scientists have actually measured it. He and I saw lights coming from the bottom of Lake Titicaca."

I took another bite of salad as my mind struggled to fill in the missing pieces.

GLOBALIZED MYSTERY

India
June, 2001

It seemed impossible that I was leaving for India. But my plane ticket read flight to Atlanta at 11:25am from Asheville. Coincidently, Teryn, was booked on the same flight to Tucson for a week of astronomy camp. Steve cheerfully carried our luggage as his wife and son departed, one to the far East, the other West. Not prearranged, yet we ended up together, mother and son, taking our next steps. At 51 years, I was introspective, at 13 he looked to the stars. It was the first time Teryn had flown alone, and my first time to the land of yogis and gurus. Our eyes locked, his gaze shifted downward. My throat tightened. The hardest part of my life is saying good-by. Tears blurred my vision. I hugged him bravely, "You'll have a great time."

My chronic worrier asked, will I ever see him again? Planes crash. India is a mystery. Ladakh is the top of the world. On the other hand, my optimist self reasoned, maybe, just maybe, this continent would give answers to my endless search for social justice and spiritual enlightenment. For months I had been reading and re-reading a book by Helena Norberg-Hodge called *Ancient Futures: Learning From Ladakh*, a study of a sustainable society in northern India. Somewhere at the top of the Himalayas, Rachel and I hoped to witness this spiritual civilization where humans lived harmoniously with each other and nature. The ancient future.

My flight delayed, giving time to reflect on how little I knew about the cosmic continent I was destined for. Like all good revolutionaries, I knew about Gandhi's peaceful civil disobedience against the British but my impressions were from the American movie-version of his life, not books. An engine roared. I glanced at my watch. "Teryn is in the air, breath more deeply." Thirty minutes later the seat belt sign was still off. Yawning, I thought about Tibetan Buddhism, my other connection to India, and the Tara thanga that hung on my wall.

6:30 am in London. Tense and tired, I slurped globalized Star Bucks coffee in the Heathrow airport, waiting for Rachel to burst around the corner with her high energy chatter. Yes, it was the same Rachel responsible for inspiring Vecino, our building brigade to Nicaragua, now my traveling companion to Ladakh, in northern India, where a Buddhist culture had survived in a balanced ecosystem for thousands of years without a war.

Like England, this airport felt old. I noticed only because the Charlotte airport was shiny, with light and the sparkle of recent history. Loads of Indians passed by me, underlining the reality of my destination. I sat carefully eyeing the door, waiting, and waiting. Rachel did not arrive. Now my stomach churned with anxiety. Was this an omen? Will we be out of sync the entire trip?

Delhi to Mussoorie

We were in a taxi. "It is the best time to come." said Rachel, "at 11:30pm in the dark. To avoid the masses of people and the heat."

Indian workers frequently ripped off tourists, so I let Rachel deal with everything—the bargaining process, taxi rides, luggage handlers. Much to my surprise we were driven to a YWCA, a Christian ashram-clean, with fan, air conditioner and a shower with hot water, calming to my brittle nerves and tight muscles.

We awakened at 5:30AM and headed for the train station. The Indian faces looked washed out, both from rain and exhaustion like the grey skies above. Men swarmed us, each wanting to carry our bags. Fighting my way through them behind Rachel, I almost tripped over some very sick people lying on the sidewalk, including a boy with half an arm. Rachel was haggling over prices, while my fear was rising as the porters shouted at us. This is a scam, I thought, this porter thing. The taxi driver could have dropped us off much closer to avoid them altogether. Suddenly my huge, black bag was whisked onto a man's head and I chased after him to the old, worn out train station, as tired looking as the airport.

I hated to worry about theft, because all it did was pump my overworked adrenal glands. I was reminded that these tickets are pre-paid and reserved, making them off limits to the poor. Therefore, it was unlikely that the middle class Indians across the aisle with suitcases of their own would steal ours. Relaxing into a seat, I welcomed the tea and biscuits and Rachel's attention. In our own ways, both of us had fought for the rebel Sandinistas in Nicaragua, only to watch their promise of political and economic justice collapse. Another failed revolution. Now, my Daniel Ortega tee shirt lay at the very bottom of a cardboard box at the very back of my closet.

We decided to be sisters, since her only blood sister drowned in India as a child, and mine were both inaccessible: Jenifer, who was locked up in a mental institution, Elizabeth, who pretended I didn't exist. Surely our time together in India would be tranquil. Surely, together we would find a healthier community in Ladakh.

The bumpy train traveled fast, blurring miles of Indian country side. Rural villages strung with electric power lines and cell phone towers on the horizon slapped my eyes wide in disbelief. Rachel believed that cell phones had revolutionized communication for common people. "Now one person in a village with a cell phone can charge other villagers a small fee to call relatives."

In contrast, I remembered my fury over the cell tower behind my own house. How I kicked the fence and complained bitterly to the county commissioners of the blighted landscape. The same technology can feel evil in some places and great in another. I blinked at the Hindi graffiti scrawled all over village walls. What are they saying? Do all humans scribble common messages? People harvesting by hand beside smoke stacks for brick-making flew by, blending with little, dried grass tee pees along fields of corn, rice, sugar, mangoes and poplar-looking trees. Plowing water buffalo reminded me of China over 20 years ago. But the power lines hanging right over fields and villages disturbed me and I voiced concern about people getting cancer. "Why can't they learn from us?" I shuddered, complaining to Rachel, projecting the death count. The train's sound system played grating high pitched vocalists that slid and whined as we crossed several dry river beds. "Can't we ask them to turn that off?" I groaned. It was my jagged critic back in full force. Miles later I uncovered my ears to hear Rachel describe the approaching holy city of Hardwar where all Hindus must come at least once in their lifetime to bath in the Ganges River. "Twenty million a year manage to show up." she pointed out. I felt nauseous thinking about the water quality of that famous river. Temperatures outside the train were in the high 80's and low 90's. I gawked at the Muslim women wearing black, at the Sikh men in turbans with long curled-under beards, and stainless steel wrist bangles. Other men peddled rickshaws, or raced by on motorbikes, while women in beautiful colored dresses bundled crops, washed and dried clothes near water or carried crops on their backs. More cell phone towers whizzed by.

In Dehra Dunn, a busy city of over 400,000 people, Rachel's friends, Mo Mo and Tsering, met us in a comfortable car. I tried letting go of expectations. Dazed from jet lag and the assault of Delhi, I was riveted awake as we turned towards Mussoorie. Mo Mo drove very fast. Sacred cows meandered wherever they pleased, indulging on garbage or peacefully sleeping in the median. I laughed imagining,

New York City with cows strolling out of the subways. Pedestrians, cars, motor-cycles, bicycles, and trucks all funneled into the same lane in a chaotic, harrowing, swerving jumble of madness with no stop signs or traffic lights. I wondered if all Westerners are introduced to the Rocky Horror Indian Show in this manner?

Mo Mo and Tsering's home was a concrete, single floor box with a front porch facing the mountains. Due to an uneven water supply, the bathroom had buckets of water next to the toilet to wash down the waste. There was no running water from the bathroom sink. A young boy sat in the kitchen next to a propane stove, a servant who primarily helped Tsering with her cooking. "Is he an untouchable?" I asked offended. They assured me that the caste system was now illegal and he could leave at any time. "You mean like racism is illegal in the US, but is still practiced," I commented. They nodded.

"And we have challenged Mo Mo on his sexism, but I'm sure he wouldn't lift a finger to do housework of any kind," joked Rachel.

"Too bad, 'cause he looks pretty Western with that pierced ear and Harley Davidson tee shirt," I added. Mo Mo grinned back from behind the bar he had constructed in the middle of their living space, a room filled with all kinds of cross cultural expressions-from plastic ninja turtles to Buddha's, Native American postcards, and modern art posters of the Indian landscape. Turning up the ste-reo sound of Willie Nelson's *On the Road Again*, he downed his third drink and offered me one. "This is my favorite kind of music. On my trip to the States I listened to it constantly."

"You're kidding." I said. He turned it louder.

Tsering showed me their big television, computer and phone. Steve and I hadn't watched TV since 1992. Electricity was available, but there were constant surges. As I sat writing, their lights came on and off several times. "Mussorie has expanded too quickly with no planning," Mo Mo said, "but last night we watched a video of *Jumanji* with only a couple of interruptions."

"*Jumanji*?" I repeated slowly in disbelief. Globalization had traveled farther than I thought. The lights flashed on and off again. "To the multinational corpo-rations," he toasted me. "We need them." He slid a copy of *Mummy II* into the video player.

"Pour me another drink, Mo Mo, please." I tried not looking distraught. So much for innocence I thought, following Rachel to the next door neighbors.

"Now of course, tigers are nearly extinct, but there are still leopards around," commented a young man receiving a haircut from a local barber who did house visits for a few extra rupees. His treatment also included a scalp massage. I felt relieved in an atmosphere where I could barely hear the screaming video. A

Bollywood flick was on TV. Sheepishly, after ten minutes of Indian vaudeville I went back to watch *Mummy*.

Traveling in a rickshaw, a three wheeled bicycle with a seat for 2 passengers behind the driver, we squeezed through very crowded streets of cars, buses, people with baby carriages, pedestrians, and of course an occasional cow. We were headed to the Tibetan Children's and Technical Training center far on the opposite side of the bazaar, founded by the Dalai Lama after the invasion of Tibet by the Chinese. I watched a young Tibetan artist in training, painting a Tara thanga. To think I had named my son after the Buddhist goddess of active compassion. I gazed at the artist's brush spreading green paint. Therapist Gwen had told me, "The artists who paint these are Buddhist monks who pray as they paint. Their vibrations are transmitted directly into the cloth through the paint. That is why during meditation you are able to receive these higher frequencies" This young boy was peaceful, but hardly an enlightened monk. Disappointed, I puzzled at the discrepancy, and left for the next building, a Buddhist Temple, with a picture of Buddha and the Dalai Lama inside.

The next morning we had breakfast with Rachel's friend Carol, an expatriate married to a Brit. Ordering a meal from a untouchable house cook felt almost sinful, but Carol put me at ease with stories of her life in India while I ate the delicious English style breakfast. Soon her talking became a flood. "Hindu fanatics rioted when MacDonald's served beef burgers. Fundamentalists torched a father and son because they were members of a Christian community." Christian? The spring equinox was my last spiritual event. "The right wing wants India to return to an all Hindu Nation State,"she chattered on. Nervous, I changed direction.

"Tell me, what do you really think about India's future?" I asked. She was silent, and then sighed deeply. "I don't have much hope for this country. India is now one billion people. The AIDS epidemic will be full blown within a year, and India is in denial. Nothing is being done. And the caste mentality gives people no hope for a better life. The Hindu karma, holds people down. One third of the country is hardly living. They accept their lot in life and don't have much motivation. Cows are treated better than women. The cast system is illegal but the untouchables are obviously darker skinned Indians who work the menial jobs. Lighter skinned women are desired by the Brahmin men." Glancing toward the kitchen, she continued, "I dislike the servant class. In fact, I feel almost like a victim of my employees. They become very dependent, and make themselves extended family regardless of how you feel about it. I couldn't wait to get a washer/dryer, because I prefer machines to people. If I could leave, I would. But my husband likes it here."

"Well, I think the United States has a type of caste system," I mumbled. "It is subtle but very real. The difference being that Christianity encourages people to rise up and achieve money, status and fame, and as a result, many working class people do." End of my mandatory criticize America speech. I wondered again why I had been born an American? How could I ever complain about anything again? How could I possibly want more material things? I was so rich and free compared to the millions here.

The return trip to Delhi from Mussorie was one solid mass of slums with people along the road, tiny one person businesses with hovels behind them on both sides of two lanes, hour after hour, one town becoming the next and the next and the next. The car's air conditioning blew warm air into the back seat where three of us sat semi-conscious. Bolivian traffic in La Paz had paralyzed me but this was beyond ridiculous. The much desired breakfast was on the other side of the road, but since there were no crosswalks, lights, stop signs or policemen, getting across was nothing short of miraculous. Complete and total pandemonium of cars, trucks, cows, bicycles, tractors, elephants, buses and some pedestrians all shared two lanes with no median. If you were lucky and fast enough to leap half way across, it was possible to turn sideways before an animal or vehicle mowed over you. Before I could react, Tsering ran with me through the maze up to the counter and back with a bag of Indian pastries. A man with his arm twisted backward at the elbow hanging from a ligament, approached me as I opened the car door. Startled, I almost handed him the sweets, but thought again and ducked into the car, slamming the door as his face pressed the window. Rachel gave him money. The rest of us looked away.

"Are there no doctors who can fix him?" I pleaded loudly as we pulled away. "No, the only public health here is sterilization, which is free of course. India wins again," he grinned. "Kendall, survival is really the only agenda in India. Think about yourself and your own family. Some make it into the middle class. Look." He pointed in the direction the car was turning. Mo Mo's humor was all that kept me going, a survival tactic he had cultivated living in a society that had no safety net, no public assistance, no social service sector whatsoever.

We drove into an oasis amidst the sweating horror of Hades. It was not an illusion but an elegant restaurant full of well dressed, well fed Indians all driving cars. Who are they? Are they returning from work? On a lunch break? It is two separate realities, parallel universes one block apart. My wavering brain stared at a chubby woman with a chubby baby.

Within yards of the oasis the beggars were back again sprawled on the curbs, banging on the car windows. My sensibilities are appalled by our drive around Delhi. We exchanged money at a fancy hotel, where a picture of President Bill

Clinton hung beside other dignitaries. From this ritzy hotel, $250/night, we are suddenly at a stop light. Barefoot in the middle of a very busy two lane road with her hands out stretched for money, a little girl about six years old approached us. She was inches away from my hand. On the car's other side, a crippled boy on a board with wheels, rolled toward us with an outstretched hand. Neither Mo Mo nor Tsering gave them coins. "If you give them money it keeps them in the beggars trade," they told me. Rachel is silent. I am lost in thought and our taxi moves on. So I am supposed to belief that these children have real options? Education, access to medicine, parents who care, all the ingredients it takes to be successful? Is there an answer? Does anyone know? My stomach turned as I looked at the cows grazing in the divided highway in between this human zoo. A fleshy well fed rump hung out into the traffic, his placid oblivious jaw chewing happily as motorists simply drove around him.

In ten minutes we were in middle class Delhi, next to a green park with benches and flowers. My drenched cotton clothing stuck to my skin. I was afraid of fainting, but welcomed the idea of collapsing into the park grass. Around the corner people were eating ice cream in an air conditioned shop. My patience was gone. Irritable and lonely for home, I kept repeating my mantra … *there must be a reason I came here, there must be a reason I came here.*

"Just take me to Ladakh, Rachel!"

Ladakh: A Globalized Gompa

Security was very tight traveling near the Pakistan border to Ladakh even before the attack on the World Trade Center because of the strategic location of Leh, the capital. After the x ray machine, each of us was frisked by a woman security guard, and then required to re-identify each suitcase as our own before loading. I was irritated at all the fuss, being an American conditioned to efficient, relaxed service, but when offered a snack of juice, tea and a sandwich for a one hour flight, I felt very privileged. Five years later, I now appreciate the need to search passengers for nail clippers and shoe bombs.

Ley, was shockingly dirty, smelly and polluted. *Fare well to Shangri-La.* The book I read only half prepared me for the massive cultural transformation taking place in this part of the world. Spewing black diesel fuel, trucks, cars, and motorbikes flooded the narrow roads. Older men and women dressed in traditional Tibetan costume strolled beside Muslims in turbans and Buddhist monks with shaven heads, red robes, and sandals. Kids in blue jeans, windbreakers and sneakers ran beside a man in robes wearing a modern sunhat and sunglasses. Potholes and gutters filled with rushing grey water made walking difficult. Stray, sickly-looking dogs with no energy to bark roamed the streets as well as a few meandering cows eating garbage, plastic bags and depositing cow pies everywhere. The electric wiring on the streets was bizarre, hanging loosely off poles decorated with Buddhist prayer flags. "Can you imagine how many deaths and accidents are caused here for lack of building codes," I shouted to Rachel and Tsering who were walking much faster than I was, heightening my worst fear—getting lost. Grumbling about altitude sickness and fatigue I called, "Remember the guide book's advice? *Rest* for the first day." I jumped over a ditch in the face of a rumbling motorbike, my lungs straining.

I was delighted to learn that the Jasmine Guest House had indoor plumbing, even though the bathroom sink had a drain pipe resting above a hole in concrete and a shower with a slanted floor, minus a shower curtain. The surrounding gardens bloomed with green, cool-weather crops. "I wonder if Steve has picked the last of my peas and Swiss chard?" I sighed thinking of the spring flowers back home.

The endless stairs to the Japanese peace pagoda donated to Ladakh in 1983 circled to the top where we viewed the basin rimmed with velvet snowy mountains. There, the Buddhist teachings were displayed in striking colored reliefs of gold, blue and orange in the round, the three stages of reality, birth, life and death. Winded, I was just beginning to absorb Buddha sleeping in Nirvana, awakening into life, defeating the devils, and turning the wheel of Dharma to lessen the suffering of all souls when suddenly Rachel wanted to leave, to accomplish another visit. I felt a scream rising and had to squelch an urge to push her off the edge of the peace pagoda. I was still far from Buddhahood, unfortunately.

And by the next evening, on a thin mattress over a board on a rock hard pillow I lay with the runs, fever, chills and cramps, cursing India in all its filth, muttering over and over, "this didn't happen in Peru, this didn't happen in China. My rational mind told me that it was because in both those countries I was protected from the germs by tourist trip agendas. Shitting water for a day, I slept and read when alert enough, and relied on Rachel and Tsering to feed me bananas, yogurt, antibiotics and electrolytes. Like a whirling dervish, Rachel assured me, "Tomorrow we leave for Dha."

June 19th

Too many bags, too many pills, too many items, and the difficulty of organizing it all—hormone cream, lotion, vitamin pills, anti-septic wipes, tooth brush, dental floss, grapefruit seed extract, and most recently the antibiotics, in the correct sequence so I could apply or take it orally. All the items a privileged Westerner can afford. The water was never safe to drink, so we continuously treated our bottles, each being in a different stage of purification or being cleaned with a different pill for better taste. "This is driving me absolutely crazy. No wonder some people just give up and eat or drink whatever they want," I sighed, disgusted with the entire process.

Peeing in India was the second most challenging event, and I learned why Indians shake with their right hands. My thighs were too weak to support my body above the ground over the pit, requiring that I steady myself with both hands in the dirt on either side. I always missed the hole, no matter how large it was or how low I squatted. Inevitably urine soaked the dirt or cement floor around the toilet before I could shift my body. There was never any toilet paper, and I quickly learned that if I didn't carry my own I would be using my left hand like the Indians. "Tsering," I joked, why don't you develop a class called 'the yoga of using toilets' for us mid-life female travelers? You could hold classes in the airport."

"Ok," she swiveled her head, "I put it on my website."

Traveling to Dha

We began our journey out of Leh at 9:30AM in a comfortable jeep with lots of leg room. I still felt weak.

The landscape was a lunar desert, much like the American Southwest, with subtle, subdued shades of red, brown and purple encircled by brilliant white capped mountains. We passed men and women digging drainage ditches with shovels and hauling rocks by hand, building the highest roads in the world. Public health signs in English painted on roadside rocks proclaimed, *We Toil Today for Your Tomorrow, The Harder You Work, the Luckier You Get, Cleanliness is Next To Godliness.* I laughed, then wondered who could actually read them.

Our driver, Norbu, lived outside Ley in a small village where we stopped at a tea stand. We headed Northwest on a very winding road high above the now muddy Indus River, bright blue in the winter season. Apricot trees grew beside poplars, next to fields of wheat and barley, and gardens of turnips, spinach, and cabbage, all irrigated by the Indus. "Without the ice capped mountains this valley watered by only 3 inches of rain per year, would be a desert," I read out loud from the guide book. Small green oasis's dotted the riverbed with Buddhist temples waving prayer flags built right into the sand. Stupas were everywhere.

We visited Alchi, a pleasant village with a Gompa of plain structures outside that opened four feet below to reveal a magnificent drama of Buddha statues, incense smells and frescoes commissioned and painted by 11th century artists.

Offering bowls placed before the Buddhas helped sustain full time monks in their duty as keepers of the tradition and faith. I found worshiping 'idols' perturbing. Are they honoring a greater God or the giant beings themselves with multiple hands peering out among snakes, elephants, monkeys and erotic devas?

All the heavy military vehicles around tourist jeeps like ours testified that this was one of the world's most politically contentious areas, but I was so focused on the landscape I didn't realize their significance. The dry, stark landscape was beautiful, a barren desert like Salt Lake City, my birthplace. My American middle class comfort level and middle age overtook me when I saw our dusty bedroom with a spot of blood on the pillow at Lamayuru. Rachel didn't blink, but I desperately wanted to leave all this underdeveloped mess. "Who cares if this is the oldest known gompa in Ladakh dating to the 10th century. It looks like a prisoner's asylum," I said. Rachel gave me that politically incorrect look. "Besides, I feel too tired to hike up to the gompa."

My body wanted comfort and Western food, but instead we climbed to the Kagyupa order, overlooking a massive mountain. Inside the colorful, soft beauty of the interior, thirty young boys between the ages of 8-12 seated at benches, were chanting, reading from scriptures beneath the watchful master monk. Some faces look healthier than others, their heads bobbing over prayer books, chattering until the master reprimanded them. Incense mixed with musty smells hung over this mysterious, alluring drama. But the longer I watched the ritual of chanting and 'brainwashing' the more convinced I became that it was only repression and denial of childhood. No different than mean nuns and Catholic schools. Outside we saw workers building a "Monastery Hotel" for the festival tourist season. "... but Coca-Cola always follows modernization," Rachel argued vehemently with an Indian journalist from Delhi as she photographed and drew sketches for a travel magazine. "You westerners always bemoan change and the loss of tradition while we Indians can't wait for more to happen," she snapped.

Lamayuru to Dha, via a winding switchback road above canyons plunging into the Indus. "It is the Grand Canyon of Ladakh!" I squealed. We picked up a couple of officers who tossed their luggage on top and sat entangled in the backseat of our jeep. One told us he had been in the army three years, and was recently stationed outside Ley. I remembered the journalist mentioning that in 1999, the Indian army had launched an attack on Pakistan from Dha.

I was yanked out of my burbling about the view. My God, we were now three miles from the fighting along the Pakistan-Kashmir border! Everyone, including Steve had warned me not to go here. Why had they given us permits? My thoughts of war began scarring my view of the landscape.

After the soldiers jumped out, we picked up a little girl and her mother, a road worker from Nepal. She pointed to the very thin, dark-skinned young men shoveling tar, sand and gravel out of a tar pit over a fire built directly on the road. Their mouths were covered with scarves to protect them from the fumes. The gruesome work made me feel weak and dizzy as I watched. We choked inside the jeep, reaching for our bandanas and rolling up windows. I winced at the tanks and canisters of tar and kerosene stored and disposed of in one large open field, blighting the magical scenery. Several miles later we felt lucky that she invited us for tea at her home located at the bottom of some concrete stairs directly off the road. I was blinded until I removed my darkened eyeglasses. Cross legged on the floor sat her husband with a two year old boy on his lap. We drank tea, mostly milk and lots of sugar, sitting on the edge of their bed while a family chicken entered through the door walking up to a tiny dish of grain at beak level, pecking happily. Welcomed in their kitchen, I assumed they gathered her eggs outside. They told us before the winter came in late September their family would return to Nepal.

"Norbu," I asked our driver, "with millions of unemployed Indians, why do they hire Nepalis?"

"No one wants *this* job," he said.

It got hotter as we approached Dha, a tiny village of 20 families living in a rocky-stone filled field with apricot trees, poplars and beautiful fields of barley, waving in the wind.

Snotty, dusty children appeared in front of the guesthouse, a dirtier place than the one last night at Lamayuru. We had a choice between a room with glass windows but no screens, and a windowless room. The heavy wool rugs on the floors appeared to have been last cleaned in 1996 when this family opened their house to guests. Thank God we brought our own sleeping bags. We survived the night without bat invasion, and followed a young boy with a small herd of burrows, goats and scrawny lambs over a rocky path. Two young monks wearing robes and sneakers opened up their gompa. Tsering bowed to the looming Buddha statues. Rachel and I nodded respectfully.

Our young boy-guide described the bombing of this village during the 1999 border war with Pakistan. He pointed to a hole in the ground next to the canyon at our feet. "Four people were killed," he said, "and others had to flee down into the lower villages." Pointing to a huge, rocky circular set of walls, he continued, "The foundation for our new buildings was abandoned by our village at the time of the Pakistan attack. When the people returned, they were afraid to continue."

On a stony courtyard in the village between a cluster of structures sat an old, wrinkled smiling man dressed in traditional flowered clothing and jewelry. I stopped short, stunned by the appearance of a Nike hat on his head. People lived here without phones, indoor plumbing, electricity, but this symbol of multinational capitalism was already here. The contrast made me dizzy.

Tsering waved her hands, "They want us to come in for tea." Water boiled on a kerosene stove. Three beautifully dressed women, of three generations sat in the dark interior, the youngest with her baby. Each woman had a flowered headdress of flowing cloth draped down her back, two thick long braids on either side of her face and necklaces of beads and stones around her neck or in her ears. A man on my left snored loudly, another male nodded from the doorway. Dreading a repeat of the tourist sickness, I politely took a glass, and pretended to sip as we sat around their table.

This was a women's circle of communication beginning with Tsering's translation and progressing to Rachel's sign language, and my enthusiastic nodding. Rachel's hands sculpted a globe in the air. One fist was the United States, the opposite fist was India. I could not tell if they had ever heard of our great country or grasped the great distance we had come to share this tea break. I was touched to be in the presence of three confident, happy women unaware of the modern world, with bright white teeth, clear, smooth skin and eyes, proud to be wearing their native holiday dress, assuming we were honored by their presence. Was it matriarchy that produced their relaxed, stress free appearance? Organic food? A small communal village? Or isolation from the rest of civilization? I poured my tea out the window so as not to insult them, excited at their curiosity, longing to capture their graceful strength on film. We took photographs enthusiastically promising to send them copies, later realizing the impossibility of that. Years later I still look at their faces from half way around the globe smiling back from the photo on my study shelf. Instantly I feel connected to an invisible thread of healthy sisterhood so opposite myself and my modern neurotic blood sisters.

Top of the World at Lake Moriri
Thursday June 21st

We left Dha, returned to Ley and decided to head south to Lake Moiri, by way of a very high mountain pass, Taglang La, at 16,000 feet. After a shower and sound sleep I actually felt refreshed and prepared for another six hour jeep ride. Rachel was now sick, but wouldn't admit that we dined in places we should not have. I felt better somehow that even she, born in India, and a resident for a year in Musoorie, had fallen ill. She was weak but the fact that our equipment was new, that we had two men with us, a driver and a cook, plus food for two days gave me added confidence. After sitting behind the unbearable, belching black diesel from the back of the army trucks we all felt nauseated. Norbu told us that in May, the government was forced to use compressed natural gas after the sky was too dirty for pilots to fly out of the Delhi airport. Norbu honked and honked in response to our choking complaints. Some drivers eventually pulled over to let him pass, others he risked passing, lurching dangerously close to the cliff's edge. Already short on breath, I gasped wondering if we would be better off breathing the toxins. I uncovered my eyes just in time to laugh at another queer road sign, *Divorce Speed if you are Married.* "Norbu, how many single men die on this road?"

Once at Taglang La, we stopped the jeep at a Buddhist Prayer Flag marker. Strings of different colored flags tied down at either end with sticks and rock piles fluttered in the June wind. Rachel had bought four strings of prayer flags in Ley and carried them in her bag just for this moment. Our Hindu cook watched the four of us tie the flags together stringing them up, bright red, white, blue, green and yellow next to the faded ones placed by other travelers. Tsering told us our prayers were for the next year, sailing down from one of the highest points on earth to bless the rest of the world. Tears overwhelmed Rachel. My camera lens clicked rapidly but my beating heart went faster, so full I thought it would burst from this much sacredness.

"*This is why you came to India*" an inner voice murmured. "The gompas are little but stale museums preserving dinosaur lineage."

After a very strenuous, bumpy, almost impassable seven hour jeep ride from Ley we camped in a mysterious, desolate nomadic land near Lake Moriri altitude, 14,000 feet. We arrived exhausted though not as drained as the earlier trip, since the temperatures were lower and the air moister. We passed herds of animals, yak, zso, cows, sheep and Indian goats whose wool is turned into beautiful shawls, herded by a tough nomads who sometimes lay on the side of the road, or stood among their animals. Tiny villages growing wheat and barley cradled in deep green fields with rushing irrigation streams appeared after miles of red and purple landscape. Water was irrigated everywhere in channels from the snow run off, sometimes dammed up into pools.

Without cars, airplanes or machine sounds of any kind, the stillness at Lake Moiri was powerful. Wind, birds and braying donkeys off in the distance blended with the sound of gentle waves lapping the shores of a large body of clear blue water. We carefully read the rules and regulations posted at the mouth of the wildlife preserve which merged with the fields of crops grown by local villagers. Another sign listed all the variety of birds. Almost alone we walked freely in the half marsh, half dry plateau like area with shrubs, flowers, herbs, and patches of barley stretching down to the lake. This is the stillness all of civilization is now seeking in its harried commuter, consumer bustle, I mused. Yet I found it scary. Where was life? The cold brackish, slightly salty lake water had nothing in it. No fish. No plants. Not a single bird diving for food. "No humans bathe or swim here," said a villager to Tsering. "Sometimes the army brings small boats."

Through the binoculars I noticed a large structure near the lake on the edge of the reserve. Later, we learned a lama had purchased land here for a retreat/meditation center. "There seem to be fakes in India catering to Westerners everywhere," I commented cynically to whomever was listening. "Even in this remote stillness. Will he be wearing sunglasses, Nike sneakers and holding a can of Coke? You bet," I answered.

Rachel convinced us to camp down on a grassy spot by the lake, and set up two brand new American nylon tents, one for the three of us and one for the two guys. Norbu passed us a bottle of Kashmiri rum and before I knew it, Rachel woke me up to go bird watching. But even at 5:30am there were very few birds and after a night of bitter cold we were unprepared for, I was stiff, blurry eyed and disappointed in this failed expedition. We walked aimlessly, the binoculars banging uselessly around my neck. I collapsed next to the lake, shivering and wondering what to do next.

"Om Tara Tu Tare … when in doubt," I chanted to Rachel, "I always sing the Tara prayer. I am meditating to a warmer place, to the island of Maui, to the warm, summer of 1987 where I chanted in the crater of Mt Haleakala."

I sat with closed eyes under a wool hat, wind breaker, my fingers in a fist wrapped in mittens waiting for a response from Rachel. "Rachel?" But she had gone, leaving me to face the four directions alone. Could I bear the responsibility of praying for humanity from the Himalayas? I wanted to merge with the stillness but my chilled body was too cold to sit much longer. Standing up, I wandered aimlessly in a walking meditation beneath grey clouds watching geese, then horses, then donkeys plodding down the slopes, passing one lonely women tilling the ground.

I must have looked strange from afar, spinning in circles like a drunk. Moving toward the water I noticed a yak horn lying in the river bed just below the surface of the shallow estuary. Like an eagle, I swooped down pulling the tip out of the sand, thrilled at the treasure. Hugging the yak's horn to my breast I looked up to see Tsering and Rachel staring at me from the campsite across the flat valley, motioning wildly with their hands. Irritated I walked toward them, calling, "Is something wrong?"

"We thought you were lost, Kendall," their voices echoed over the lake to the mountains behind.

Spinning in circles I howled back, "I am, I am! I am lost. Can't you see?"

That afternoon I felt exhausted hiking in such thin air. Rachel looked tired but Tsering, a Tibetan used to high altitudes was prepared to climb higher. I had food and water but as soon as they disappeared over the next range my heart beat quickened, convinced a spying snow leopard from a nearby cave crouched, planning its attack, or that a native man crossing the mountain, a bandit with evil intentions, would rape or murder me. What was I supposed to do now? "Meditate," said my higher self. "You are here at the top of the world alone with the silence. Everyone you know back in the States would envy this moment. All the new age gurus, spiritual seekers, yogis, all the wanna-bes of the new paradigm would die to be right where you are at this moment." I settled into lotus position, my eyes closed. Follow your breathe. Follow your breath I told myself, scanning the back of my mind for the information in *The Isaiah Effect* by Greg Braden, words about how to pray written by the early Essene masters in the Dead Sea Scrolls 2,500 years ago. It was something like, *to bring peace to those we love in this world we must first become that very peace.* For a few seconds I visualized a future healed world, *as if it had already happened.* Each moment grew longer and longer. I was face to face with silence. No airplanes, no cars, no wind, no birds. Total silence. I listened, terrified. All I heard was my own breathing. This must be the void, I thought.

It was summer, but we were completely unprepared for the following night's bitter, cold wind. At 6am I wore three sweaters, Rachel's hat and gloves, and wished I had a down jacket. My fingers smelled of garlic from rubbing the essential oil all over my feet to stimulate blood flow. We had layered a yak wool blanket on top of foam mats, slept in our clothes, including hats and socks, and burrowed deep into our sleeping bags. Living here in the winter was unimaginable. I was a foolish, weak American compared to these hardy people who live here year round. "Don't bring too much," Rachel advised from Boston. "We can always buy clothes there." Unfortunately, Indians don't sell winter clothes.

Before we left I scooped water out of the lake with a film canister. "Hopefully it will bring me the purity and stillness I need back in the States," I explained to Tsering. Around the first bend in the road after Lake Moriri disappeared behind us, we met up with some Buddhist nomads. Nomads! Living ancient history! We descended on them like aliens from another planet, ohhhhhhing and ahhhhhing over their tents and their animals. There stood one man shearing his yak, while another combed out the fine soft wool. Then I noticed their clothing was modern and some of the tents were equipped with solar reflectors, like ones we had witnessed in other gompas and villages in Ladakh. The nomads seemed used to invasions like ours, which explained their strategic location next to the road. A profitable tourist attraction. Their happy, very dirty children were accustomed to posing for photographs.

After trading rupees for white goat's wool, we were invited inside one tent to see their gas stove. They had no toilets, but as Rachel pointed out, who needs plumbing when it's always pack and move on with the animals?

"I can see you live in perfect balance with your surroundings," I gestured to three of the nomads making a scale with my fists. "E-co-logy," I slowly enunciated. No comment. Conversation was futile. I felt a woman tugging at my sleeve. She wanted to sell me a foxtail for another 600 rupees. I smiled, admired, shook my head and hustled back to the safety of the jeep, slamming the door to keep out the cold morning air.

At the top of the world I was weary, but Rachel's mania spurred us onward. Two days later we looked utterly absurd sitting in the airport, in front of a huge pile of bags. Thirteen in all, including sleeping bags, mats, odd shaped packages, and backpacks. But we didn't make it out, not that day. "Three women went shopping in India," I could hear Mo Mo laughing when Tsering called him. "And you had to take everything back to the hotel because the army commandeered your plane out of Ley?" Departure delayed.

Journal

> *This morning it is raining. No plane available. That means more time shopping. That means more packages. It is a spiritual confusion that Rachel doesn't make any easier since she loves to shop for herself and all her friends. They are egging me on. "Oh Kendall, this is good for your mother, oh, good for your son ... good for your daughter ... I squint through the glass at jewelry forgetting that I have already spent at least one hundred dollars in Mussorie on silver. I imagine giving my friends presents for Christmas, birthdays....*

On day three, we left Ladakh with sixteen bags.

America

Back home, a few days later, it was the fourth of July. The sparkly, clean gas station/convenient store looked beautiful and felt cheerful. Almost sacred. I was shocked at how happy I felt walking in to pay for gasoline. I was usually irritated that I had to buy gas at all, that we were still using fossil fuels, selling so much junk food. But today, I hummed. "… and crown thy good with brotherhood from sea to shining sea." Astounded at my new found patriotism, and the clarity of my American identity, I breathed with gratitude and love, grateful to be going home to a Yankee husband with roots as deep as the waters of Lake Winnipesauke, and children who adored me.

However, it appeared that I had more to learn about India and the new world economy.

Out-Sourcing

"Mom, the world is flat again," Teryn explained taking a huge bite out of his salami sandwich.

"Wait a minute, we didn't send you to the North Carolina school of Science and Math to learn that," I pleaded, pouring three scoops of sugar into my coffee.

"Yeah, this author we're reading says the new technology is allowing people and corporations to compete or collaborate across continents. Consumer goods for us can be produced more cheaply in Third-world countries, and services here can be farmed out to lower-paid technicians over there."

My face gave away my opinion.

"The Indians love it. They're getting rich, Mom."

"Teryn, the untouchables aren't getting rich. Do you know that in India a dark skinned man sitting on a fence in a pasture beckoned me over. Just to squeeze a white person's hand was like being touched by a goddess. And how is all this good for people like me?" He paused to check his text message.

"Supply chaining gets you all that nice stuff in you guest cabin for cheaper, Mom. And your banking, telephone and credit card services are all done by someone over in India."

"I know but what about people my age, who lose jobs to out sourcing? What about us?" I asked slightly angry.

His cell phone rang. "Hold up" he waved his hand to me.

"Hey, I don't know," he shrugged. "Go back to school. Learn new skills. I know it's tough Mom, when you can't even learn to use your Ipod."

Later

"May I speak with Kindale Halee," the Indian voice asked for the 50th time.
  "Who is this?"

"I'm calling from American Express about overdue charges on your credit card, Ms Hale."

"Look, I've told you for the last eight months that I do not have an American Express card. Never did, never will. Stop calling me." *Slam. Slam. Slam. And Slam!*

It felt like an entire village of out sourced Indian workers were passing my name around, determined to make me pay $70. Relentless, they called at breakfast, dinner, and on Sundays. Eventually at 11pm.

'This is sexual harassment," Steve told the Indian debt collector one evening from our bed. I leaned over the receiver and spoke in a deeper voice, "It's against the Hindu religion."

"Excuse me, sir?"

We hung up laughing.

New Year's World Fellowship, Conway, New Hampshire, 1986.
Back row, center: Kendall, Moriah and Steve.

Teryn and Kendall,
Vermont, 1989.

Teryn,
Fairview, 1994.

Norris-Hale family, Sharon Spring farm, 1998.

Our house at Sharon Spring, Fairview, NC, 2007.

Bear Wallow Mountains from our window

Building a sweat lodge, Fairview, NC, 1998.

The Portal, Peru, 2000.

Peruvian women with llamas, 2000.

Prayer flags: Rachel, Tsering, Kendall and Norbu, Ladakh, India, 2001.

Solar panels, Ladakh, 2001.

Tribal women, Ladakh, 2001.

Canteens taken on The March on Washington,
Alys and Myron Hale, West Lafayette, Indiana, 2002.

"I Have a Dream"   Vietnam Memorial Wall

Whetstone High School reunion, Columbus, Ohio, 2003.

Kendall, Whetstone High School reunion, Columbus, Ohio, 2003.

Pro Choice rally, Washington, DC, 2004.

Iraq Memorial Wall, Asheville, NC, 2005.

Bring the Troops Home, Washington, DC, 2006.

Top row: Steve Norris, Teryn Norris-Hale,
Front row: Moriah Norris-Hale, Kendall Hale,
Folly Beach, SC, 2006.

My Dad, Myron Hale, Karl Marx's grave, London, England, 1992

Kanji = Crisis
Opportunity in Danger

AGING WITH THE SMOKIES

20th Wedding Anniversary
August 21, 2002

> *Kendall, I can't imagine a richer or more passionate dance in the last 20 years than the one I've done with you. From Mission Hill to Esteli to Sharon Spring; from Moriah and Teryn; from demonstrations and fund raisers and political campaigns to sweat lodges, saunas and a walk in the Smokies; along with all our friends and music and poetry and gazebos and animals—What a dance we do. I love you, Steve.*

Faces look out from tree bark with humanoid features—knobs, lumps, swellings, growths, a little like my own middle-aged body with lines, stretch marks, sagging skin, blemishes, spots. Trees are honored in some places, by some people for the number of lines around their trunks. A measurement of beginning and end. A life of accomplishment with growth spurts, wide spaces, mid life, and old age. These are circles of experience and knowledge expressed in vertical height, approaching the heavens, pushing the boundaries of earth's biosphere.

I watch Steve counting the rings of a huge trunk, a copy of the Tao Te Ching poking out the top of his backpack. "Three hundred and fifty," he grins. I take a photo of him and his knife, marking his own lifetime, first his birth, then his own personal passages, from the center outward to 59 years. I flash on him as a very old man of 90, still smiling, strong in spirit, a little like the tree trunk, with a few more wrinkle-rings. He once told me that aging was about 'learning how to become one with God.'

The Cherokee called it Shaconage, 'land of the blue smoke'. Two hours from our house is an emerald rainforest of spruce, fir, yellow buckeye, white basswood, Eastern hemlock, yellow birch, and tulip tree. This land mass is one billion years old, the Appalachian Revolution geologists call it, when older land masses were pushed on top of younger ones. Backpacking through this queendom, my body breathes the magnificence of trees and the delicacy of flowers. A centipede traveling across my path is awesome; a daddy long legs looks elegant on plant stems; at home both would be smashed in toilet paper. Captured by the sexual splendor of blossoms, I photograph an orange flower named Turk's Cap, the camera an excuse to draw me closer, to focus on her graceful glory. My eyes follow a trunk upward gazing at the branches of a three hundred year old grand, gnarled tree, twisting upward 150 feet to the smoky haze.

Three categories of people use this park. The tourists and many locals who come for day hikes/picnics/fishing and tubing, or in RV/tent campers, none of whom go very far. The horse-people, prefer being carried by animals, miles into or across the park on horse trails. Their experience is deeper, more extended. The backpackers' feet carry them inside this green paradise, and connect directly to the inherent intelligence of nature without TV, computers or cell phones. Loggers removed all they wanted in this place of the blue smoke, yet I witness rejuvenation. Hope surges at me in all directions. Settlers brought cows to pastures left by loggers, followed by trees that replenished as new growth beside the old. White quartz stones appear in small splinters, then in larger clusters. Now the forest floor is carpeted in ferns, mosses, and ground covers that transform every 100 feet or less weaving a new pattern of undergrowth too complex for human eyes.

I am in awe of the equipment I have purchased that gives my 52-year-old frame an opportunity to disappear from my life into this wild place. We are surviving at a very high standard of living. Our tent and sleeping bags are efficient, dry and warm. An ultra light tarp, umbrellas, water purification tablets, plastic bottles, plastic zip lock bags for food, plastic garbage bags, a propane stove, a new pack, a snake bite kit, light weight rain jackets. Wonderful, organic food. Excellent hiking boots. Not to mention the medication that keeps my knee pain under control plowing through the underbrush. When the 22-pound backpack feels like torture, and my lungs labor, the rhododendrons throw petals at our feet, pink and white blossoms blinking a reminder that the shelter or campsite is really just moments ahead.

I'm in a trance, vibrating in earth energy. Nature's sexuality is entrancing. The flowers seem so feminine, the petals so vaginal. Yesterday's hike seemed womb-like, tunneling into earth's core where the water falls, collects and runs to rivers and oceans. Today we pass an incredible phallic mushroom. What a plant signature! Could this fungus be good for men? It is a perfect replica of an erect penis. I break it off, determined to take it home to our garden, for Steve. I place it in a plastic bag, but by morning it is soggy and much less virile.

Which brings me to the subject of the man made vibrator. The sinful present arrived with orchids, much to my embarrassment, the week before our anniversary.

Steve and I had been paying for sex therapy without health coverage. Out of pocket: one hundred and twenty dollars a session. My problem was that sex just didn't zing me anymore, and I knew that even a single-payer health care system was not going to fix me. Maybe if mid-life women knew that the Canadians, Cubans, and the Europeans had a magic sex formula in their universal health care systems that included free Viagra, vibrators, or a one night stand as part of sex therapy, the movement might get somewhere. A young bucking bronco with a flat stomach, thick hair, big muscles and a big you know what, might pump up my hormones for one night, and I'd feel jazzed, really jazzed. But still, when the music ended, I would be a woman with elephant skin married to a *very* middle aged man that I loved.

"You need a younger lover," Steve complained when I asked for harder and faster.

"Get some of that Viagra everyone's talking about. As much as I hate to admit, those natural Chinese herbs only get you half way up, darlin'."

"I need to feel wanted by you, desired. It's not very romantic when you stand in my study door fully clothed with a book in hand asking, 'Are we having a date tonight Steve?' I need a little more help now."

Exasperated, I asked, "But how?" Temptress 101, uhhhmm, I thought, must have cut that class. Shaking my head, I turned from the light of the study doorway to the dark hallway, groping toward the bedroom into the memory of rape—claws of the exorcist. Scarred by the devil, the scratches were still alive.

So went the conversation of two people married 25 years, still trying hard not to be members of the American Association of Retired Persons, (AARP) but enjoying the phrase, 'two seniors, please', at the movies.

"Have you ever tried a sex toy?" Inquired the therapist.

"Never." We both answered. She took out The Good Vibrations Catalog.

"I've never even seen a vibrator," I confessed. "It isn't natural. In fact, I'd be surprised if anyone I know had ever used one."

"Most people don't have leave them out on the coffee table," she smiled with that secret therapist look. "You can have this. Practice, have fun together." Reluctantly I put the naughty booklet in my purse, after a few quick peeks at the pink hip 'n' hop vibe, the purple powerhouse bullet, and the waterproof turbo glider, and hid it safely in the bottom dresser drawer so that no one, especially me, could ever see it. I was still a good Puritan.

"Who in the world would send me this?" I glared at Steve, pulling out a plastic, blue penis with ripples glittering from top to bottom.

"Happy birthday," he grinned.

"Oh my God! Steve, please don't tell anyone. *Please!* I'll never forgive you if you do!"

"It's been weeks since our last couples therapy, Kendall, so I ordered it on line." He laughed louder than usual, and believe me, when Steve laughs everyone in a theater can hear him. "There's more, keep unwrapping." He was having a great time.

"Eee Gads, as Mom used to say." It was a second model, a white plastic prick with little whirly gigs growing out the side, like a science fiction rocket ready for take off.

"Did NASA find this on Mars? Do I have to use it?"

"No, they grow in the Great Smokey National Forest. I'll show you when we get there. Yes, use it. It comes with an instruction book. Then teach me."

Back in the wilderness, six days without a mirror to remind me how imperfect I am—how very middle aged. I can't check to see if another brown hair has turned, or if the depression on the end of my nose has grown over, or if I really do look 52. Six days to stop checking how flat my stomach is. To stop measuring myself against cultural norms. Without gel or spray, my hair is pulled into a knot on top of my head. My lips are their own color. I'm wearing a magnetic brace around my right knee, and a pair of lightweight hiking shorts with zippers at the edges to add legs to when the weather or terrain changes. I feel great.

In the midst of all these trees, Fraser fir, spruce fir, red spruce, American beech, and red maple, a tough heart shaped vine climbs with such determination she pulls at my heartstrings wrapping, tugging me deeper into the motherland, the bosom of creation. My guidebook says this vine may grow 100 feet into forest trees to a diameter of 4 inches. Here she is again. Tara, the Green Goddess, so everlasting, so compassionate.

We are hiking along the North Carolina/Tennessee border on the Appalachian Trail and unexpectedly a jet fighter wreckage appears to my left. Checking the guide book we learn that in 1984 a fighter plane crashed into this smoky illusion. It is eerie to imagine the pilot in the haze, the sudden explosion, and watch Steve tear off a piece of the metal remains.

Last week a radio reporter told us the ozone levels in the Smokies were the highest since 1995. Shaconage is now covered in blue chemical mist weaving veils that shroud then expose, then shroud our view from a fire tower replaced by a more precise satellite. I turn one fourth of a circle, facing each direction, around and around, watching each view transform under the shifting blanket. A lesson in appearance. Nothing here is definite. We sit under a tree near a shelter to meditate with gratitude on our twenty years of marriage. Prayers we hope will resonate with truth inside this land of the blue smoke.

Steve begins to recite his favorite lines from *Lao Tzu:*

> *Yield and overcome; Bend and be straight;*
> *Empty and be full; Wear out and be new;*
> *Have little and gain; Have much and be confused.*
> *Therefore the wise embrace the one*
> *And set an example to all.*
> *Not putting on a display, They shine forth.*
> *Not justifying themselves, They are distinguished.*
> *Not boasting, They receive recognition.*
> *Not bragging, They never falter.*
> *They do not quarrel,*
> *So no one quarrels with them.*
> *Therefore the ancients say, "Yield and overcome."*
> *Be really whole,*
> *And all things will come to you.*

I ask that all the apus (mountain spirits) I have visited be connected in marriage if they wish to be. The apus of the Andes, the Himalayas, the Rockies, the White Mountains, the Sierras, and Esteli, Nicaragua. We breathe together, "Shaconage, oh Shaconage, the earth, the air, the fire, the water, Return, return, return, return".

MORNING AFTER THE
ATTACK ON BAGHDAD

March 20, 2003

The cashier at Ingle's is wearing an American flag tie. The red stripes and glittery stars make me squint.

"You ignorant fool," I thought turning my head toward the grey rain outside the front store windows. I had just delivered a CD my son left in his computer to the office at his high school. At 7:30am Teryn pleaded as I dropped him at school, "Mom, can you bring it to me? It's really important! I really need it."

Fumbling with new buttons I found a CD war game inside. "What! This can't be it," I cried out loud. "He's using this as part of his report?" Recalling the rumbling bomb blast sounds emanating from his room that morning, I cringed, imagining him demonstrating to his classmates how to launch a nuclear weapon. The cashier asked me if I needed help with my groceries. 'No, I'm fine," I smiled weakly, avoiding his tie.

"Are you sure?" His bright grin was begging to get out of the store. "OK," I said resentfully, as he wheeled my bags to the car.

Moriah must be on her way to Puerto Rico with her new tattooed boyfriend. As the missiles aimed at Saddam killed innocent children, she was on a college spring break. At twenty one, I was a revolutionary running beside my draft dodger friends smashing windows on State Street in Madison, Wisconsin.

"Yes, there are armed soldiers on the subways. I will probably be safer in Puerto Rico than here. Mom, we have to go on with our lives," she advised me on her cell phone from the upper West Side. Yes, we go one with our lives, as they lose their lives, I thought, knowing the media will not be permitted to send back photographs of naked, maimed children as they did from Vietnam. The pictures that catalyzed millions of us into action.

Today, my guinea hens were running wildly across the spring grass, honking like geese, always on the look out, expecting an emergency. Their frantic calls matched my feelings this morning driving to yoga class in the March rain. Spring was always the happiest time of year for me with a brimming pond, pink magnolias, singing frogs back from their muddy winter dormancy, scattered yellow daffodils across the pasture, old plastic bottles washed up from our dog's secret holes.

This morning was ominous. Steve pounded his fists into a pillow last night in the blue room down the hall, my cat woke me up four times. I dreamed of our family terrorized by the attack. We were together. I comforted Teryn, as a younger boy, telling him the bombs wouldn't reach us here. In the dream, Moriah was comforting Steve who was clutching his head in despair.

No blood for oil. No blood for oil.

Something Bad is Happening

Hiking in the forest behind Hickory Nut Gap farm, I panted heavily, walking on tip toes up the steep trail leading to the overhang where all of Fairview filled your vision wider than an omni theatre screen. "Ahhhhhh." I sucked in the humid, green jungle—terra firma, terra firma. We had named Teryn after Tara, the Buddhist goddess of active compassion. Teryn did not feel honored. He was an airy Gemini, a mathematician from a Norris lineage embarrassed by the crazy story of the golden rainbow on Maui.

Walking alone here was safe, far from terrorist threats and the latest corporate scandal. A bird rustled. A nut fell. My feet crunched in the stillness. Trying to focus on myself, my path, my journey, even my career, was hard. I could feel my daughter all the way from New York. Sky scrappers jumped from tree trunks, bridges spanned the tops of ferns. I saw her beautiful face rippling across a clump of white flowers. Tears sprang instantly to my eyes, blurring the memory of a Mother's Day card she had sent in May: a collage with two feet anchored on large stones: *Mom, you are the foundation of my vision.* Moisture dripped down my chest reminding me that yoga really wasn't a complete exercise program. Moriah. A tear ran off my chin. What was she going to do? How will she stay safe? I felt terror remembering 911 and her vivid description of the smoking twin towers she viewed from her Harlem fire escape.

In the summer of 1999, my spirits soared when I gathered with Moriah, her friends and thousands more to hear a concert with Bob Dylan and Paul Simon. We boomers reveled in nostalgia, and the young prayed for a muddy rainstorm to re-create the visions birthed at Woodstock Nation. Moriah already knew Dylan's lyrics better than I. Later we followed her Fairview-New York tribe to the bi-yearly Black Mountain Lake Eden Arts Festival, stomped with contra dancers, listened to winner poetry slammers, admired beautiful craft creations. Ecstatic when Richie Havens called it "the son of Woodstock", we danced to ethnic rhythms in a cross generational jubilee.

But later that week our shared music squealed a furious discordant sound of annihilation, slapping hard upon our eardrums.

"I feel that something bad is happening," sobbed Moriah. A poet and writer, she was now visiting home. Steve had gone west to set another house, leaving his side of the bed empty. We talked; she shook in the dark night.

"It could also be a flashback about our move to Asheville," I whispered stroking her back. "Memories from the first year in Asheville, the suicide, Skittles' death, moving from Boston to the "dead trees" (Moriah's childhood name for the Blue Ridge Mountains.) I rubbed lavender oil on her back as she choked beside the toilet. Massage skills always come alive for disaster and exhaustion. I could feel the tenderness on the bottom of her feet, the ovary points. I was thankful I no longer menstruated. I don't miss the bloated feeling, the aches, the short fuse, the snapping words of emotional rock and roll. The extreme sensitivity. My crystal wand shone a green light over the spinal reflex, the color of balance. "It feels good," she said.

That night we needed Rescue Remedy, but I had given my last bottle to Teryn last summer in case math camp got too stressful, his roommate too unbearable, or if he missed my cooking just a tiny bit. So at midnight I found the cherry plum for feeling crazy, the mimulus and aspen for fear, the sweet chestnut for 'the ground is shaking beneath your feet'. Moriah took the drops under her tongue, from the glass of water with a mixture of all the essences—their healing frequencies captured in a glass bowl under the sun.

Her body relaxed, the sobs were softening. My love with the help of these flowers, has soothed and quieted the catastrophe of sadness and fear. My generation converted all our fear into anger at our government. Simple. Today, the information age talks at our children twenty four hours a day: terrorists, war, global warming, peak oil. One long emergency.

The Patriot

I was preparing to give our annual free concert with the Blue Ridge Orchestra on the 4th of July. Last year my mother replied with compassion to my complaint about being a once-upon-a-time revolutionary, now the star of America's most patriotic holiday.

"Well, it happens to everyone."

"At least the program has only two patriotic songs," I added noting the difference between 1972 and 2002. The phone went dead for the third time.

Mom's voice again. "Old age is such a waste of time. I can't hear, I can't walk, I can't write. I can't even use the phone without cutting you off. Whatever happened to the Golden Years? I wish I would die."

I laughed at this game of dial tone. No mother, called her back, busy. Waited a minute. She answered, cut me off. She realized I would not call back.

"Hello, Kendall, are you there?"

"See, you can still use the phone," I joked.

"I would call Moriah, but I have absolutely nothing to say," Mom said in her crackly voice.

Finally, maybe she would just listen. It's too late. She couldn't hear.

"Just tell her you love her", I spoke loudly.

"What?" she said slightly louder.

"Tell her you …" The phone was dead. Within two years Mom would be too.

COLUMBUS REUNION

August 28, 2003

Six of us arrived in Columbus, Ohio on the fortieth anniversary of the March on Washington to celebrate our high school reunion. I hadn't attended any reunions or communicated with these women, my best teenage friends, since graduation thirty five years ago. After three days of sharing memories, I discovered that my adolescence was not as dark as I remembered. My friends had noticed my budding talents—my sense of justice, my passion for peace.

"Honestly, I always wanted to be like you," Clair smiled, "because you seemed so calm, like you had it all together."

"Yeah," added Libby, "You looked self confident and self assured."

"That's because I didn't tell you how love sick I was, or how low my SAT scores were." I grimaced. "They kept me out of the honor society, you know."

"Me, too," nodded Linda. "It wasn't honorable to protest the Vietnam war."

The clean, new all white campus of our memories now had a few boarded up windows, cracked, leaky ceilings and African American football players in the halls. Soon we found ourselves in the history wing between two large photos dedicated by the class of 2001. One photo of Martin Luther King at the march on Washington the other of a weeping man, his face contorted in grief as he leaned into the wall of the Vietnam War Memorial. "Some of our classmates' names are on that wall," someone said. My chest tightened in a sad numbness as I pondered the two major social events that planted the seeds of my political awakening.

Across from the school office a glass bookcase held a tribute from the Whetstone Braves to American Indians: a tribute of amethysts, crystals, a mandala, and a prayer stick overrode my discomfort with the old name. Ten feet above the football trophies were photographs of the school's top scholars, most of them girls.

A shriek welled from my core. My fingers squeezed the silver charm bracelet I had put on that morning to celebrate my return to Whetstone. A gift from my mother in 1967 these charms had dangled from my teenage wrist in these halls thirty-five years ago: a violin, a horse shoe, a Mormon Tabernacle with a choir inside, a Whetstone pendant, a lighthouse from the North Carolina outer banks, and a primitive Easter Island statue. The impact of the changes I could feel and see unexpectedly gave me a sense that some of the things I'd done had mattered, that all the years of activism had manifested right here, in this building—students with different color skins, girls at the head of the class, respect for Native Americans, all of it headed by a woman principal.

Peering through the window of the locked door of the orchestra practice room, I held the violin charm tight in my palm. My violin. She had been a best friend—a life saver, her beautiful, red chestnut body vibrated passionately through my jaw bone into the teenage existential void of my heart. Off and on for almost fifty years she sang under my fingertips—classical, eclectic folk, then sweet long silences re-awakened when I joined the Blue Ridge Orchestra in Asheville. Could it be that Mr. Suzie at 65 or 70 was still waving his arms over the same music, bellowing at the trumpets, hurling his baton over the violists' heads, determined to win first place again at state competition?

Outside on the school's front lawn, red, white and blue ribbons hung from tree branches. A large sign, *Welcome Back, Mr. Jarvis, Our Hero*, gave tribute to one of the first veterans to return from Iraq. Damn! Some things never change. Like war. I bit my lip trying to stay calm, then shook my head and bracelet in disapproval at this patriotic display. Jingle! Jingle! "Let's cover it up," I said to the group. Gleefully we grabbed magic markers and scotch tape out of the car, created a new sign, *Welcome Back '68 Sisterhood, Our Heroes,* and posed for group pictures. I stood wearing my green Girl Scout beret, my sash of Girl Scout badges draped behind me on the sign and my precious tattered jean jacket covered with political buttons from 1966-1985: DARE TO STRUGGLE, DARE TO WIN, BOYCOTT GRAPES, WOMEN AGAINST SEXUAL HARASSMENT, PEACE AND JUSTICE IN SOUTH AFRICA. Crazy with laughter at my costume, the sisterhood helped me reclaim our school in the name of feminism, peace and justice. "Hooray," I screamed. "Columbus is no longer a wasteland of reactionary forces!" Giddy I collapsed into the grass and rolled over and over, as if to better spread the history of our movement across the Whetstone property. Light sparkled on the charm bracelet as I waved it over my head, the Mormon Tabernacle Choir careening and swaying over me.

KARMIC EDGE IN THE CHOCOLATE RIVER

2005

I poured my mother's ashes into the Wabash River. Balancing on Steve's arm, I slid my feet inch by inch along a log sticking over the water. Steve gently tossed in a red rose from her garden. Downstream, two fisherman tipped their caps. The plastic bag that held her for over a year in my parents' house was finally empty. I had imagined her ashes being swept up dramatically on a wave so she could join the Mississippi into the ocean but most sank to the muddy bottom. A few sprinkles swirled into an eddy. Nervously I watched the ashes and the rose bobbing in the direction of the fishermen who quickly reeled in their lines.

Devastated I stepped back to shore.

"Dad was supposed to be here. Liz was supposed to be here. Jenifer was supposed to be here. What an ending! God!" The tips of my shoes were as wet as my eyes.

Steve cried. Wiping his eyes, he said, "You gave her an incredible memorial service. Everyone thought so. As she wanted, we returned her to the river."

It was six months after Mother's journey downstream when I found the braids, my braids, in a plastic bag at the bottom of a wooden chest under baby clothes and prom dresses next to my mother's bed in my parent's house.

My waist length hair admired so by my mother had hung like a chocolate river over my back until Dad's barber cut it all off when I was four. Before then, my mother braided my hair every morning with purple and pink ribbons, combing out the six strands every night back into the river down my back. Kneeling by the chest, I rubbed my thumb and index finger over the thick, silky auburn hair, and hardened bits of rubber band fell off. The braids frightened me because I could feel Mom's fingers weaving the strands once attached to my head. And because they were beautiful and seemed alive, like two kittens curled in sleep. I feared the touch of my healing hands might awaken them from fifty four years of deep, dark solitude.

The Mother Line
July, 2005

Luminous eyes behind thin, framed glasses low on his nose, the astrologer warned me that my trip to Salt Lake City might be mercurial. He held the computer mouse with one hand and stroked a black dachshund under the chair.

Staring over his shoulder at the chart on the computer screen, I listened to him describe why I was fated to be a seeker/warrior.

"We have free will, but not really," he smiled. "A certain percentage of people have active karmic/genetic ties to a group of ancestors. You are among them."

I bit my lip, admitting with ambivalence that both parents were descendents of Mormon pioneers who crossed the great plains.

"Your ancestors had deep faith. You are here to seek beyond their beliefs but guided by their faith. Sitting on top of a lineage of people, you are on a karmic edge. The truths you discover will bring all of those souls forward with you."

He had given me an answer to the question: why do I need so badly to believe in a revolutionary purpose or in a spiritual ordering of the universe?

An awesome task. Had I even come close?

I knew that Cheri, my uncle's eldest of ten children, was key to the motherline. Dad would soon be gone. Jenifer, my middle sister, lived in an institution for the mentally ill, and Elizabeth, the youngest victim of family madness, did not speak to me. My family of origin would soon be obliterated, and that thought paralyzed me.

Cheri embodied the perfect female Mormon success story. She was married forty years to a wealthy executive, mother of nine children, a housewife and scout leader. And now the old Marxist yoga instructor needed her. So Moriah and I went to Utah.

Below a gigantic orange moon sinking between the mountains, fires were burning on both sides of the highway as we approached St George, Utah. Lightning struck deep into the red desert sand, as if to welcome us to Zion—or to announce the apocalypse. My cousin drove fearlessly past all seven hills of flames and smoking sagebrush straight to her second house, to the safety of our desert roots.

While Cheri busied herself in the kitchen, I was drawn to a wall of photos. Are you the Swedish parents our great grandmother ran away from? I wondered at a stern looking man in his Sunday suit with his hand on the shoulder of his serious looking wife. Another pioneer woman in a lacy, white high necked blouse sadly held a stillborn baby dressed in a hand made gown. I felt renewed pride. My Mormon ancestors had survived the treacherous crossing of the Atlantic Ocean and an unimaginable trek across the Midwestern plains for spiritual reasons.

"It was the truth," Cheri called to me. "They heard the Mormon missionaries and no distance was too far to go, not even across the ocean."

"The Salt Lake valley must have been a terrible shock when you were expecting to find a Kingdom on Earth. Poor, worn out pioneers," I whispered to them, gazing intimately, so close my nose brushed the glass surface. "Tarred and feathered by angry mobs who burned down your temples, shot your animals, cursed your land. Well, you rest in luxury now," I assured them, turning around to admire the interior southwestern adobe décor, sandstone tiles, and a blown glass vase full of white cloth flowers opposite a piano.

Flopping into the plush couch, Moriah turned on the TV news: "Terrorist attack in London kills...." Cheri had gone to bed. "Don't tell her," I whispered to Moriah. "I'm here to mend family ties not discuss truth or the world crisis."

"You don't have to hide in the car," Cheri called to me from the door the next morning. I slouched deeper into my seat fearing that my tanned bare shoulders and upper chest might startle the Mormon women tending the gas station in Colorado City. Cheri had accidentally driven toward the infamous polygamist community on our way to Zion National Park. Intrigued, we all wanted to investigate.

I paid for a chocolate bar, blinking at the women's pale necks and blemished faces poking out of high neck lines. Long skirts and long sleeves completed the cover up. In the parking lot a husky farmer and two little boys also clothed from head to toe, took a quick look as our SUV rolled slowly down the hot asphalt.

"Those poor kids. It's 104 degrees. And look at their houses, Mom? Isn't it totally weird? Moriah shook her head as we slowly steered past large unfinished structures with lopsided roofs, half built porches, semi painted exteriors, missing gutters. All purposely left undone to avoid paying taxes to the state of Utah. Moriah quickly added, "And remember that teenage girl who escaped by hitchhiking out one night. She said they would force her to marry an old man, and be one of several wives."

Several years later Warren Jeffs, the president and prophet of this community, the Fundamentalist Church of Jesus Christ of Latter Day Saints, was convicted as an accomplice in the rape of a fourteen year old girl. Jeffs forced her to marry her nineteen year old cousin who pulled her from under her mother's bed where she lay hiding for three weeks and ordered her to, 'be a wife and do your duty.' Jeffs and his followers believed the Mormon Church had committed mortal sin when they made polygamy illegal in 1890 for Utah's statehood.

"Can you imagine all the girls and women who had to submit to the whims of a bunch of white men who created a religion around incest and sex with minors?" Moriah asked me two summers later while she was in graduate school. Just the thought made us wish Mormon founder Joseph Smith had never dug up those gold tablets from the dirt, the ones responsible for his strange vision.

Cheri had left me a copy of the Book of Mormon on the kitchen counter the evening before we left. "You seem to be on a spiritual gathering. I don't want you to dismiss it," she pointed to the dark blue paperback. She condemned the practices of this strange polygamist sect, but seemed unconcerned that many people viewed her the same way, a mother of nine who had never tasted wine, Coca-cola or coffee. In neither of her beautiful picture perfect houses could I find a tea pot, so each morning Moriah and I heated water in a saucepan.

"Polygamy was necessary when so many pioneer men died," she continued. But, I protested silently, Brigham Young had a beehive of more than thirty wives.

"You know," I said cautiously, "My father's brother was ex-communicated from the Mormon Church for being a polygamist." Pause. "He had an affair."

"We believe in personal revelation," Cheri reminded me as we walked barefoot between Zion National Park's looming sandstone cliffs stretching closer to heaven than all the cathedrals in Europe.

"Good, because I think I had one," I said. "Liz and I are estranged you know. It made Mom's last five years even worse. She wanted to be part of a healing between us and I'm convinced she helped co-create it through the dream dimension. A few months after she died, Mom visited me wearing her old blue bathrobe but looking forty years younger with a full head of dark hair. In the dream I was speaking with Liz on the phone. Then I noticed Mom emerging from the back of the room. 'Elizabeth, look who's here! It's Mom.' She never made eye contact but clearly wanted me to see her. As she turned to go, I ran to her, "Don't go yet, you must say hi to Liz."

Cheri looked peaceful when I said, "I woke up feeling healed."

We followed some hikers into the river from the scorching hot trail. The cold water felt as sharp as the dream.

"My good dream. Sister Jenifer was the nightmare, Cheri. The last episode went something like this."

Winter, 2002

She was screaming. "Kendall, Kendall! Help me. Kendall, Kendall. Save me!" My sister Jenifer stood on the barred second story balcony of the Indiana state mental institution. Her arms stretched out from her obese body, reaching through the iron bars. Horrified, I looked at my husband's face, begging to drive the '88 Volvo back to Asheville as fast as possible. Images of people shuffling in slippers, talking to walls, banging, crying, cursing or numb from drugs flared in my brain.

"Steve, I can't move. I cannot go in there." I said. He held my arm, walking us toward the entrance. Jenifer's experimental drug cramped her stomach forcing her to collapse forward in pain every few seconds as we talked in the group living room.

Her front tooth was chipped. She told us, "My roommate attacked me when the staff was gone. Pushed me onto the floor. But I don't smoke now. I'm wearing the patch."

The two Jenifers haunted me: a gorgeous, blonde teenager in a bare sleeved, flowered dress, tanning in the back yard—and a 200 pound, drugged woman behind bars with make up layered over the torture lines of her face.

"She has the Miles curse," Cheri explained. "Mental illness drove Aunt Patty to suicide and totally disabled Jenifer. My sisters had manic-depressive episodes, and my brother rarely leaves his apartment in downtown Salt Lake."

"Cheri, hers was a crazy gene that nearly drove us all insane," I said. "Hundreds of phone calls. For years. Sometimes about imaginary men following her around in cars. Or a thief stealing her bag of drugs. Or that the house was burning down. It ended with a terrifying phone call from Jenifer to me after midnight: Call the police, Dad's been shot in the head!"

"Mom and Dad finally committed her."

August, 2005

"Dad, we had a reunion at the Miles headstone in the Smithfield Cemetery. We posed with our arms linked as if forty years ago was last week. Blood runs deep, I guess." My tears splashed into the phone. "Yeah, we visited the Miles hardware store, the one Mom always talked about, and saw her paternal Grandmother Annie Smith Miles' house. She was one of the original Mormon pioneers and lived through the last Indian war in Utah. Dad, did you know she died in 1950, the year I was born?"

"Your mother was very proud of her family story," he answered, his eight-three year old voice almost inaudible as he spoke from the Medicare unit in Indiana.

I could picture his hospital bed, his fragile head against the stacked pillows, the bedpan on his wheeled tray.

"I was in tears listening to the Mormon Tabernacle Choir sing pioneer folk songs. I kept seeing four year old Annie Smith Miles walking across the plains with her parents and baby sister on the wagon train. And your great grandfather, Aroet Hale. Eighteen years old and walking a thousand miles from Nebraska to Salt Lake City in 1847, with his two younger brothers and sister in tow, all of them orphaned by malaria."

"Parts of the Mormon story are very moving," he agreed. "I'm happy you went sweetheart … I'll call you tomorrow."

"Dad…. Dad? Dad," I continued, "Mom's death allowed me to finally discover, I mean really discover who these people were. When they were twenty years old they went on a long march for freedom. You know, my whole life feels like a long march, for the same ideals and more."

Did I hear a raspy breath?

"Dad, guess what? Salt Lake City has a really far-out mayor, named Rocky Anderson. A lapsed Mormon, of course. He has mandated that all the city buildings use compact fluorescent light bulbs, replaced all SUV's in the city fleet with hybrid cars, doubled the city's recycling capacity in one year, started a program to recapture and use methane produced at the city's water treatment plant and landfill for electricity generation."

Pause. He had disconnected.

Sigh. "He marches against the war in Iraq and attends Gay Pride marches too," I added, grimly holding the receiver up to the ceiling.

"I love you Dad."

Everything Changes, Nothing Changes
Sept 24, 2005

The signs above our heads declared, "Make Levees, Not War," "Iraq is Arabic for Vietnam," and "I never thought I'd miss Nixon." I could see the Washington Memorial in the distance, now part of the Republican firewall.

I was shocked and grateful when cousin Cheri sent me a large donation for the Iraq Memorial Wall we were fundraising for in Asheville, reminding me that just because President George Bush had learned nothing from Vietnam didn't mean my conservative relatives in Salt Lake City had not. Steve dug footers for the wall with his track hoe, and supervised young college age volunteers on site. One hundred and two engraved stones with names, ages and hometowns were cemented into the Peace Park wall including Casey Sheehan's name, son of

Cindy Sheehan, the woman who declared that "emperor Bush had no clothes." Nearly two thousand American soldiers and hundreds of thousands of Iraqis were dead from the mindless fantasies of our inept politicians. Thirty six years after celebrating the end of the Vietnam War and several hundred miles from Asheville, we were marching again.

"I really don't miss the tear gas," Steve smiled.

"Yeah, I can't even jog, never mind run," I realized, reaching for my cosmic-ring cell phone. "Hi, Teryn," where are you?" It was his first demonstration. "Have you passed Billionaires For Bush? Did you see the Condoleezza Rice impersonator? I thought I'd die laughing."

For the first time in our lives we flew into Washington for a demonstration rather than travel by bus, another indication of our age.

"This is what democracy looks like," we screamed at the White House with 300,000 other protestors, September 24, 20005.

And this was what we looked like: Steve had almost no hair and few teeth. I had osteoporosis, and too many memory lapses. We had changed but the Amerikan Empire was still young, powerful and stupid. My twenty-five year old self wanted to strip off my clothes and stand naked with the born again voluptuous hippies waving from the sidewalk. Or join the young men sitting on the shoulders of the granite general draped in peace paraphernalia. A Che Guevara banner surrounded by a contingent of drum beating Latino kids made me long for the revolution that was sure to come. *How couldn't it?*

"I guess I belong over there with the Raging Grannies, huh Steve?"

"No, not till you have a grandchild." He looked wistfully at the muscled dad jogging past pushing his two year old in a baby carriage covered with Out of Iraq, anti-Bush buttons.

West Lafayette, Indiana

As Dad slipped away, the past got bigger and brighter.

I remembered how much I treasured being alone with my him at breakfast. It was all I got after years of yearning for a daughter/father weekend, or something, anything other than a car trip to and from a college campus, an airport or my grandmother's funeral. He turned me down for the last time when I suggested a raft trip in the Grand Canyon. "I can't swim, remember?" He told me a joke instead.

But he made wonderful omelets with coffee and toast. After fifteen minutes of yoga—down dog, tree pose and warrior postures I heard the floor boards creak and scampered upstairs.

Back from ten weeks in Nicaragua in 1986, I was home safe again at the kitchen table. Dad was at the stove. "Why do you take so many risks, Kendall?" he asked quietly stirring the eggs.

"I have radical passions," I blurted back hotly. Inhaling, I hesitated. "You know why, Dad." Half joking I answered, "Because Mao said, *To know the taste of a pear you must first change the pear by eating* it."

He looked thoughtfully at the fry pan. "You mean," he laughed cracking another eggshell, "You can't make an omelet without breaking some eggs."

March, 2006

Dad was dead, and I was a Democratic precinct chair in Fairview. The sixties me was disgusted that I was organizing a forum for the sheriff's race. How in the hell did I end up like this? I was supposed to be a member of the American Central Committee by now. But Dad was dead, I was saluting Mom's flag at the precinct meetings, and the Democratic candidate running for Congress in our district was really a Republican.

The grieving me so wants to be my Dad's little girl—too cute face, framed in braids and pink ribbons, his beautiful ballerina balanced on his knee. All I want is to hold his hand again, to look three feet up at his protective, strong face and blue eyes. To know that as long as he is teaching about democracy the world will be OK. But he is somewhere else and I am left with his tattered flight jacket and his doctoral dissertation placed carefully inside his 1950's leather briefcase. Wondering.

How many more pears do I have to eat, Dad? *Really?*

Return to Berkeley

Thirty-five years later, from Teryn's summer sublet a block from Telegraph Ave, I re-entered Berkeley, California as an empty nester. Today he was working at his climate change job and I was the house guest/tourist. Yesterday I had floated through the now upscale Haight Ashbury where young professionals live, walked through drizzly Golden Gate Park, hung off the city hills on trolley cars with people from Michigan, Illinois and hundreds of other places. But today I was going to find it, the little green square on the map, labeled for real, People's Park. Holding the map I turned the corner past a groovy, paisley looking coffee shop that might have been open in the 70's, and ran right into a huge demonstration. The kind you least expect. One right out of history.

Could it be? It was. A mural depicting both the free speech movement and the early cry for people's power, over twenty feet long and ten feet high. Here at last, a public tribute. A memorial to us?! It felt more exciting than the Lincoln Memorial. A quiet quivering like the start of an earthquake flushed to my skin's surface. For several minutes I stepped closer then further from this wall of raw emotion, remembering twenty two year old Mario Salvio, the avatar of free speech.

"It happened a long time ago," he said from behind, "Before I was born."

"When were you born?" I turned to look at the voice's face. Well under thirty. Spiky hair, black framed glasses, a yoga tee shirt. How could I explain to this youngster, a self appointed tour guide, why a mural of the free speech movement at the University of California made me pace back and forth, eyes watering over every detail in the painting of the 1964 event that rocked America? The right to political activism on campus. Clubs, cops, clenched fists. Negotiations. Victory.

"It was one hell of a fight, I guess. I know an old guy ..."

My lips trembled listening to *him* tell *me* all about it. I pulled it together.

"Stop! Stop. I was there. I mean my family was." He got quiet.

"Yeah," I slid my hands over the bumpy concrete surface of their slightly faded faces, "Without these 800 students—my brothers and sisters, we could have lost it. All of it."

"All of what?" he turned and actually looked at me, an elder, a movement stateswoman, wearing sandals and a two week old pierced nose that still bled if I blew it. I didn't, so the tears ran down my neck.

"Wow, like you are **there**, man." He gently put his hand on my shoulder, as if he knew exactly how to handle sixties flash backs. "Breathe deeply." He flared his nostrils again and again. "Breathe deeply, like, you know, like in yoga class."

I snorted loudly. "Our constitutional right to free speech."

"You know about the Patriot Act, don't you? It's all part of the same battle, the battle to speak the truth, to protest. Just like these students did, all of you must defend our civil liberties," I waved my shaky hand toward the university campus, then toward Moe's Book Store, the one place I clearly remembered from 1969.

"You look wiped. Would you like to sit down in our park? Come, on." He scurried down the sidewalk three or four yards ahead of me, checking back over his shoulder just to be sure I hadn't jumped right into the mural.

I really did need a place to sit, but there wasn't a single bench in sight. Everyone in the park except for the basketball players, was snoring under a bush or slouched against a shopping cart full of rags, blankets and empty plastic bottles. The others were talking to trees and street lights, or jumping back from attack ghosts stationed behind the public bathroom. I sniffed the old familiar scent. Weed. A group of scrubby men huddled under the once upon a time free speech stage.

Ignoring the people in the park I said brightly,

"Can you imagine 1969, man, what it was like when a young army of 20,000 marched into this park, waving American flags, kites, balloons and paper airplanes. They planted flowers on the barbed wire fence the University put up and on the helmets of the National Guard. It was a fight against urban renewal. People's power, you know."

"What's wrong with urban renewal," he looked puzzled.

"I know, I didn't get my parents either. World War II and all that."

"Well, at the moment, all I remember is that the university tore down some old houses here," I pointed to the grass, "but left it vacant for two years. So the community wanted it for a park. The mayor of Berkeley and Governor Ronald Reagan called out police, and guards, and it was a stand off for seventeen days. One protester died. Someone just like you."

I was unraveling again. An ancient looking hippie from the weed huddle shuffled toward us in a smoky haze.

"Shit, I gotta go., uh, what did you say your name was?"

"Jonah."

"Thanks, Jonah. Uh, thanks for listening. Some things are better in print. Read about it. Better yet, Google it. Bye…. Never forget what happened … Bye"

Hopeful, I smiled, gave him the fist. Then shouted, "Think karma. Think karma yoga," and hustled back to see Teryn, his friend Aden, and the future breakthrough generation on Telegraph Ave.

Folly Beach, SC, 2007

"Moriah, maybe you could create a climate change therapy," I giggled, kicking the sand as we walked toward the dolphins. Owanda (named by Teryn after a character in an Orson Scott Card novel) pulled her leash, excited by sand crabs venturing into the cooler eighty degrees of the late afternoon breeze over Charleston. Asheville's summer drought and record number of days over ninety were anxiety producing warning signs: *we're not in Kansas anymore.*

A large crab scuttled over a dune escaping Owanda's black nose.

"It wouldn't be much different than counseling trauma victims, Mom," she answered.

Do dolphins take off for cooler water we wondered, scanning the flat blue ocean channel for fins? Last summer a group of dolphins did a surprise beach attack forcing flipping silver fish onto the sand for dinner inches from our bare feet, fearless, intent only on feeding themselves. Hoping for a repeat show, we drank beer with bread and cheese glaring at every enemy jet ski that approached from either side of our yellow beach blanket. Our angry environmentalist arms motioned to the alien sea monsters: Go away! Go away!

After a long odyssey, Moriah had grown so much bigger than my imagination by diving into a sea of graduate students to explore one of my lost careers. *They call the wind Moriah,* the song is uniquely her own, now a crescendo of strong beauty, a therapy language harmonizing with poetry, literature, and music rooted in northern cities and southern mountains, blowing her home to our family, her lover Ben, and the dolphins. Karma of the whale goddess.

"Hey," yelled Teryn running towards us ahead of Steve plodding slowly down the shoreline wearing his treasured peace symbol tee shirt. "I've got something to show you." I stared, puzzled at his empty hands. In a powerful twist he yanked off his white tee shirt exposing his back."

"Oh no, you didn't," I moaned looking at a two strange dark symbols on his upper right shoulder. "What the heck is that?" I touched his skin tentatively.

"It's a tattoo, Mom," Moriah said excitedly. "Cool, Teryn."

"Teryn, I warned you not to get one. I see so many people on my massage table with really ugly, faded, blurred shit they totally regret, that is permanent and means nothing to them at age forty."

"Mom," Teryn said, "I will never outgrow this, it…."

I cut him off. "It was one thing for Moriah to get that hideous, silver, tongue ring, against her better judgment, that dangled out of her mouth like a snake's tongue which she eventually had removed because it, well, it was repulsive."

"OK Mom, who got her nose pierced? Not me!" Moriah laughed.

"Let me finish," Teryn protested. This is a Chinese symbol for crisis, *Kanji.* Two characters, *opportunity in danger.* That's what climate change is."

"What's all the fuss about," Steve asked observing my all too common worried, angry expression.

"That," I pointed at Teryn's back.

With a huge laugh, he joked, "I guess it's time for me to follow the evil ways of my son and get this old peace symbol tattooed onto my chest so I don't have to wear this anymore." Before we could stop him, he tore off his shirt and plunged into the ocean, swimming out to meet the dolphins.

My Steve. Our hero, the peacemaker.

Evolving the Light

I have told you my story, how the strands of my life like the braids neatly tied in ribbons unraveled into anarchy as I tasted one pear and then another, devouring life in its glory and cruelty. My mother chose my name from a movie, *Lady in the*

Dark, and I wish I could tell you I found the light. But I would be lying. I only found pieces of it, because that's all there is. But when the light appears, sparks fly and the girl with braids runs wild down the beach with an ipod rocking out to greet the other young net warriors—Teryn, Moriah and the break through generation, blogging their way to power, preparing to crash the gates. The gates my generation only dented. But oh, what a dent!

I still dream that the socialism of the future will have a very different character from the failed old model. After all, I am Zion's step daughter born in the Mormon vision of "a city in which the people are unified and are 'pure of heart', with no contention and no poor among them." A little bit like Damanhur and the Temples of Humankind in northern Italy, the largest eco-village in the world that appears to embody feminist democracy, earth centered spirituality, renewable energy—everything I want in the New Jerusalem. And it is possible to get there, but only when the majority, not just the working class liberates itself from our reckless, wasteful political economy. I wish I could promise you that some day the US government will have a Peace Department. Or that you will survive the devastation of global warming. Or that if you look as hard as I did the right formula for paradise will appear. But no, never. Formulas and dogma belong permanently under deleted messages.

But I do know it is possible to find moments of personal peace like those Buddha found sitting under the Bo tree. I've seen that tree, and I know. It has six huge trunks with the same roots, like the childhood braids growing from my crown. Each leaf is heart shaped. And when the wind blows, the message of the clapping leaves is Divine.

I *can* promise you that.

Lao Tzu Tao Te Ching

Free from desire, you realize the mystery.
Caught in desire you see only the manifestations
When you lack expectations, you reach what is hidden,
Unexpected, true, mysterious, the Way, the Tao.
Do the work and let it go.
For letting it go is what makes it stay.

Afterword

Writing *Radical Passions* led me to the language of values, politics, and art, the framework that shaped the life I inherited and the responsibility I consciously and unconsciously chose as I reacted to events that shaped our nation's destiny. My parents, veterans of World War II and the anti-communist witch hunt of the McCarthy era, taught me to protect and defend our country's democratic ideals, to fight for human rights and justice for all. Their biting critique of how greed and discrimination failed minorities, women and the working poor alerted me to America's failures at an early age.

Religious and intellectual freedom were highly prized by my ex-Mormon parents—my mother became a Unitarian, my Dad an agnostic. They lived simply and consumed only what they needed. Art, music and literature filled our household, and each family vacation, included a trip to a museum of one kind or another.

These family values were the foundation of who I became and who I am today. Thankfully I survived and grew from the powerful sixties revolution and the right wing backlash of the next thirty years into a new territory of spiritual practice and energy healing. I have learned that day to day politics is really an expression of deeper moral, psychological and spiritual issues driven ultimately by emotions rather than intellect. My conclusion—only when more of us can embrace forgiveness, awareness, kindness, generosity and selflessness to all living beings will our civilization be prepared to take the next evolutionary step forward to a politics guided by love rather than hatred.

Presently I am hopeful and grateful for the opportunity to work with a diversity of people waking up to the challenges presented by climate change that will demand a powerful paradigm shift from all of us as we learn to live in balance on this earth.

Kendall Hale
Fairview, North Carolina
January, 2008
www.radicalpassions.com

Thanks

Writing this book took over ten years without a dime of support except our family income. I can never thank my husband, Steve, enough for his invitation to write and to his patient listening and unwavering belief in me. And to both my children for their loving participation in my life and writing.

Thanks to the women of *Written Out of History*, Nancy Teel, Bette Steinmuller, Linda Stern, and Beatrice Nava who made possible the idea of writing creative nonfiction, and insisted that writing our collective history would make a difference. Thank you to Janice Eaton Kilby who copy edited and wordsmithed with great love and attention, Elena Dodd who pointed me forward, Laurie Alberts, for her insightful comments and feedback, Georganne Spruce and Max Elbaum for the final read, and to Joseph Taylor, for his guru computer skills.

Thanks to all my friends who heard me say over and over again, "I'm almost finished with my memoir, will you buy a copy?" And to all the souls who incarnated with me in these times to whom I am forever grateful.

About the Author

Kendall Hale is a massage therapist, yoga instructor, and wellness retreat owner who lives on a farm in the Blue Ridge Mountains near Asheville, North Carolina. She embraces justice and peace with her family and community as a grassroots activist, musician, and vocalist.

978-0-595-48387-7
0-595-48387-9